Performance Management in International Organizations

Marco Amici • Denita Cepiku

Performance Management in International Organizations

palgrave
macmillan

Marco Amici
University of Rome Tor Vergata
Rome, Italy

Denita Cepiku
University of Rome Tor Vergata
Rome, Italy

ISBN 978-3-030-39471-4   ISBN 978-3-030-39472-1   (eBook)
https://doi.org/10.1007/978-3-030-39472-1

This Palgrave Pivot imprint is published by the registered company Springer Nature Switzerland AG.
The registered company address is: Gewerbestrasse 11, 6330 Cham, Switzerland

CONTENTS

–

List of Figures

LIST OF TABLES

Introduction: The Increasing Relevance of International Organizations, Key Challenges, and Management Aspects

Abstract This first part will introduce the topic of the book, starting from the increasing relevance of international organizations due to the need for states to cooperate to manage the main transnational and global challenges. Nevertheless, the rising importance of international organizations increased their level of intrusiveness in the national sphere raising democratic, legitimacy, but also management issues. While democracy and legitimacy of international organizations is a rather investigated topic, by contrast, their management aspects received little attention by scholars although both are linked to each other.

Keywords International organizations • Legitimacy problem • Management deficits

The increasing transnational interdependence fuelled by the need for tackling the current global challenges are questioning the predominance of state actors in ruling the world. In the last fifty years, the number of non-state actors dealing with rulemaking and regulatory functions experienced a remarkable increase. At the same time also states went through a process of disaggregation passing from 50, in 1945, to almost 200 in 2010 (Cassese 2012). Such a trend diffused the concentration of power to other

© The Author(s) 2020
M. Amici, D. Cepiku, *Performance Management in International Organizations*, https://doi.org/10.1007/978-3-030-39472-1_1

actors of global governance, favoring the emergence of different kinds of non-state entities in the international arena. This coupled with the rising challenge of governing globalised markets where trade, finance, health, and environmental issues are interconnected led to the creation of 265 inter-governmental organizations (IGOs),[1] almost 8000 International—non-governmental organizations (INGOs)[2] as well as a large number of international regulatory regimes, multilateral agreements, and private institutions with regulatory functions. All such pieces of global governance (Karns et al. 2010) contribute to shape the administration of the world.

Among these, the inter-governmental organizations (IGOs) experienced the most spectacular growth in number, size, and competences, becoming those entrusted with higher responsibilities for shaping and managing global challenges (Karns et al. 2010). From one side, such growth reflects the need for states to cooperate to manage the main transnational and global challenges. However, on the other side, the rising importance of international organizations increased their level of intrusiveness in the national sphere. According to Zürn (2004: 261), the need for "enlarged and deepened cooperation in the age of globalization led to new and more intrusive international organizations respect to the traditional ones", raising democratic, legitimacy but also management issues. While democracy and legitimacy of international organizations is a rather investigated topic (Zurn 2004; Mehde 2007; Schneller 2010; Weilar 1991; Schimmelfennig 1996; Stokes et al. 1999; Bohman 2005), by contrast, their management aspects received little attention by scholars although both are linked to each other (Bauer 2007; Balint and Knill 2007). As much as international decision-making substitutes decision making at the national level, as much international organizations are in need to justify their authority in the exercise of power (Mehde 2007). The international organizations now address issues that were previously decided at the national level, and their decisions are increasingly affecting people within states (Woods and Narlikar 2001). The increased binding character of the decisions taken by the international organizations, as well as the extended span and scope of their content impact on individuals, firms, or states, put pressure on the justification of their power. Often such international organizations are perceived as undemocratic, favoring "unjust" solutions, as well as mostly inefficient, resources waste and ineffective, as not being able to transform policies into actions (Stutzer and Frey 2005).

Although the debate over the legitimacy of international organizations is very complex, triggering endless discussions among lawyers, sociologists, and political scientists about the introduction of national legitimacy mechanisms in international organizations, less attention was devoted to the concept of the output legitimacy (Schimmelfennig 1996). This latter focuses on the positive results that any state or administrative entity brings about (Schimmelfennig 1996). Following this perspective, the legitimacy of a political system depends on its capacity to achieve the citizens' goals and solve their problems effectively and efficiently, leading to conclude that the extent the actions taken by the international organizations are legitimized depends on the results of such actions. In other words, "if an institution exhibits a pattern of egregious disparity between its actual performance, on the one hand, and its self-proclaimed procedures or major goals, on the other, its legitimacy is seriously called into question" (Buchanan and Keohane 2006: 422). According to this approach, legitimacy is invariably linked to performance, and improvements in performance lead to an increased legitimacy of the organization as such (Mehde 2007). If this is true, then performance becomes a crucial aspect, especially for the more intrusive international organizations (Zurn 2004). From a management perspective, performance depends on how inputs are processed to deliver outputs and how these latter impacts in the organizational environment producing outcomes. Thus, performance improvements are linked to the modernization of the management structures dealing with inputs, outputs, and outcomes. According to Pollitt and Bouckaert (2017), a huge amount of public management reforms mushroomed in many countries' administrations together with comparative studies and analysis highlighting common trajectories and reform models.

By contrast, the management reform of international organizations attracted minimal attention and was hardly subject to comprehensive investigations (Balint and Knill 2007). Until very recently, international organizations were often considered as mere platforms or devices in the hands of the member state governments, useful for transnational decision-making only. They were not perceived as administrative bodies, and the research focus was primarily on the political structures (Mehde 2007). In such a context, linking their management reforms to an increase in performance and organizational legitimacy was "consistently neglected in the analytical framework of global governance and its alleged democratic deficit" (Mehde 2007: 168). Despite this, reforming international organizations should be now a primary concern, considering their recent spectacular growth, in the number, size, and competences, as well as their chronic management problems, quickly transforming into pathologies unless correctly addressed (Dijkzeul and Beigbeder 2003). Nevertheless, evidence shows that many international organizations recently started modernizing their internal management structures in an attempt to be more effective and more efficient (Bauer 2007).

Several international organizations embarked on lengthy reform programs with very ambitious aims. The United Nations committed to "adapt the internal structure, the operational processes and the culture of the United Nations to the expectation of greater efficiency, effectiveness, openness, and problem-solving readiness of the constituency" (United Nations 1997: 2). Similarly, the European Commission management reform aimed "to equip the Commission to fulfil its role in addressing the challenges facing Europe with maximum effectiveness" (European Commission 2000: 1), as well as "making sure that every action taken delivers maximum performance and value-added" (European Commission 2014: 3). On the same line, the World Bank's reform aimed at making the Bank more effective in delivering its regional program and in achieving its basic mission of reducing poverty (World Bank 1997).

In this context, reforming the management structures became a priority.

- However, to what extent the rhetoric of the reform statements has been translated into action? Compared to national public administrations, how have the peculiarities of international organizations influenced the management reform processes? Have the same management ideas and reform paradigms spread in the public sector organizations, also influenced the reform trajectories of international organizations?
- More specifically, regarding performance management, how could issues of low measurability be overcome? What are other adaptations to the traditional performance management systems needed?

Research on these types of organizations could help unveil implementation obstacles or undesired effects of management reforms. The book intends to contribute to the debate in order to shed light on the processes and substance of management reforms in international organizations. The study relies on the analysis of the existing literature as well as on a case study analysis to assess and compare the trajectories and contents of management reforms in international organizations.

After a focus on the increasing role of international organizations in the global context which calls for an equal increase of their legitimacy by performance improvements (Chap. 4), we will analyse the main characteristics of the managerial reforms including the factors influencing the processes as well as the substance of the managerial reforms (Chap. 5).

Following this, we will focus on the analysis of the performance management systems in public sector organizations to discuss similarities and differences for their application to the international organizations (Chap. 6). In the last part, two case studies of management reforms carried out in a selected number of international organizations will be analysed, namely the European Union (EU) (Chap. 7) and the Organization for Economic and Development Cooperation (OECD) (Chap. 8).

NOTES

1. See The Yearbook of International Organizations (YIA) statistics for "conventional intergovernmental organizations", 2013, UIA.
2. See The Yearbook of International Organizations (YIA) statistics for "international non-governmental intergovernmental organizations" 2008, UIA.

REFERENCES

Balint, Tim, and Christoph Knill. "The limits of legitimacy pressure as a source of organizational change: The reform of human resource management in the OECD." University of Konstanz. Department of Politics and Management. Chair of Comparative Public Policy and Administration. Working Paper n. 1. (2007).
Bauer, Michael W. "Introduction: Management Reform in International Organizations." In *Management Reforms in International Organizations*, eds. Bauer M., Knill C., Nomos, 2007.
Bohman, James. "From demos to demoi: Democracy across borders." *Ratio Juris* 18, no. 3 (2005): 293–314.
Buchanan, Allen, and Robert O. Keohane. "The legitimacy of global governance institutions." *Ethics & international affairs* 20, no. 4 (2006): 405–437.
Cassese, Sabino. *Chi governa il mondo*. Il Mulino, 2012.
Dijkzeul, Dennis, and Yves Beigbeder, eds. *Rethinking international organizations: pathology and promise*. Berghahn Books, 2003.
European Commission. *White Paper "Reforming the European Commission"*. 2000.
———. *Communication from the President Mission letter to Commissioner to Competition*. (2014).

Karns, Margaret P., Karen A. Mingst, and K. W. Stiles. "Chapter 1: The Challenges of Global Governance". *Karns, Margaret P./Mingst, Karen A.: International Organizations. The Politics and Processes of Global Governance*, Boulder (2010): 3–34.

Mehde, Veith. "Creating a missing link? administrative reforms as a means of improving the legitimacy of international organizations." In *Management reforms in international organizations*, pp. 163–175. Nomos Verlagsgesellschaft mbH & Co. KG, 2007.

Pollitt, Christopher, and Geert Bouckaert. *Public management reform: A comparative analysis-into the age of austerity. Oxford University Press*, 2017.

Schimmelfennig, Frank. *Legitimate rule in the European Union.* Center for German and European Studies, University of California at Berkeley, 1996.

Schneller, Lena. "Conceptions of Democratic Legitimate Governance in the Multilateral Realm: The Case of the WTO." *Living Reviews in Democracy* 2 (2010).

Stokes, Susan C., José María Maravall, James A. Stimson, and Jon Elster. *Democracy, accountability, and representation.* 1999.

Stutzer, Alois, and Bruno S. Frey. "Making international organizations more democratic." *Review of law & economics* 1, no. 3 (2005): 305–330.

United Nations. *Renewing the UN: A Program for Reform.* 1997.

Weiler, Joseph HH. "Problems of legitimacy in post 1992 Europe." Aussenwirtschaft 46, no. 3 (1991): 4.

Woods, Ngaire, and Amrita Narlikar. "Governance and the Limits of Accountability: The WTO, the IMF, and the World Bank." *International Social Science Journal* 53, no. 170 (2001): 569–583.

World Bank. *The World Bank Annual Report 1997.* 1997.

Zürn, Michael. "Global governance and legitimacy problems." *Government and Opposition* 39, no. 2 (2004): 260–287.

CHAPTER 2

Roles, Types, and Definitions of International Organizations

Abstract The second chapter reviews the main theories and academic perspectives applied to the study of international organizations. We start by explaining the different meanings associated with the term international organization. Then we focus on how the role of the international organizations has been conceptualized across the different academic disciplines to highlight the current literature gaps and future research trajectories.

Keywords Roles and functions of international organizations in the global arena • Management deficit • Literature gap

2.1 THE CHALLENGE OF DEFINING INTERNATIONAL ORGANIZATIONS

The term "international organizations" refers to a wide variety of formal structures with both common elements as well as specific peculiarities, which call for clarification. As noted by Brechin and Ness (2013: 17), scholars of international organizations "seem to typically focus on intergovernmental organizations, and at times, seem to use the term interchangeably. This can be confusing". In the same vein, Dijkzeul and Beigbeder (2003: 7) claim that "sometimes the term international organizations is used to include multinational corporations, bilateral organizations, multilateral organizations, and international non-governmental

© The Author(s) 2020
M. Amici, D. Cepiku, *Performance Management in International Organizations*, https://doi.org/10.1007/978-3-030-39472-1_2

organizations (INGOs)." "Other times, only UN organizations are covered by this term." Most commonly, the term international organizations is used to refer to "all forms of non-state actors working at international or global levels" (Brechin and Ness 2013: 17). According to this, intergovernmental organizations (IGOs) can be considered a subset of the international organizations' category together with international non-governmental organizations (INGOs). The reference work on this topic is the Yearbook of International Organizations published yearly, since 1999, by the Union of the International Associations (UIA). It contains the list[1] of all types of international organizations according to different criteria.[2]

As for the types, the most relevant distinction is between intergovernmental organizations (IGOs) and international non-governmental organizations (INGOs). The first attempt to categorize the intergovernmental organizations (IGOs) was implicitly made by the Economic and Social Council of the United Nations with the Resolution 288 (X) on 27th February 1950. This latter stated that "any international organization which is not established by intergovernmental agreement shall be considered as a non-governmental organization for the purpose of these arrangements." Such definition, however, does not directly explain what international organizations are and what is considered an intergovernmental agreement. Further complications arose from the fact that by the time more and more international agreements included a constituent state of a federal system, or an inter-governmental organization itself—acting as one of the parties of an inter-governmental agreement together with a government (YIA 2015). Finally, these agreements have also been signed on behalf of governments or by their agencies for purely technical issues. Such agreements may not fully engage the government and thus including such entities in the non-governmental organizations category (YIA 2015). Therefore, according to the Union of the International Associations (UIA), an organization can be included in the intergovernmental category if it is established by the signature of an agreement engendering obligations between governments (YIA 2015). Further conditions include that IGOs must be composed primarily of sovereign states, although they can also include other intergovernmental organizations and the establishment of a permanent Secretariat performing ongoing tasks. Karns et al. (2010: 5) provided a similar definition of IGOs as "organizations whose members include at least three states, that have activities in several states, and whose members are held together by a formal intergovernmental agreement." Even more challenging is finding a common and acceptable definition of international non-governmental organizations (INGOs). For Karns et al. (2010: 5) non-governmental organizations (NGOs) are "private voluntary organizations whose members are individuals or associations that come together to achieve a common purpose." Consequently, international non-governmental organizations (INGOs) are NGOs with an international dimension. Nevertheless, according to the editors of the Yearbook in International Organizations, defining the international dimension of an organization can be challenging. In practice, there are seven aspects of organizational life, acting as indicators of eligibility of an organization in the INGOs category. They include aims, membership, structure, officers, finance, relations with other organizations and activities.[3] On this basis, the UIA includes in the INGOs category those NGOs with an international dimension, active in at least three countries, with a constitution allowing for periodic elections of the governing body and with no attempt to distribute profits among their members (Dijkzeul and Beigbeder 2003). Another element differentiating IGOs and INGOs is that the first enjoys a legitimate legal status recognized in constitutions, international conventions, and host agreements, while the INGOs are created under national law (Dijkzeul and Beigbeder 2003). Finally, INGOs can take different forms according to the emphasis and typology of their members, among them the transnational NGOs (TRANGO), the business and industry NGOs (BINGOs), the donor organized NGOs (DONGO) etc.

Based on such classification, Bauer (2007) proposes a different categorization of international organizations focused on the type of decision-making systems adopted. In his view, international organizations whose members are predominantly sovereign states can be considered as "public international organizations." They differ from "private international organizations" whose members are mainly private actors. Public international organizations can have an intergovernmental or supranational character. This latter refers to the different decision-making system adopted by international organizations. In supranational organizations, member states transcend national boundaries or interests and take the decisions by majority voting system, while in intergovernmental organizations state governments play a more prominent role, and unanimity applies. Consequently, following the Yearbook of International Organizations, the "public international organizations" are those international organizations (Bauer 2007: 14):

1. based on a formal instrument of agreement between the governments of nation-states;
2. including three or more nation-states as parties to the agreement;
3. having intergovernmental or supranational character;
4. possessing a permanent secretariat performing ongoing tasks.

Another debated aspect concerning the definition of international organizations is the reference to international bureaucracy. In fact, some authors (Barnett and Finnemore 2004; Reinalda and Verbeek 2004), use these terms interchangeably, giving them the same meaning, while others (Biermann et al. 2009; Cortell and Peterson 2004; Bauer et al. 2017) use them distinctly, considering international bureaucracies the administrative body of the international organizations. In their study on the influence of the International Environmental Bureaucracy, Biermann et al. 2009: 6) define international bureaucracies as "hierarchically organized group of international civil servants with a given mandate, resources, identifiable boundaries, and a set of formal rules of procedures within the context of a policy area." On the same line, Cortell and Peterson (2004) link the term international bureaucracy with the "administrative support apparatus" within the international organizations. In the public administration tradition, international bureaucracies are also called international public administrations (IPAs). Bauer et al. (2017: 2) define international public administrations (IPAs) as "the bureaucratic bodies and administrative interactions of international organizations [...] with a certain degree of autonomy, staffed by professional and appointed civil servants who are responsible for specific tasks and who work together following the rules and norms of the international organization in question". IPAs constitute an integral part of the international organizations, although distinct from their political bodies (Eckhard and Ege 2016). As stressed by Trondal et al. (2013: 4), "international bureaucracies consist of the permanent secretariat of international organizations. They are organizationally separate from the plenary assemblies of international organizations and have a formal autonomy vis-à-vis the member states [...] they typically have a fixed location, they have a formalized division of labour [...], they have regular meetings, and they are staffed with permanent personnel recruited on the principle of merit". Such definitions mark a clear line between international bureaucracies and international organizations. According to Biermann et al. (2009), these latter can be seen as "institutional agreements that combine a normative framework, member states and a bureaucracy," a sort of over-reaching structure with a bureaucratic body inside. For example, the Organization for Economic and Cooperation Development (OECD) is composed of three different bodies. The Council and Committees, made up of the representatives of the member states, dealing with the, decision making and the Secretariat, made up of 2500 international civil servants that supports the activities of the committees, and performs the administrative tasks in response to the priorities decided by the Council. Similarly, the International Labour Office staffed of 1900 officials, is the permanent secretariat within the International Labour Organization (ILO), as well as the European Commission, which can be considered as the executive body of the European Union, and so forth. Although functions and tasks of the permanent secretariats can vary across international organizations, their role and influence are on top of the agenda for scholars interested in studying the bureaucratic interior of international organizations (*see infra*). Ultimately, a terminological distinction needs to be made between international organizations, their bureaucratic part, and the term international institutions. This latter is largely used by sociologists to stress the fact that the organizations are not only made of formal structures and written norms but encompass systems of norms and values. As noted by Biermann et al. (2009), in the wider policy debate, it is common to refer to the World Bank or the International Monetary Fund as Bretton Woods institutions. Nevertheless, the term "institutions" refers to "systems of norms, rules and decision-making procedures that give rise to social practices, that assign roles to participants in these practices, and that guide interaction among participants" (Biermann et al. 2009). Similarly, Krasner (1984) defines international regimes as "a set of implicit and explicit principles, norms, rules and decision-making procedure, around which actors' expectations converge in a given area of international relations." Both definitions share the common focus on an abstract set of principles and values that do not possess material entity on their own (Biermann et al. 2009). Conversely, international bureaucracies have a physical structure, employ people, have buildings and properties to serve administrative functions (Biermann et al. 2009). Finally, the use of the term "organization" denotes a stricter link with management studies. Here is much broadly conceptualized as formally established systems of social interactions to achieve certain goals (Blau and Scott 1962) or "systems of coordinated and controlled activities that arise when work is embedded in complex networks of technical relations and boundary-spanning exchanges" (Meyer and Rowan 1991: 41). Table 2.1 shows the different types of classification.

Table 2.1 Types of classification of international organizations

1st classification type	2nd classification type		3rd classification type		4th classification type	
Classification focused on the status of their members	*Classification focused on the status of their members and the decision making system adopted*		*Classification focused on internal structure*		*Classification focused on academic traditions*	
Inter-governmental organizations (IGOs)	Organizations whose members include at least three states, that have activities in several states, and whose members are held together by a formal inter-governmental agreement (yearbook of international organizations/types A-D)	Public International Organizations	*Organizations based on a formal instrument of agreement between the governments of nation states; including three or more nation states as parties to the agreement; having intergovernmental or supranational character; possessing a permanent Secretariat performing ongoing task* (Bauer 2007)	International organizations	Institutional agreements that combine a normative framework, member states and a bureaucracy (Biermann et al. 2009)	International organizations	Formally established systems of social interactions to achieve certain goals at international level (management perspective) (Blau and Scott 1962)/ Institutional agreements that combine a normative framework, member states and a bureaucracy (political science perspective) (Biermann et al. 2009)

Type	Definition
International non-Governmental organizations (INGOs)	NGOs with an international dimension, active in at least three countries, with a constitutions allowing for periodic elections of the governing body and with no attempt to distribute profits among their members (yearbook of international organizations)
Private international organizations	Organizations acting at the international level whose members are mainly private actors (Bauer 2007)
International bureaucracies/ International Public Administrations (IPAs)	*Hierarchically organized group of international civil servants with a given mandate, resources, identifiable boundaries, and a set of formal rules of procedures within the context of a policy area (Biermann et al. 2009)*
International institutions	Systems of norms, rules and decision making procedures that give rise to social practices, that assign roles to participants in these practices, and that guide interaction among participants (sociological perspective) (Biermann et al. 2009)

Source: own elaboration

Relying on the concept of networks defined in literature (Agranoff and McGuire 1998; Ferlie et al. 1996, 2011; O'Toole 1997; Milward and Provan 2003; Provan and Milward 1995, 2001; Provan and Sebastian 1998), international organizations can also be seen as networks of organizations. According to O'Toole (1997: 45), networks can defined as "structures of interdependence involving multiple organizations or parts of thereof, where one unit is not merely the formal subordinate of the others in some larger hierarchical arrangement" or as a form of organizing essential governance functions across independent actors (Elliott and Salamon 2002). The key features of networks include:

- the orientation towards addressing complex policy problems that cannot be solved by one actor alone, and require the collaboration of several actors (Mandell 2001; Agranoff and McGuire 2003; Koppenjan et al. 2004);
- high interdependencies between actors, which means sharing resources owned by different actors, in terms of financial, instrumental, and human resources (Hanf and Scharpf 1978);
- complex interactions between actors because each actor may have different expectations and because each actor has its perception of problems, solutions, and strategies (Hanf and Scharpf 1978; Agranoff and McGuire 2003; McGuire and Agranoff 2011).

Considering international organizations, the concept of networks can be applied at two different levels. The first level is focusing on the networks the international organizations are members. In this case, the international organization is a network member. The second level is considering the international organization, a network of organizations where the nation-states are the network members. In fact, international organizations display the key characteristics of networks (O'Leary and Bingham 2007; Rhodes 1996: Klijn and Teisman 1997; Agranoff and McGuire 2003). Among them:

- International organizations are composed of other organizations (nation-states), each with its interests and objectives that have to be met.
- Both common and different missions exist. Hence, states' missions can at any time clash with the mission of the entire network/international organization;

- Diversity among network members' cultures exist which may present conflict management challenges within the network itself;
- Different methods of operation, diverse degrees of hierarchy and management control exist, which may affect what a network can and cannot achieve and the speed at which it is accomplished;
- Network members have different stakeholder groups and different funders;
- Network members have different degrees of power, despite network rules which may give an equal vote to each member;
- Networks typically are formed to address multiple issues and complex problems that are not easily solved by one nation-state;
- Interdependency regarding the distribution of resources between various network members, the goals they pursue and their perceptions of their resource dependencies;
- There are continuing interactions among network members to exchange resources and negotiate shared purposes.

Building on such premises, in the rest of the book—if not otherwise stated—with the term international organizations, we will refer to Bauer's definition of public international organizations. The term includes all international organizations of intergovernmental or supranational character, whose members are predominantly states,[4] although our analysis will main target their internal bureaucracy.

2.2   Types, Scopes, Numbers and Functions of the International Organizations

Despite the attempt to use standard definitions to categorize international organizations, their universe is considerably heterogeneous due to their relevant differences in size, geographical scope, tasks, and functions. As for the size, the international organizations can include few members, three as in the case of the North America Free Trade Agreement (NAFTA), or a large number as the United Nations, which counts 193-member countries.[5] Their geographical scope varies extensively from a specific area as the case of the regional organizations as ASEAN or the African Union, to worldwide organizations having members from all countries. Furthermore, there are single tasks organizations like the Organization for Petroleum Exporting (OPEC) as well as multipurpose organizations as the European

Table 2.2   Types of international organizations

Geographical range	International Organizations
Global	United Nations (UN)
	International Labour Organization (ILO)
	Food and Agricultural Organization (FAO)
Regional	ASEAN
	European Union
	Africa Union
Sub-regional	East African Community
	West Nordic Council
	Arab Maghreb Union
Purpose	*International Organizations*
Multi-purpose	United Nation
	European Union
Single-purpose	Nuclear Energy Agency
	International Organization for Migration (OIM)

Source: based on Karns et al. (2010)

Union or the United Nations. Consequently, their functions differ, as well. The most common include sharing and collecting information, monitoring trends, providing forums for collective decisions and, settling disputes (Karns et al. 2010). Again, how international organizations serve such functions vary extensively according to their rules, financial resources, level, and degree of bureaucratization (Karns et al. 2010). In the following table, a summary of the different main characteristics of international organizations is proposed (Table 2.2).

As far as the number of international organizations is concerned, different prominent sources show very different figures. The number of international organizations according to the leading online and textbook sources vary significantly, ranging from 126 international organizations listed by the US Department of State to 325 by the correlates of the war database (Davies and Woodward 2014). More detailed data on the number and typologies of international organizations are provided by the Union of International Associations (UIA) in its yearly publication "The Yearbook of International Organizations." According to the 2018/2019 edition of the YIA, the number of international organizations (type A-D/ Conventional international bodies) is 285.[6] Nevertheless, the methodology adopted by the UIA to classify the different typologies of international organizations is far from being consistently applied. Davies and Woodward

(2014) found several incongruities in the classification of international organizations respect the criteria defined by the same organization. Nevertheless, although the exact number of international organizations can be questionable, all scholars agree on the fact that since the Second World War, the number of international organizations increased steadily with an exceptional rise in the twentieth century. The growth of the state system favoured by the decolonization process was among the main reasons (Karns et al. 2010). As stressed by Cassese (2012), after the Second World War, states went through a process of disaggregation, passing from 50 in 1945 to almost 200 in 2010. As argued by Cupitt et al. (1996) the birth rate of international organizations "correlates positively with the number of states in the international system". Contrary death rate is low as shown by the fact that of 34 international organizations created in 1914, 18 were still functioning in twentieth-century (Cupitt et al. 1996). A second relevant reason is the need to give adequate answers to the emerging global challenges coming from financial, health, security, and environmental sectors. Dealing with global issues increases state interdependence and calls for more effective solutions, able to cope with transnational problems. This issue opened the vast debate about the increasing role of international organizations in the world system, to which this book aims to contribute. Before dealing with the core content of the book, in the following paragraphs, we will briefly discuss the main academic perspectives adopted to study the role and processes of international organizations in literature, to locate our contribution better.

2.3 Conceptualizing the Role of International Organizations

The increased importance in number, scope, and size of international organizations does not seem to correspond to a similar theoretical and empirical attention by scholars. Several authors (Bauer 2007; Balint and Knill 2007; Ness and Brechin 1988) complain about the lack of a comprehensive and systemic approach to the study of international organizations, especially concerning their internal management. According to Dijkzeul and Beigbeder (2003: 9), "over the last two decades, the debate on international organizations has been characterized by a continuous lament that more and better studies are required." The lack of a comprehensive theory explaining the behaviour of international organizations is still probably the main evidence. The reasons, according to Bauer (2007), are probably "due to the fact that international organizations topic falls between the boundaries of several social sciences sub-disciplines", namely international relations, organizational sociology, public administration, and business administration. The intensity, scope, and research focus of such disciplines vis à vis international organizations varied considerably along time. The study of international organizations by international relations scholars, for example, after the second world war witnessed a considerable development (Ness and Brechin 1988) "to such an extent that international organizations were viewed not so much as a subfield but as practically the core of the discipline" (Rochester 1986: 779). On the same vein, Bauer (2007) notes that international organizations have been the focus of scholarly interest for many years.[7] Such interest was characterized by little or no interaction between the different disciplines, which dealt with the study of international organizations separately. According to Ness and Brechin (1988: 2), the "gap between the study of international organizations and the sociology of organization is deep and persistent" adding "for reasons unknown, international organizations [...] have not been studied much from a sociological perspective". One year before, Jönsson (1986: 39) had noted that "the relations between organization theory and the study of international organizations [...] has largely been one of mutual neglect." Similarly, Dijkzeul and Beigbeder (2003: 16) considered the "lack of interaction among scholars from the disciplines of international relations, business administration and public administration," one of the general shortcomings in the study of international relations. They did not find any relevant interactions between international relations theory and management and organization theory—apart from few exceptions (Allison 1971; Jervis 1976; Cox and Jacobson 1973)—concluding "disciplinary myopia often persist."

Each discipline has been concerned with a particular aspect of international organizations, thus preventing, so far, a systematic understanding of their role and functioning. Similarly, Bauer et al. (2017: 4) stress how "historically there has been a kind of mutual disregard preventing interdisciplinary debate. Public administration was not interested in international bureaucratic issues, while international relations did not look systematic at the intra-organizational features of international organizations". Bauer (2007) points out how international relations and comparative politics restricted their research interests on the relations between sovereign states and international organizations and how these latter affect domestic politics and policies. The main theoretical traditions in international relations, although with different visions, mainly looked at international organizations as a sort of device or platform for transnational decision making, ignoring their bureaucratic interior (Bauer 2007). At the same time, organizational sociologists focused their research interests in the study of the functioning of modern organizations, but scarcely noting the existence of the international organizations (Ness and Brechin 1988). Gordenker and Sanders (1978) suggest that possible reasons for the lack of integration between political scientists and sociologists' work lies in the fact that these latter only focused their attention on business firms and governments which do not provide applicable models for international organizations. The disciplines studying both internal functioning of organizations and their relationships are business administration and public administration. Despite this, Dijkzeul and Beigbeder (2003: 10) acknowledge that "attention to international organizations from a business administration point of view is minimal" as the focus is on "private enterprise and international organizations falls outside the realm." Similarly, in Public Administration, the main research focus is on no-profit and national public organizations, although international organizations are not as marginalized as in business administration (Dijkzeul and Beigbeder 2003). In their relevant contribution to understanding the functioning of international organizations, Dijkzeul and Beigbeder (2003) suggested more considerable attention on actual management issues of international organizations, including the management of resources and the achievement of results. In fact, according to them, the conventional type of study suffers from three important shortcomings. These latter include (Dijkzeul and Beigbeder 2003):

- the insufficiently appropriate theory about the actual functioning of international organizations;
- a lack of interaction of scholars from the disciplines of international relations, business administration and public administration;
- a choice of units of analysis, concepts, and research methodology that blocks attention to such issues as implementation, internal functioning and deviations from mandate, but emphasizes such issues as decision making and the role of states.

Despite such a complex picture, the time has come to re-connect the research programs of the different academic disciplines towards a more integrated approach to the study of international organizations (Bauer et al. 2017). In the following paragraphs, the different perspectives of the study of international organizations will be briefly explored.

2.4   THE INTERNATIONAL RELATION PERSPECTIVE

The focus of studies on international organizations by political scientists largely contributed to the lack of a systematic understanding of their functioning for a long time (Barnett and Finnemore 1999). In fact, despite "a variety of theories explain why [international organizations] have been created [...], research flowing from these theories paid little attention to how international organizations actually behave after they are created" (Barnett and Finnemore 1999: 699). Historically the most prominent international relations scholars devoting considerable time to the study of international organizations were political scientists. As stressed before, the period of 1945–1960, was defined by Hoole[8] an intellectual era dominated by the study of the United Nations system by international relations scholars, followed by the rise of regional integration studies associated with the development of the European Economic Communities (EEC). As noted by Dijkzeul and Beigbeder (2003), in the seventies, the research focus shifted to transnational politics, networks of independence, and international regimes. This latter continued to receive considerable attention also in the eighties while the attention paid to international organizations as formal organizations declined (Dijkzeul, Beigbeder 2003). Considering the relevance of international relations perspective for the study of international organizations, the main theories and school of thoughts will be briefly discussed. This analysis will serve to highlight their different and sometimes opposite views about the role and functions of international organizations in shaping international decision-making. The first group of theories belongs to the realist tradition associated with ancient thinkers like Machiavelli and Hobbes but including modern scholars as Carl von Clausewitz, Hans Morgenthau, Jonathan David Kirshner, and Reinhold Niebuhr. Realists focused their research on issues related to national power, believing that nation-states are the main actors in international relations, interacting in a world without any central or sovereign authority. In brief, they assumed that the international system is anarchic, and no actors above states could regulate their interactions. States were the only and most important actors in the arena, behaving rationally and aiming at surviving. Consequently, they considered international organizations as creatures of the states and not an interesting object of analysis per se, as they had little independent influence on states. Hence international organizations are not important arenas for member states' interactions and are certainly not autonomous actors in their own (Nielsen and Tierney 2003). According to Mearsheimer (1995: 82), a prominent realist scholar, international organizations "reflect state calculations of self-interested based on concerns about relative power; as a result, institutional outcomes invariably reflect the balance of powers." At the same time, realists recognize that sometimes powerful states could find alliances—rather than institutions—useful for achieving their purposes (Mearsheimer 1995). The classic example is the creation of NATO led by the United States to balance Soviet power. The main realist point here is that NATO "did not force its member states to behave contrary to balance-of-power logic" (Mearsheimer 1995: 82). Relevant empirical studies analyzed the exercise of power behind the international organizations (Stone 2011), showing the extent to which powerful states buy off the cooperation of smaller states in international organizations (Martin and Simons 2012). Similarly, Reynaud and Vauday (2009) document how lending in international institutions depends on the geopolitical interests of the major powers. On the same line, Kaja and Werker (2010) estimated in sixty million dollars, the additional funding for developing countries sitting in the board of the World Bank, while Kuziemko and Werker (2006) discovered that a country sitting in the UN Security Council expects an increase of 59% of bilateral aid by the United States. A recent development in realists' tradition is soft realism, which explores how the states use international organizations to achieve their objectives (Martin and Simons 2012). According to He (2008) states use international organizations to engage in "institutionalized balancing" behavior, as the use of pressures and threats for securing their interests. Similarly, Gstöhl (2007) argued that the most powerful countries increasingly use international organizations to achieve their preferred outcomes over debt relief and terrorist financing. Despite it is impossible to ignore such basic insights of realists theory, on the other hand, as Martin and Simons (2012) suggest challenging questions arise. If governments are not likely to be bind by the rules, they agree in the context of international organizations, why spending time and resources to negotiate them? If international organizations are merely considered as little more than a power play, why work through multilateral institutions at all? Alternative answers can be found in the Liberal family of theories, which recognizes greater attention to the role and functions of international organizations, although with variations. Within the liberal family, institutionalism assumes that the active role of international organizations can generate an independent effect on state behavior (Keohane and Martin 1995). According to Mearsheimer (1995: 82), international organizations have the power to affect states' decisions, "to reject power-maximizing decisions and to accept an outcome that might weaken their relative power position." The classical divide between realists and institutionalists lies" whether the international organizations can have independent effects on state behavior, or whether instead institutional outcomes reflect great powers and are essential tools that great powers employ for their selfish purposes" (Mearsheimer 1995: 82–83). Institutionalist theories include different approaches, differing in the way they proceed. The functionalist approach, proposed by Mitrany (1933, 1948) starts challenging realist positions assuming the desuetude of the state as a form of social organization. As Rosamond (2000) points out, instead of the self-interest of nation-states, functionalists assume as motivating factors the interests and need shared by states and non-state actors, in the process of global integration triggered by the erosion of state sovereignty. Mitrany (1933, 1948) considered nationalism as the main reason for conflicts and argued that states should be bound together by a network of international agencies that built on common interests and had authority in functionally specific fields (McCormick, 1999). Mitrany (1933, 1948) also sustained that these agencies would be executive bodies with autonomous powers and would perform some of the same tasks of national government, only at a different level (McCormick 1999). According to this approach, the creation of international organizations would lead to greater world integration in relatively noncontroversial areas in several economic sectors or sector of industry. The success in sector integration will enhance cooperation in other sectors; consequently, state sovereignty declines and will be replaced by international organizations (McCormick 1999). At the same time, greater integration would also produce cognitive and value changes; people would realize the complexity of world affairs and consequently will reject simple-minded solutions (Ness and Brechin 1988). Such awareness would erode the limited national loyalties often assumed as the basis of the war. This vision was further elaborated by neo-functionalists (Haas, 1958), which focused more on the regional rather than the global integration. Building on Mitrany's work, Haas (1958) and Lindberg (1963) laid down the first basic principles of regional integration through spillover effects, considering territorially based organizations as crucial agents of integration. According to Lindberg (1963: 10) the spillover effect can be described as a process by which "a given action related to a specific goal, creates the situation in which the original goal can be assured only by taking further actions, which in turn create a further condition and a need for more action". Consequently, functional international organizations would have created to oversee and direct this process. In other words, as much the level of the regional economic integration is high, as much regulation will be needed and consequently greater will be the authority delegated to centralized institutions (Caporaso, 1998). The main empirical evidence of neo-functionalists theories is the European integration process, which aims at bringing peace in the European continent through a process of regional economic integration first. When created the European Coal and Steel Community (ECSC) in 1951, Robert Schuman affirmed that the ultimate aim of ECSC was "making future wars between France and Germany [...] not merely unthinkable, but impossible." (Heilbron-Price 1995: 1). Scholars associated with liberal intergovernmentalism, like Paul Taylor, Robert Keohane, and Andrew Moravcsik, lately challenged the neo-functionalists view of international organizations, as the engine of European integration. Born between the eighties and nineties, the liberalism intergovernmentalism approach combines the importance of domestic policies in shaping international organizations' role and the recognition of the importance of state actors in international relations. This view downgrades the role and functions of the EU institutions. According to them, the EU integration process moves further not by the crucial role of their institutions but because of intergovernmental bargains reached at the European level. Moravcsik (1993) argues that integration advance as a result of a combination of factors such as the commercial interests of economic procedures and the relative bargain power of major governments (Moravcsik 1993). On a similar line, some recent studies challenged the validity of this theory contesting the link between regional economic integration and institutionalization. For example, Grieco (1997: 172) argued that "contrary to functionalists' expectations, in some area of the world there have been increase in interregional trade without a corresponding increase in institutionalization [...] Moreover in some cases we can observe growth of institutionalization, in the absence of increased trade encapsulation". Equally, in response to realists' positions and drawing on the work of classical functionalists, Keohane (1984), together with Krasner (1983), paved the way to the rational functionalist approach[9]—also known as institutional liberalism.

This latter rooted on the basic assumptions that international organizations provided a way for states to overcome problems of collective actions, high transactions costs and information deficits and asymmetries thus providing an effective answer to the puzzle posed by realism for the problem of international collective action (Martin and Simmons 2012). Similarly, Abbott and Snidal (1998: 8) explain that according to the rational functionalist approach, states use international organizations for "producing collective goods, collaborating in prisoner's dilemma, solving coordination problem". Consequently, the strong point of this approach lies in the ability to explain the reasons for the creation of international organizations and their maintenance, although proved weaker in explaining the effects on state behavior (Martin and Simmons 2012). Within the realm of rationalist theories, the relationship between international organizations and the member states is better explained by the principal-agent model, which provides further insights on the conditions and modalities under which international organizations acquire autonomy to pursue their preferences and how the government can control them. The principal-agent model explores the possibility for international organizations to become actors in their own, although subordinated to states (Nielsen and Tierney 2003). In this model, principals (in our case, the governments) hire an agent (an international organization) to perform several duties (functions) that will benefit all members (Nielsen and Tierney 2003). In the literature, the main functions performed by the agents generally concern monitoring and information sharing to all participants, solving problems of incomplete contracting, adopting technical and complex regulations, and agenda-setting powers (Pollack 1997). Nevertheless, as noted by Koch (2006), the principal-agent model proves that international organizations can acquire autonomy by their member states through delegation. However, this latter is considered defective and deviates from the expected behavior. Consequently, this model provides to member states mechanisms and tools to ensure that international organizations act in the way they intended (Koch 2006). In sum, while international relations scholars were initially focused on explaining why the international organizations were created and how member states can control them, they gradually started looking at the functioning of their internal mechanisms. Recent studies on principal-agent model (Elsig 2010; Haftel and Thompson 2006; Brown 2010) started to take into account the international secretariats of international organizations analyzing the administrative features including the role of the independent staff, the ability of international secretariats to initiate and recommend policies (Haftel and Thompson 2006) and in general on how international organizations are able to act autonomously (Grigorescu 2010; Brown 2010). Nevertheless, as pointed out by different scholars (Yi-Chong and Weller 2008; Bauer et al. 2017), the main failure in the principal-agent literature remains the lack of a proper definition of the bearer of agency within the international organizations. In other words, the tendency of the principal-agent approach not to differentiate between the administrative and political parts of the organization. As argued by Ege and Bauer (2013), we need a more explicit distinction between the political and administrative levels in the study of international organizations, although some scholars have recently started to distinguish the two intra-organizational levels following a principal-agent approach (Elsig 2010). Finally, in political science, the visibility of network analysis has been recently grown (Ward et al. 2011). In this perspective, international organizations can be seen as "policy networks." Studies related to "policy network" have the main goal to understand how policy actors achieve desired policy objectives in terms of outcomes through the creation and sharing of networks. The majority of these studies is focused on policy innovation (Berry and Berry 1990; Mintrom 2000; Walker 1969), policy change and agenda-setting (Dahl 1961; Kingdon 1984; Jenkins-Smith and Sabatier 1999) and new institutional economics (North 1990; O'Toole 1997; Schneider et al. 2003; Williamson 1975).

2.5   THE SOCIOLOGICAL PERSPECTIVE

A different perspective on the study of international organizations was taken by sociologists, who introduced the analysis of the social context in understanding the relations of international organizations. Different groups of theories and approaches confronted over time. The first group that, moving from sociological assumptions, started to challenge the international relations rationalist approach was the *sociological constructivists*. According to the constructivist approach, international organizations act gradually independent and contribute to enforce or create norms that shape behavioral patterns for states. In this framework, international organizations are seen as norms entrepreneurs, entities for norm diffusion, having monitor and sanctioning duties as well as being organs for legitimating disputes. Constructivists are focused on how the framing of rules and norms place constraints on the different players of the international arena. As argued by Arend (1999: 142), "international organizations can alter the identities and the interests of states as a result of their interactions over time within the auspices of a set of rules." This leads to the important consequence that the complexity of social interaction cannot allow international organizations to be treated as an exogenous or pure object of choice (Ruggie 1992). At the opposite, according to the constructivists' approach, international organizations are crucial for furthering normative convergence, considering their role in creating, reflecting, and diffusing normative understanding (Martin and Simmons 2012). For Finnemore and Sikkink (1998), international organizations can be viewed as chief socializing agents in their role of pressuring targeted actors to adopt new policies and laws and to ratify treaties and by monitoring compliance with international standards. Similarly, Keohane and Nye (1972) observed that international relations are increasingly be governed by norms and rules, having a fundamentally moral character. They defined such moral norms and principles "regimes" and studied the relations between regimes and international organizations. According to Ness and Brechin (1988: 12), the concept of regimes is an extension to the international arena of Durkheim's discovery generally applied to society that "any contractual arrangement depends upon an underlying set of non-contractual norms that alone permits contracts to be made." The functioning of regimes in the international arena can follow two directions, according to Ness and Brechin (1988). From a sociological point of view, regimes representing underlying normative structures, permit the creation of international organizations, and as much as the regimes strengthen as much the perseverance and effectiveness of the international organizations' increases. A different and opposite mechanism is described by international relations functionalists that believe that international organizations promote and create regimes. Consequently, greater is the incidence and persistence of international organizations stronger will be the regime (Ness and Brechin 1988). Although the two directions are mutually exclusive, both link regime characteristics, formation, and performance of international organizations. Such variation in the way international organizations act for reaching their objectives is a crucial aspect that marks the difference between political scientists and sociologists' functionalists. While political scientists' functionalists consider international organizations the tools that will increase peace and prosperity in the world, sociologists' functionalists produced a more skeptical and even cynical view of organizations, giving the field something of an expose character (Perrow 1986). Both groups share the Weberian approach to organizations "as rational collectivities with limited goals and an orientation to action" (Ness and Brechin 1988: 9). However, sociologists consider international organizations not just a mechanical tool serving altruistic purposes. The interaction of international organizations with the environment and their members produce a distinctive character in each international organization that change over time (Ness and Brechin 1988). This can lead to a transformation of international organizations from rational tools to collectivities seeking powers and interests their creators not always intended (Ness and Brechin 1988). In fact, following Mitrany's view, international organizations acted precisely and accurately as the creators intended (Ness and Brechin 1988). Consequently, the international relations functional theory assumed that all international organizations were similar, ignoring the differences in terms of performance of the different international organizations. Evidence can be found in the quantitative cross-national tests[10] of functional theory, where the main indicator used for measuring the importance of international organizations is their number (Ness and Brechin 1988).

As described above, such a simplistic view is challenged by functional sociologists. According to Ness and Brechin (1988: 11) "it is logical to derive from functionalism propositions about variance in organizational performance" as well as "it is possible that organizations differ radically in the extent to which they aim […] toward promoting stability, peace, and integration of the international system". This leads to the consequence that more sophisticated and specialized tools need to be used to understand how different organizational performance affects the role of different international organizations in achieving their objectives (Ness and Brechin 1988). Thus the internal structure of international organizations started to gain particular attention in the organization theory. The focus moves towards assessing the role and features of the international bureaucratic bodies performing administrative tasks within the international organizations. In this regard, the most prominent work is Barnett and Finnemore's book "Rules of the World: International Organizations in Global Politics," published in 2004 and aims at creating a common framework for evaluating different kinds of authorities in international organizations (Ege and Bauer 2013).

As noted by Eckhard and Ege (2016), the debate over international bureaucracies gained substantial momentum after 2005, certainly due to the publication of Barnett and Finnemore's book, which marked a seminal point in recognition of the importance of the bureaucratic branch of international organizations. In the view of Barnett and Finnemore (2004), the importance of international bureaucracies is not linked to what they are allowed to, but to a different kind of authority, they can use and exercise vis à vis the member states (Ege and Bauer 2013). This allowed the authors to focus on the organizational elements leading to potential dysfunctional processes and pathological outcomes (Ege and Bauer 2013). Based on such contribution, Ege and Bauer (2013) identify four broad topics around which sociological studies can be divided; organizational change, the interaction of international organizations with the environment, pathologies and powers, and administrative leadership. Among them, Koch (2006) tried to explain the process of *autonomization* in international organizations stressing the need to adjust the focus on these latter rather than on state-international organizations' relations. In his study, he focuses on the internal dimension of international organizations. He defines the automatization process as the "the degree to which the core gets independent from the environment, including the inner environment i.e. member states influences as well as the outer environment i.e. all other non-international organizations elements" (Koch 2006: 21).

Similarly, Barnett and Coleman (2005) focused on the analysis of change in international organizations, highlighting as the international bureaucracies themselves may be strategic agent for organizational changes depending on their level of internal security and the congruity of internal culture with external pressure. These findings were also supported by the studies on organizational reform in the UN peacekeeping missions (Hultman et al. 2016). Other contributions focused on the powerful role played by administrative leaders of international organizations sitting at the top of the bureaucracy and performing administrative and political tasks (Cox 1969; Johnstone 2003). This strand of publications following Barnett and Finnemore's book share some similarities with the principal-agent theory discussed in the previous paragraph as both tend to not differentiate between the administrative and the political part of the organization (Bauer et al. 2009). Nevertheless, as noted by Ege and Bauer (2013), the principal-agent approach tends to view international organizations as solely political institutions, while sociological institutionalists refer to bureaucracy when dealing with international organizations, neglecting their relations with the political part within the organization. Finally, in the perspective of international organizations as networks, another interesting trend of organizational sociological studies focus on "social network analysis," and it is grounded in the sociological tradition and sociometric studies (Moreno 1934; Nadel 1957; Dahl 1961; Dahrendorf 1959; Granovetter 1973). Using both case studies and quantitative approaches, some of the most investigated topics are related to the consequences of network structure on attitude similarity, job satisfaction, power, and leadership distribution (at the micro-level) and the impact of network structure on joint ventures, alliances and knowledge sharing (at the macro-level).

2.6   THE PUBLIC ADMINISTRATION AND MANAGEMENT PERSPECTIVE

Public administration and public management could potentially offer a more detailed picture about the internal functioning of the international organizations considering their focus on linking internal administrative structures with internal processes and outputs, although it does not seem the case (Bauer 2007; Dijkzeul and Beigbeder 2003; Jönsson 1993; Cooperrider and Pasmore 1991).

In public administration, public entities and international organizations share a common focus, i.e., the administration of collective goods. According to Bauer (2007: 12), "given the perspectives of international relations and comparative politics, public administration appears to be the natural discipline to consult in order to learn about international organizations as bureaucratic entities." Despite this, in public administration, "international organizations do not receive much research attention." The main reason is that public administration scholars limited their study to the public administration of nation-states (Bauer 2007), which is after all their main market (Dijkzeul and Beigbeder 2003). Also, in the case of comparative public administration studies, the focus remains on national public administration systems (Peters 2001; Pollitt and Bouckaert 2004). According to Bauer et al. (2017), this has two unfortunate consequences; from one side, we miss how international public administrations matter for global governance, and from the other, how insights regarding international public administrations may productively inform the public administration research. The crucial issue at stake is whether studying the management of international organizations falls into the public administration theories and approaches developed so far for national public administration, or if there are structural implications that could impede such analogical application. Bauer (2007: 12) points out how "at first sight, the political environment of international organizations seems to differ in important aspects from those of national or subnational administrations." Similarly, Stutzer and Frey (2005) stress how issues as participation, representation, responsiveness, communication appear to be less pronounced in the international sphere than in the case of public administration. However, such differences appear "more as a matter of degree rather than of kind" (Bauer 2007: 12), and time has come for public administration concepts and theories "for going international" (Bauer et al. 2017: 5). Considering the rising importance of the collective decisions in which international organizations are involved and the emerging role of the international bureaucratic bodies that support international organizations to adopt such decisions, the public administration scholars increased their attention towards the international bureaucracy research (Ege and Bauer 2013). As noted by Trondal et al. (2013: 1), "international bureaucracies constitute a distinct and important feature of public administration studies."

As public administration discipline is interested in public policies and in those entrusted to execute it, then it is also necessary to deal with such process at the level of international organizations and international public policies (Bauer et al. 2017). According to Trondal et al. (2013: 1), "a public administration turn" in the study of international organizations has recently increased the research on the internal functioning of international organizations, paving the way to a third generation of studies on international organizations. In the first generation of studies, the most important actors on the world scene were nation-states, and international organizations were mainly dealt with as black boxes. While in the second generation, international bureaucracy gained attention by public administration scholars, and several research works focused on their bureaucratic interior (Trondal et al. 2013). Nevertheless, the increasing number of empirical studies on the functioning of international organizations increased the systematic understanding of how and when international organizations matter only to a limited extent, as we still lack comparative studies for reasonable generalizations (Ege and Bauer 2013: 143). On the same vein, Biermann et al. (2009) and Trondal et al. (2013) point out the lack of comparative studies of international bureaucracies.

Consequently, according to Trondal et al. (2013: 2), a third-generation of studies on international organizations is needed to "normalize the study of international organizations," calling for "a public administrative turn" to characterize international organizations' studies. This new generation should be based on the long academic and theoretical development within the public administration area, requiring that new questions be asked and new concepts applied to the field of international organizations (Trondal et al. 2013). Nevertheless, the public administration discipline is commonly viewed as an interdisciplinary field that could be defined as the need to address conflicting political, legal, and managerial values and processes (Rosenbloom 1983). Applying a public administration turn to the study of international organizations means also balancing the three above mentioned approaches. There are, however, legitimate concerns among scholars that the public administration often ignores one or more fields (Wright 2011).

As put by Wright (2011), public administration seems to be isolated from the mainstream management literature and practice, ignoring its valuable lessons. Among the reasons for such isolation, the most common is the field's believe in the uniqueness of public organizations and employees that keep of limited values the attempts of learning how lessons from mainstream management can be applied (Allison 1983). However, several research studies suggest the contrary evidence (Boyne 2002; Rainey and Bozeman 2000), and even if differences persist, they do not justify ignoring the considerable evidence that the most prominent mainstream management theories on leadership, motivation, and performance provide (Wright 2011). If management aspects are marginalized in the public administration discipline, whose primary focus remains on national governments, it is likely to expect that the management aspect of international bureaucracies will be even more.

As noted by Biermann et al. (2009), management studies have largely neglected international bureaucracies. The attention of management studies to international organizations is minimal because the focus remains on private and commercial firms (Dijkzeul and Beigbeder 2003), although different forms of organizations share similar problems concerning the organization of the internal structures and the way resources are managed to achieve a common goal. At the same time, differences exist between profit organizations and no-profit or public bureaucracies and need to be acknowledged. The international bureaucracies can be considered as international public administrations (IPAs) based on an international treaty and with a legal mandate, consequently less subject to changes in political priorities (Biermann et al. 2009). One of the most significant difference concerns the criteria for performance evaluation: whereas for-profit organizations is the commercial profit, for international public administration there is a multitude of qualitative objectives to be measured in terms of effectiveness (Biermann et al. 2009). Nevertheless, as mentioned above, the differences in the nature of the organization do not prevent us from studying how lessons from management theories and practices can be applied to international public administration (IPAs). As put by Dijkzeul and Beigbeder (2003), looking at the international organization with public management lenses "facilitates a more balanced look at organizations which has often been noticed by authors who lament the lack of attention to international organizations." Yet, although the internal functioning of international organizations has been subject to several research studies as mentioned above, only a few studies (Geri 2001; Levy 2003; Glöckler 2007; Alesani et al. 2007; Balint and Knill 2007) applied management insights to international bureaucracies. More considerable attention to the management aspects of international organizations was raised in combination with the increased interest in topics such as civil society (Carothers and Barndt 1999) and governance. Starting from the eighties, this caused a deviation from the traditional (top-down) public administration towards a new model where implying more attention to nongovernmental actors and implementation problems (Dijkzeul and Beigbeder 2003). At this point new policy instruments and managerial tools gained considerable attention under the New Public Management (NPM)—which builds on the understanding of public administration as service units that need to improve efficiency and effectiveness (Geri 2001; Barzelay 2001)—and Reinventing government (Osborne and Gaebler 1992) paradigms of reform, especially in the Anglo-Saxons world (Dijkzeul and Beigbeder 2003). Nevertheless, the attention to the new paradigms remained confined at the national level waiting to be translated in the international context. Those who tried to connect the recent debate opened up by the new paradigms of reform to the managerial reforms and modernization process in international public administration (Bauer and Knill 2007), mainly focused their attention on the triggering factors explaining the occurrence of a management reform, rather than investigating on the substance of the reform implemented. In other words, except few cases (Geri 2001; Balint and Knill 2007; Davies 2002; Dijkzeul 1997), the main focus is on the analysis of the reasons and the processes behind the managerial reform, rather than on the implementation of the managerial practices, related to budgeting, accounting, performance and human resource management. As noted by Bauer (2007), compared to process, contents of management reforms in international organizations is a less investigated topic. For this reason, we think that the "normalization of international organizations studies" needs to include also a more balanced approach of public administration discipline towards management aspects of international organizations, to complement and integrate the research findings so far achieved in this field.

Considering the perspective of international organizations as networks, the public administration and public management field focused on the analysis of the "public management networks." The primary aim of this community is to understand (1) whether networks exist and how they function (Mandell 1988), (2) how network managers can successfully manage these and what competences and skills are needed for this purpose (Agranoff and McGuire 2001; Gage and Mandell 1990) and lastly, (3) the impact that networks have on service delivery and customer satisfaction (Agranoff and McGuire 2003; Provan and Milward 1995). Nevertheless, such perspective has been poorly applied to the study of the internal dynamics of the international organizations.

NOTES

1. The Yearbook contains a directory of names and addresses, as well as profiles of organizations (historical and structural information, specifics on activities, events, and publications as well as biographies of important members), www.uia.org
2. Criteria include Type A, B, C.
3. For the full list, see Karns et al. (2010), page 18.
4. The study will focus on the characteristics and the dynamics of this type of international organizations although as suggested by Huntington (1993) comparing studies on public and private international organization could be as much revealing.
5. As of 21st of January 2019 http://www.worldometers.info/united-nations/
6. If we consider all types (A-U) of inter-governmental organizations listed in the Yearbook of International Associations (2018/2019 edition), the total number increases to 5.627. However, this number includes also dissolved or apparently inactive organizations (879), multilateral treaties, and inter-governmental agreements (2.454) and organizations emanating from places, persons, and bodies (930), which escape from the classical definition of international organizations used in this text. Nevertheless, different research works as Bauer and Knill (2007), and Trondal et al. (2013) consider all types of inter-governmental organizations listed in the YIA (types A-U) as "international public organizations."
7. See Barnett and Finnmore (1999, 2004), Rochester (1989), Dijkzeul and Beigbeder (2003).
8. See Rochester (1986).
9. Some call the school of thought rational functionalism instead of liberal institutionalism. Liberal institutionalism is also very close to—but not syn-

onymous with—regime theory and neoliberalism. To complicate matters even further, Robert Keohane, a political scientist largely responsible for the development of liberal institutionalism, considers his ideas part of institutionalism or rational institutionalism, even though those schools disagree with him on certain points.

10. See Wallace and Singer (1970).

REFERENCES

Abbott, Kenneth W., and Duncan Snidal. "Why states act through formal international organizations." *Journal of conflict resolution* 42, no. 1 (1998): 3–32.

Agranoff, Robert, and Michael McGuire. "Multinetwork management: Collaboration and the hollow state in local economic policy." Journal of Public Administration Research and Theory 8.1 (1998): 67–91.

Agranoff, Robert, and Michael McGuire. "Big questions in public network management research." Journal of public administration research and theory 11, no. 3 (2001): 295–326.

Agranoff, Robert, and Michael McGuire. "Inside the matrix: Integrating the paradigms of intergovernmental and network management." International Journal of Public Administration 26.12 (2003): 1401–1422.

Alesani, Daniele, Mariannunziata Liguori, and Ileana Steccolini. "Strengthening United Nations accountability: between managerial reform and search for legitimacy." *Management Reforms in International Organizations, Baden-Baden: Nomos* (2007): 97–115.

Allison, Graham T. *"Essence of Decision Making: Explaining the Cuban Missile Crisis."* New York, Harper Collins Publishers (1971).

———. "Public and private managers: are they fundamentally alike in all unimportant respects." *Public Management. Public and Private Perspectives. Palo Alto, Cal.: Mayfield Publishing* (1983).

Arend, Anthony C., Anthony Clark, and Clark Anthony Arend. *Legal rules and international society.* Oxford University Press on Demand, 1999.

Balint, Tim, and Christoph Knill. "The limits of legitimacy pressure as a source of organizational change: The reform of human resource management in the OECD." University of Konstanz. Department of Politics and Management. Chair of Comparative Public Policy and Administration. Working Paper n. 1. (2007).

Barnett, Michael, and Liv Coleman. "Designing police: Interpol and the study of change in international organizations." *International Studies Quarterly* 49, no. 4 (2005): 593–619.

Barnett, Michael, and Martha Finnemore. "The politics, power, and pathologies of international organizations." *International organization* 53, no. 4 (1999): 699–732.

———. *Rules for the world: International organizations in global politics.* Cornell University Press, 2004.

Barzelay, Michael. *The new public management: Improving research and policy dialogue.* Vol. 3. University of California Press, 2001.

Bauer, Michael W, and Christoph Knill. "Management reforms in international organizations.", Nomos, (2007).

Bauer, Steffen, et al. "Understanding international bureaucracies: taking stock." Managers of Global Change: The Influence of International Environmental Bureaucracies (2009): 15–36.

Bauer, Michael W, Christoph Knill, and Steffen Eckhard. "International Public Administration: A New Type of Bureaucracy? Lessons and Challenges for Public Administration Research." In *International Bureaucracy*, pp. 179–198. Palgrave Macmillan, London, 2017.

Berry, Frances Stokes, William D. Berry. State Lottery Adoptions as Policy Innovations: An Event History Analysis. American Political Science Review 84, No. 2 (1990):395–415.

Biermann, Frank, Bernd Siebenhüner, and Anna Schreyögg, eds. *International organizations in global environmental governance.* Vol. 17. Routledge, 2009.

Blau, Peter M., and W. Scott. "Richard: Formal Organizations." *A Comparative Approach. San Francisco: Chandler* (1962).

Boyne, George A. "Public and private management: what's the difference?." *Journal of Management Studies* 39, no. 1 (2002): 97–122.

Brechin, Steven R., and Gayl D. Ness. "Looking back at the gap: international organizations as organizations twenty-five years later." *Journal of International Organizations Studies* 4, no. 1 (2013): 14–39.

Brown, Robert L. "Measuring delegation." *The Review of International Organizations* 5, no. 2 (2010): 141–175.

Caporaso, James. "Regional integration theory: understanding our past and anticipating our future." *Journal of European Public Policy* 5, no. 1 (1998): 1–16.

Carothers, Thomas, and William Barndt. "Civil society." *Foreign policy* 117, no. 117 (1999): 18–24.

Cassese, Sabino. *Chi governa il mondo.* Il Mulino, 2012.

Cooperrider, David L., and William A. Pasmore. "The organization dimension of global change." *Human Relations* 44, no. 8 (1991): 763–787.

Cortell, Andrew, and Susan Peterson. "Historical Institutionalism and IO Design: A Synthetic Approach to IO Independence." In *Conference on Theoretical Synthesis and the Study of International Organization, February, Washington, DC.* 2004.

Cox, Robert W., ed. International Organization: World Politics. Springer, 1969

Cox, Robert W., Jacobson H. J., *The Anatomy of Influence: Decision Making in International Organization,* New Heaven, Yale University Press, 1973.

Cupitt, Richard T., Rodney L. Whitlock, and Lynn Williams Whitlock. "The (IM) Morality of international governmental organizations." *International Interactions* 21, no. 4 (1996): 389–404.

Dahl, Robert A. The Behavioral Approach in Political Science: Epitaph for a Monument to a Successful Protest. American Political Science Review 55, no. 4 (1961): 763–772.

Dahrendorf, Ralf. Class and class conflict in industrial society. Vol. 15. Stanford, CA: Stanford University Press, 1959

Davies, Thomas. *"The Administration of International Organizations: Top Down and Bottom up."* Ashgate, 2002.

Davies, Thomas, and Richard Woodward. *International organizations: A companion.* Edward Elgar Publishing, 2014.

Dijkzeul, Dennis. "United Nations development co-operation as a form of international public service management." *International journal of public sector management* 10, no. 3 (1997): 165–189.

Dijkzeul, Dennis, and Yves Beigbeder, eds. *Rethinking international organizations: pathology and promise.* Berghahn Books, 2003.

Eckhard, Steffen, and Jörn Ege. "International bureaucracies and their influence on policy-making: A review of empirical evidence." *Journal of European Public Policy* 23, no. 7 (2016): 960–978.

Ege, Jörn, and Michael W. Bauer. "International bureaucracies from a public administration and international relations perspective." *Routledge handbook of international organization* (2013): 135–148.

Elliott, Odus V., and Lester M. Salamon. *The tools of government: A guide to the new governance.* Oxford University Press, 2002.

Elsig, Manfred. "The World Trade Organization at Work: Performance in a Member Driven-Milieu." *The Review of International Organizations*, 5 no. 3 (2010): 345–363.

Ferlie, Ewan, Louise Fitzgerald, and Andrew Pettigrew. The new public management in action. OUP Oxford, 1996

Ferlie, Ewan, et al. "Public policy networks and 'wicked problems': a nascent solution?." Public Administration 89.2 (2011): 307–324.

Finnemore, Martha, and Kathryn Sikkink. "International norm dynamics and political change." *International organization* 52, no. 4 (1998): 887–917.

Gage, Robert W., Myrna Mandell, and Dale Krane. Strategies for managing intergovernmental policies and networks. Praeger, 1990

Geri, Laurance R. "New public management and the reform of international organizations." *International Review of Administrative Sciences* 67, no. 3 (2001): 445–460.

Glöckler, Gabriel. "From Take-off to Cruising Altitude: Management Reform and Organizational Change of the European Central Bank." In Management Reforms in International Organizations, pp. 85–96. Nomos Verlagsgesellschaft mbH & Co. KG, 2007.

Gordenker, Leon, and Sanders Paul. "Organization Theory and International Organization." In *International Organization: A Conceptual Approach*, Paul Taylor and A.J.R. Groom, eds., New York, Nichols Publishing Co., (1978): 84–108.

Granovetter, Mark S. The Strength of Weak Ties. American Journal of Sociology 78 no. 6 (1973): 1360–1380.

Grieco, Joseph M. "Realist international theory and the study of world politics." *New thinking in international relations theory* 167 (1997).

Grigorescu, Alexandru. "The spread of bureaucratic oversight mechanisms across intergovernmental organizations." *International Studies Quarterly* 54, no. 3 (2010): 871–886.

Gstöhl, Sieglinde. "Governance through government networks: The G8 and international organizations." *The Review of International Organizations* 2, no. 1 (2007): 1–37.

Haas, Ernst B. *The Uniting of Europe*, Stanford: Stanford Univ. Press., 1958.

Haftel, Yoram Z., and Alexander Thompson. "The independence of international organizations: Concept and applications." *Journal of Conflict Resolution* 50, no. 2 (2006): 253–275.

Hanf, Kenneth, and Fritz W. Scharpf. Interorganizational policy making: Limits to coordination and central control. Sage Publications, 1978.

He, Kai. "Institutional balancing and international relations theory: Economic interdependence and balance of power strategies in Southeast Asia." *European Journal of International Relations* 14, no. 3 (2008): 489–518.

Heilbron-Price, David. "Schuman and the dynamics of the new Europe." (1995): 4.

Hultman, Lisa, Jacob D. Kathman, and Megan Shannon. "United Nations peace-keeping dynamics and the duration of post-civil conflict peace." *Conflict Management and Peace Science* 33, no. 3 (2016): 231–249.

Huntington, Samuel P. The third wave: Democratization in the late twentieth century. Vol. 4. University of Oklahoma press, 1993.

Jenkins-Smith, Hank C., and Paul A. Sabatier. "The advocacy coalition framework: An assessment." Theories of the policy process 118 (1999): 117–166.

Jervis, Robert. "Perception and Misperception in International Politics (Princeton, NJ." *Press: Princeton* (1976).

Johnstone, Ian. "The role of the UN secretary-general: The power of persuasion based on law." *Global Governance* 9, no. 4 (2003): 441–458.

Jönsson, Christer. "Interorganization theory and international organization." *International Studies Quarterly* 30, no. 1 (1986): 39–57.

———. "International Organisation and Co-operation: An Interorganizational Perspective." *International Social Science Journal* 138, no. 3 (1993): 463–477.

Kaja, Ashwin, and Eric Werker. "Corporate governance at the World Bank and the dilemma of global governance." *The World Bank Economic Review* 24, no. 2 (2010): 171–198.

Karns, Margaret P., Karen A. Mingst, and K. W. Stiles. "Chapter 1: The Challenges of Global Governance." *Karns, Margaret P./Mingst, Karen A.: International Organizations. The Politics and Processes of Global Governance, Boulder* (2010): 3–34.

Keohane, Robert Owen, and Joseph S. Nye. *Transnational relations and world politics*. Harvard University Press, 1972.

———. *After hegemony*. Vol. 54. Princeton: Princeton University Press, 1984.

Keohane, Robert Owen, and Lisa L. Martin. "The promise of institutionalist theory." *International security* 20, no. 1 (1995): 39–51.

Kingdon, John W., and Eric Stano. Agendas, alternatives, and public policies. Vol. 45. Boston: Little, Brown, 1984.

Klijn, Erik-Hans, and Geert R. Teisman. "Strategies and games in networks." Managing complex networks: Strategies for the public sector 98 (1997): 118.

Koch, Martin. "Processes of Autonomization in/of International Organizations– the case of the World Trade Organization (WTO)." (2006).

Koppenjan, Johannes Franciscus Maria, Joop Koppenjan, and Erik-Hans Klijn. Managing uncertainties in networks: a network approach to problem solving and decision making. Psychology Press, 2004.

Krasner, Stephen D., ed. *International regimes*. Cornell University Press, 1983.

———. "Approaches to the State." *Comparative politics* 16, no. 2 (1984): 223–246.

Kuziemko, Ilyana, and Eric Werker. "How much is a seat on the Security Council worth? Foreign aid and bribery at the United Nations." *Journal of political economy* 114, no. 5 (2006): 905–930.

Levy, Roger. "Confused expectations: Decentralizing the management of EU programmes." Public Money & Management 23, no. 2 (2003): 83–92.

Lindberg, Leon N. "The political dynamics of European economic integration." *The political dynamics of European economic integration*. (1963).

Mandell, Myrna P. "Intergovernmental management in interorganizational networks: A revised perspective." International Journal of Public Administration 11.4 (1988): 393–416.

———. Getting results through collaboration: Networks and network structures for public policy and management. ABC-CLIO, 2001.

Martin, Lisa, and Beth Simmons. "International Organizations and Institutions." In *Handbook of International Relations*, (eds.) Carlsnaes W., Risse T., Simmons B.A. Thousand Oaks, CA, Sage Publications, 2012: 192–211.

McCormick, John. "Environmental policy." In *Developments in the European Union*, pp. 193–210. Palgrave, London, 1999.

McGuire, Michael, and Robert Agranoff. "The limitations of public management networks." Public Administration 89.2 (2011): 265–284.

Mearsheimer, John J. "A realist reply." *International Security* 20, no. 1 (1995): 82–93.

Meyer, John W., and Brian Rowan. "Institutionalized organizations." *and Robert Wuthnow, Meaning and Moral Order* (1991).

Milward, H. Brinton, and Keith G. Provan. "Managing networks effectively." In National Public Management Research Conference, Georgetown University, Washington, DC October. 2003.

Mintrom, Michael. Policy entrepreneurs and school choice. Georgetown University Press, 2000.

Mitrany, David. *The progress of international government*. Yale University Press, 1933.

——. "The functional approach to world organization." International Affairs (Royal Institute of International Affairs 1944) 24.3 (1948): 350–363.

Moravcsik, Andrew. "Preferences and power in the European Community: a liberal intergovernmentalist approach." *JCMS: Journal of Common Market Studies* 31, no. 4 (1993): 473–524.

Moreno, Jacob Levy. "Who shall survive?: A new approach to the problem of human interrelations." (1934).

Nadel, Siegfried F. 1957. The Theory of Social Structure. London: Cohen and West.

Ness, Gayl D., and Steven R. Brechin. "Bridging the Gap: International Organizations as Organizations." *International Organization* 42.2 (1988): 245–273.

Nielsen Daniel L., and Michael J. Tierney. "Delegation to Internal Organization: Agency theory and World Bank Environmental Reform." *International Organization*, 57, no. 2 (2003).

North, Douglass C. "A transaction cost theory of politics." Journal of theoretical politics 2.4 (1990): 355–367.

O'Leary, Rosemary, and Lisa B. Bingham. A manager's guide to resolving conflicts in collaborative networks. Washington, DC: Center for the Business of Government, 2007.

O'Toole Jr, Laurence J. "Treating networks seriously: Practical and research-based agendas in public administration." Public administration review (1997): 45–52.

Osborne, D., and T. Gaebler. "Reinventing Government: How the Entrepreneurial Spirit is Transforming the Public Sector. Addison-Wesley Publ." *Reading, MA* (1992).

Perrow, Charles. "Economic theories of organization." *Theory and society* 15, no. 1 (1986): 11–45.

Peters, B. Guy. *The future of governing.* Univ Press of Kansas, 2001.

Pollack, Mark A. "Delegation, agency, and agenda setting in the European Community." *International organization* 51, no. 1 (1997): 99–134.

Pollitt, Christopher, and Geert Bouckaert. *Public management reform: A comparative analysis.* Oxford University Press, USA, 2004.

Provan, Keith G., and H. Brinton Milward. "A preliminary theory of interorganizational network effectiveness: A comparative study of four community mental healt systems." Administrative science quarterly (1995): 1–33.

——. "Do networks really work? A framework for evaluating public-sector organizational networks." Public administration review 61, no. 4 (2001): 414–423.

Provan, Keith G., and Juliann G. Sebastian. "Networks within networks: Service link overlap, organizational cliques, and network effectiveness." Academy of Management journal 41.4 (1998): 453–463.

Rainey, Hal G., and Barry Bozeman. "Comparing public and private organizations: Empirical research and the power of the a priori." *Journal of public administration research and theory* 10, no. 2 (2000): 447–470.

Reinalda, Bob, and Bertjan Verbeek, eds. *Decision making within international organisations*. Vol. 31. Routledge, 2004.

Reynaud, Julien, and Julien Vauday. "Geopolitics and international organizations: An empirical study on IMF facilities." *Journal of Development Economics* 89, no. 1 (2009): 139–162.

Rochester, J. Martin. "The rise and fall of international organization as a field of study." *International Organization* 40, no. 4 (1986): 777–813.

Rochester, J. Martin. The United Nations and World Order: Reviving the Theory and Practice of International Organization. University of Missouri–St. Louis, Center for International Studies, 1989.

Rosamond, Ben. *Theories of European Integration*. Macmillan-St Martin's Press, Basingstoke and New York, 2000.

Rosenbloom, Paul Simon. "The chunking of goal hierarchies: A model of practice and stimulus-response compatibility." (1983).

Ruggie, John Gerard. "Multilateralism: the anatomy of an institution." *International organization* 46, no. 3 (1992): 561–598.

Schneider, Mark, et al. "Building consensus institutions: networks and the National Estuary Program." American journal of political science 47.1 (2003): 143–158.

Stone, Randall W. *Controlling institutions: International organizations and the global economy*. Cambridge University Press, 2011.

Stutzer, Alois, and Bruno S. Frey. "Making international organizations more democratic." *Review of law & economics* 1, no. 3 (2005): 305–330.

Trondal, Jarle, Martin Marcussen, Torbjörn Larsson, and Frode Veggeland. "Unpacking international organisations: The dynamics of compound bureaucracies." (2013).

Walker, Jack L. "The Diffusion of Innovations Among the American States." American Political Science Review 63, no. 3 (1969): 880–899.

Wallace, Michael, and J. David Singer. "Intergovernmental organization in the global system, 1815–1964: a quantitative description." International Organization 24.2 (1970): 239–287.

Ward, Michael D., Katherine Stovel, and Audrey Sacks. "Network analysis and political science." *Annual Review of Political Science* 14 (2011): 245–264.

Williamson, Oliver E. "Markets and hierarchies." New York 2630 (1975).

Wright Bradley E. Public Administration and Management Research: Evidence of Isolation and Unrealized Opportunity 267, In O'Leary, Rosemary, David M. Van Slyke, and Soonhee Kim, eds. *The future of public administration around the world: The Minnowbrook perspective*. Georgetown University Press, 2011.

Yearbook of International Organizations, (2015), Union of International Associations (UIA).

Yi-Chong, Xu, and Patrick Weller. "'To Be, But not to Be Seen': Exploring the Impact of International Civil Servants." *Public Administration* 86, no. 1 (2008): 35–51.

CHAPTER 3

Aims and Methods of the Study

Abstract The chapter explains the adoption of the comparative case study method for our research analysis on international organizations. The choice of this method resides in the contemporary and complex nature of global public management decisions, the need to retain their holistic characteristics, and the type of research questions to address. Furthermore, given that management reform strategies are path-dependent and conducted in several rounds, it is necessary to observe a multi-year timeframe that would provide insight into the sequence and dynamics of decision-making processes and behaviours. The research case studies include the OECD and the European Union. The aim was to create more theory-driven variance in the data by selecting cases with different external and internal contexts and varying organizational size and characteristics.

Keywords Global public management • Case studies • Management reform strategies

© The Author(s) 2020   41
M. Amici, D. Cepiku, *Performance Management in International Organizations*, https://doi.org/10.1007/978-3-030-39472-1_3

3.1   THE RESEARCH QUESTIONS FOR OUR ANALYSIS

The research aim of the book is to contribute to the understanding of the internal functioning of the international organizations, and specifically their administrative bodies. The contribution sits on the debate on the functioning of international organizations following a public management studies perspective. In particular, we are interested in assessing how international organizations have been responsive to the different waves of managerial reforms hitting all public administration of OECD countries and beyond at the national level in the last decades, with a specific focus on their performance frameworks. To address such topics, we formulated the following research questions:

- *RQ 1: What are the key characteristics (in terms of contents and process) of managerial reforms adopted by international organizations as a consequence of the increasing globalization and legitimacy crisis?*
- *RQ 2: What are the characteristics of performance management systems, part of such managerial reforms?*

In the study of management reforms in international organizations, Bauer (2007) identifies two preliminary basic sets of questions for a research project aiming to deliver a meaningful empirical study. The first aims "at explaining the management reforms as such", the second asks "what difference this particular administrative reform makes—in terms of policy output or even outcome" (Bauer 2007: 17). Answering to the first set of questions means taking the management reform as the dependent variable of our research model. By contrast, replying to the second means that the management reform becomes our independent variable. In the field of international organizations, Bauer (2007: 17) argues that neither of these questions "have been systematically investigated so far" and, on a similar vein, Balint and Knill (2007) claim that management reforms in this field have been hardly subject to comprehensive investigation. In this framework, our research work will contribute to such investigation addressing the first set of questions, i.e., taking the explanation of management reforms as our dependent variable. These latter can be assessed against two main descriptive dimensions, the processes influencing and leading to a management reform program and the substance of reform, including the direction and intensity of changes (Bauer 2007). The analysis to answer the identified research questions (RQ1 and RQ2), will be conducted according to the following structure.

After a focus of the increasing role of international organizations in the global context which calls for an equal increase of their legitimacy by performance improvements (Chap. 3), we will analyze the main characteristics of the managerial reforms including the factors influencing the processes as well as the substance of the managerial reforms (Chap. 4).

Following this, we will focus on the analysis of the performance management systems in public sector organizations to discuss similarities and differences for their application to the international organizations (Chap. 5). In the last part, two case studies of management reforms carried out in international organizations will be analyzed, namely the European Union (EU) (Chap. 6) and the Organization for Economic and Development Cooperation (OECD) (Chap. 7).

3.2   THE RESEARCH METHOD

The empirical part of the book relies on two methodological pillars: the "ideal types" model and the case study analysis. The former can be defined as a methodological tool to interpret the reality supporting the analysis of the observed changes through the construction of relationships sufficiently motivated and objective probable (Weber and Winckelmann 1968). As defined by Bouckaert and Halligan (2008: 212), "ideal types are representations of modeled behavior reduced to its essence, which therefore has a pure flavor with features of models such as modules and verifiable causal links." In the theoretical frameworks developed in the studies on management reforms, the ideal types have been connected to "a vision of the desired future" or to "an ideal world that certain groups wanted to get it" by directing the trajectories of the management reform programs (Pollitt and Bouckaert 2017: 75).

Ideal types have been thus associated with ideal reform paradigms or big models, including the New Public Management (NPM), the Neo-Weberian State (NWS), and the New Public Governance (NPG).[1] These models are a powerful tool to classify observed changes and, according to Lynn (2008), "a classification suggests that something new has emerged or is emerging [...] and using generalizations to depict the new can be illuminating." Nevertheless, the use of ideal models has also raised several concerns among academicians (Lynn 2008; Ongaro 2009; Kettl 2006). As argued by Lynn (2008: 19), the first tension is between "such generalizations with the widely-accepted notion of path dependence in the evolution of national governing institutions." On a similar line, Kettl (2006: 315) notes "like much cutting-edge work in government reform, struggles to deal with the inescapable dilemma: the search for central, driving themes, on the one hand, and the need to recognize the vast variation among nations, on the other". The underlying questions are to what extent the ideal paradigms influence management reforms and whether states can deviate from historical paths of national institutional development to follow them. Moreover in the attempt to find common models in public management, reforms rest a national matter fundamentally (Lynn 2008).

A second tension could be identified among the different ideal models. As argued by Lynn (2008: 19), the succession of different ideal paradigms can be caused by "tensions between these models and underlying path dependence of legal state evolution, generally resolved in favor of the weight of history." In this context, findings need to be interpreted with caution. As put it by Pollitt and Bouckaert (2017), the paradigms depict an ideal world, while the real future vision is much more confused and untidier. The observed changes in a country management reform could be linked to preset reform paradigms, although the reasons could be elsewhere. Moreover, the reform programs often overlap each other, and no successive waves of reforms are observable. Rather new layers overlie and do not replace or thoroughly wash away the previous layers of reform (Pollitt and Bouckaert 2017).

In sum, the reality can be much more complicated than following a linear trajectory towards an ideal paradigm, and the relations between decisions and observed changes can be sometimes looser (Pollitt and Bouckaert 2017). Such concerns prevent scholars from mechanically observe and classify the changes observed according to the ideal models. Further qualitative assessments on key variables as reasons for reform, administrative culture, and legal state evolution need to integrate and complement such classification.

The use of ideal paradigms calls for case study analysis which relies on experienced realities (Bouckaert and Halligan 2008). As argued by Yin (2003), the case study analysis is the main strategy when investigators face how and why research questions, have few controls over events and when the focus is on contemporary phenomenon within some real-life context. Case studies analysis starts with the selection of a limited number of objects of analysis (international organizations in our case), and proceed with a systematic collection of observations about changes carried out in the selected sample.

In combining ideal types and multiple case study analysis, Bouckaert and Halligan (2008) provided a useful explanatory model to classify changes, highlighting the differences between formal changes and their degree of implementation. The former includes the official documents, legislation and sources containing the proposed management changes (they refer to the "country model"), the latter the concrete level of implementation of the proposed management changes observed in the organizations (Bouckaert and Halligan 2008: 213). The literature refers to the level of reform implementation as a reform implementation gap, the dichotomy between the rhetoric and the reality of management reforms, or the interaction between the desirable and the feasible (Pollitt and Bouckaert 2017).

According to this model (Fig. 3.1), the three elements, ideal types, formal changes and degree of implementation, influence each other. Ideal types can trigger or inspire formal changes (1), but the capacity of implementation of a country or organization can influence the reform agenda (2). Finally, the formal and observed changes in a management reform model can be compared against the ideal types (3) (Bouckaert and Halligan 2008: 213).

Building on such literature (Bouckaert and Halligan 2008; Yin 2003; Pollitt and Bouckaert 2004, 2017; Balint and Knill 2007; Bauer 2007) our comparative study will focus on the analysis of the management

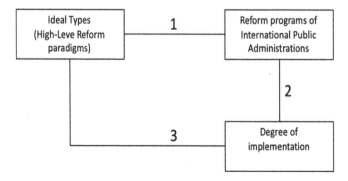

Fig. 3.1 The conceptual framework "three modes of reality" model for international organizations

changes in international organizations administrations, based on the outlined descriptive category of the process and substance of the management reform. The substance of management reforms will be the main object of our analysis. It will aim to compare the observed changes (1, 2) shaped by the management reforms processes in the selected international public administration, against the ideal reforms model, further described in Chap. 4, i.e., the traditional model, the NPM, the NWS and the NPG (3).

Consequently, the main elements of our case study is structured include:

1. A selection of international organizations
2. The operational framework of analysis
3. The documental sources

3.2.1   A Selection of International Organizations

The case study includes a selected number of international organizations, which have carried out significant management reforms, namely the European Union and specifically its executive arm, the European Commission, and the Organization for Economic and Development Cooperation (OECD), and specifically its Secretariat. They have been chosen according to the following three criteria:

The first criterion aims at selecting a balanced selection of international organizations in terms of purposes, functions, attitude of their constituent members towards managerial innovations, nature of the organization, and size (Bauer 2007). According to the first criterion:

- The European Union can be considered a multiple purpose organization, carrying out regulatory and operational functions, mostly traditional, of supranational character and medium-big size;
- The OECD is a single purpose organization, carrying out research and policy advice functions mostly traditional, with intergovernmental character and of medium size.

The second criterion concerns the intensity of the management reforms carried out in the international organizations administrations through formal reform programs in recent times. According to this criterion, the selected international organizations launched the following major management reform programs aiming to modernize their administrative structure:

- The European Union, and specifically its executive body the European Commission, carried out the following main reforms programs:
  - in 1995, the Efficient Management initiative (SEM)[2] aimed to modernize and improve finance and resource management systems and increasing coordination between financial controllers in member states and the European institutions for EU the spending programs;
  - in 1997, the Modernization of Administration and Personnel Policy (MAP 2000) aiming at decentralization and simplification of many of the procedures linked to the management and organization of personnel;
  - in 2000, the Kinnock Reform (European Commission 2000), addressing the following areas, strategic planning, human resources development, financial management, openness, and transparency.
- The Organization for Economic and Cooperation Development carried out the following reform projects:
  - in 1997, the "*Challenges and Strategic Objectives; 1997*" (OECD 1997) aiming to improve the internal working methods, streamlining the work of Committees, reforming budgetary process and management systems as well as putting a greater focus on results;
  - in 2003 the "*Reform and Modernization of the OECD (2003)*" (OECD 2003) focused on structure consolidation, simplification, and rationalization initiatives.

In addition to such main reform programs, less extensive and more recent reform initiatives have also been included in the case study analysis.

The third criterion concerns the role of international organizations as agents for the diffusion of good practices in the management of public services among national administrations. Those played an important role as promoters of modernization standards should be those more incentivized by using the management practices they promoted in their administrative structures.

According to these criteria, both the OECD and the European Union are widely recognized actors, largely contributed to the process of international diffusion of good management practices through communication and networking activities (Bouckaert and Halligan 2011; Balint and Knill 2007).

3.2.2   The Operational Framework of Analysis

To operationalize our main dependent variable, the contents of management reforms in the selected international organizations, we need to embed the conceptual framework linking the formal reform programs to the level of implementation to a more operational framework for classifying the implemented changes. To build such a framework, we rely on Pollitt and Bouckaert's work (2004, 2017) on public management reforms. They identified four main sectors of a reform program (*management sector*), finance, personnel, organization structure, and performance as well as several elements (*management elements*) within each sector. The sectors and the elements for each sector are outlined below.

1. (*Management sector*)
   (a) the Finance sector
      • (*Management elements*)
         – Budgeting
         – Accounting
         – Auditing
2. (*Management sector*)
   (a) the Personnel policy
      • (*Management elements*)
         – Recruitment
         – Contract policy
         – Promotion and Appraisal
3. (*Management sector*)
   (a) the Organization structure
      • (*Management elements*)
         – Specialization
         – Decentralization of functions
         – Coordination
4. (*Management sector*)
   (a) Performance focus
      • (*Management elements*)
         – Extension of the performance measurement system (span and depth)

Table 3.1 The operational framework for assessing the reform contents

| | *Ideal paradigms* | | | | | |
	Traditional	*NWS*	*NPM*	*NPG*	*EU*	*OECD*
Sectors/ elements	*Management sectors*					
Management elements	(indicator)	(indicator)	(indicator)	(indicator)	(ideal paradigm)	(ideal paradigm)

Based on such framework, by the analysis of the main reform programs implemented in the selected international organizations, we evaluate for each observed change in one of the management area/element, whether it corresponds to an element of the main ideal type models identified (NPM, NWS, NPG). All the observed changes will be classified according to the following table to facilitate the comparative analysis (Table 3.1).

Nevertheless, the content and characteristics of the high-level paradigms are far from being coherent and homogenously shared among the research community (Schedler and Proeller 2007). Thus, the core concepts of each ideal paradigm of reform will be examined to find the common elements for each indicator related to the different management areas and elements. Following this, based on our conceptual model, we will proceed with the descriptive analysis of the main formal changes observed (1)[3] in the different management areas and elements of our case study to explain their degree of implementation (2), resulting from available research studies, or independent evaluation reports. Finally, each observed change will be compared to the indicators associated with the ideal paradigms, as in the example below:

- (observed change) the introduction of the accrual accounting system

The observed change will be compared to the indicators set to reflect the characteristics of the management area/element in each ideal reform paradigms:

- (management area) Finance
  - (management element) accounting system:

(indicator) use of a cash-based system (traditional model)
(indicator) use of a full cash-based or combination of cash/
accrual (NWS)
(indicator) use of an accrual accounting system (NPM)
(indicator) use of an outcome-based system (NPG)

As outlined above, such operation cannot be done mechanically, as in reality, any observed change could have different degrees of compliance respect to the core element of the ideal types, as well as different degrees of implementation, potentially altering the results of the analysis. Nevertheless, to face such potential shortcomings, the following measure will be taken:

- to take into account the different *degrees of formal compliance* of each management element to the indicator set, in case of partial correspondence, we will classify the management elements as "*towards the ideal model X.*" Contrary in case of substantial adherence, this latter will be classified as compliant "*to the ideal model X;*"
- to assess the *degree of implementation*, we will rely, where possible, on evaluation and assessment studies or technical reports elaborated by third parties.

3.2.3   *The Documental Sources*

The case study analysis has been conducted through empirical investigation that is based on several selected primary and secondary literature sources. Although full details can be found in the bibliography section, below the most important are briefly reported:

1. Primary sources concern official and unofficial documents and reports directly elaborated by the selected international organizations related to the management reforms implemented, including internal working papers, reform statements, budget plans, strategic plans, financial and personnel regulations, technical handbooks on the new management instruments, and so forth. The availability of these documents varies across organizations, although most of the documents consulted are open to the public or have become unclassified.

2. Secondary literature: This category includes books, papers, reports, and external evaluation studies related to the management reform of our case study, which supported the evaluation of the observed change, as well as provided valuable elements, in case primary sources were missing. Nevertheless, the scientific knowledge of the management reforms in international organizations is somewhat limited (Bauer 2007; Balint and Knill 2007). Resources and publications on the topic are not abundant, with probably one exception, the European Commission (Bauer 2002; Bearfield 2004; Coull and Lewis, 2003; Cram 2001; Kassim 2008; Levy 2002, 2003a, b; Metcalfe 2000; Spence 2000; Spence and Stevens 2006; Stevens and Stevens 2006; Nugent and Rhinard 2015; Wille 2013). Compared to the European Commission, the OECD Secretariat received little scholar attention, being a much-cited but little-studied institution, and its role in international governance is poorly understood (Mahon and McBride 2009). Nevertheless, recently, different books have been published partially dealing with its internal functioning (Mahon and McBride 2009; Woodward 2009; Carroll and Kellow 2011).

Notes

1. The core concepts of the main big reform models will be discussed in Chap. 5.
2. The reform elements introduced by SEM initiative was assessed through the analysis of secondary sources (Schön-Quinlivan 2007; Spence 2006).
3. The (1) refers to the "three modes of reality" model described in Table 3.1.

References

Balint, Tim, and Christoph Knill. "The limits of legitimacy pressure as a source of organizational change: The reform of human resource management in the OECD." University of Konstanz. Department of Politics and Management. Chair of Comparative Public Policy and Administration. Working Paper n. 1. (2007): 117–131.

Bauer, Michael W. "The EU 'partnership principle': still a sustainable governance device across multiple administrative arenas?." *Public Administration* 80, no. 4 (2002): 769–789.

———. "Introduction: Management Reform in International Organizations." In *Management Reforms in International Organizations*, eds. Bauer M., Knill C., Nomos, 2007.

Bearfield, Nicholas David. "Reforming the European Commission: driving reform from the grassroots." *Public Policy and Administration* 19, no. 3 (2004): 13–24.

Bouckaert, Geert, and John Halligan. "Managing performance across levels of government: lessons learned or reproducing disconnects?." *Policy, Performance and Management in Governance and Intergovernmental Relations* (2011): 236–254.

Geert Bouckaert, and Halligan, J.. "Managing Performance: International Comparisons." (2008).

Carroll, Peter, and Aynsley Kellow. *The OECD: A study of organisational adaptation*. Edward Elgar Publishing, 2011.

Coull, Janet, and Charlie Lewis. "The impact reform of the staff regulations in making the Commission a more modern and efficient organisation: an insider's perspective." *EPIAScope* 2003, no. 3 (2003): 2–9.

Cram, Laura. "Whither the Commission? Reform, renewal and the issue-attention cycle." *Journal of European Public Policy* 8, no. 5 (2001): 770–786.

European Commission. *White Paper "Reforming the European Commission"*. 2000.

Kassim, Hussein. "'Mission impossible', but mission accomplished: the Kinnock reforms and the European Commission." *Journal of European Public Policy* 15, no. 5 (2008): 648–668.

Kettl, Donald F. *The global public management revolution: A report on the transformation of governance*. Brookings Institution Press, 2006.

Levy, Roger. "Modernising EU programme management." *Public Policy and Administration* 17, no. 1 (2002): 72–89.

———. "Confused expectations: Decentralizing the management of EU programmes." *Public Money & Management* 23, no. 2 (2003a): 83–92.

———. "Critical success factors in public management reform: the case of the European Commission." *International Review of Administrative Sciences* 69, no. 4 (2003b): 553–566.

Lynn, L., 2008. What is a Neo-Weberian State? Reflections on a concept and its implications. *NISPAcee Journal of Public Administration and Policy*, 1(2), pp. 17–30.

Mahon, Rianne, and Stephen McBride. "Standardizing and disseminating knowledge: The role of the OECD in global governance." *European political science review* 1, no. 1 (2009): 83–101.

Metcalfe, Les. "Reforming the Commission: will organizational efficiency produce effective governance?." *JCMS: Journal of Common Market Studies* 38, no. 5 (2000): 817–841.

Nugent, Neill, and Mark Rhinard. *The European Commission*. Macmillan International Higher Education, 2015.

OECD. *The OECD: Challenges and Strategic Objectives 1997. Note by the Secretary General.* 1997.

———. *Reform and Modernisation of the OECD. HOD (2003)3.* 2003.

Ongaro, Edoardo. *Public management reform and modernization: Trajectories of administrative change in Italy,* France, Greece, Portugal and Spain. Edward Elgar Publishing, 2009.

Pollitt, Christopher, and Geert Bouckaert. *Public management reform: A comparative analysis.* Oxford University Press, USA, 2004.

———. *Public management reform: A comparative analysis-into the age of austerity.* Oxford University Press, 2017.

Schedler, Kuno, and Isabella Proeller, eds. *Cultural aspects of public management reform.* Emerald Group Publishing Limited, 2007.

Schön-Quinlivan, Emmanuelle. "Administrative reform in the European Commission: from rhetoric to relegitimization." In *Management Reforms in International Organizations,* pp. 25–37. Nomos Verlagsgesellschaft mbH & Co. KG, 2007.

Spence, David. "Plus ca change, plus c'est la meme chose? Attempting to reform the European Commission." *Journal of European Public Policy* 7, no. 1 (2000): 1–25.

Spence, David. "15. The Commission's External Service." *The European Commission* (2006): 396.

Spence, David, and Anne Stevens. "Staff and personnel policy in the Commission." *The European Commission* 3 (2006): 173–208.

Stevens, Anne and H. Stevens. "*The internal reform of the European Commission*", in The European Commission, ed. Spence D., John Harper Publishing, London. 2006.

Weber, Max, and Johannes Winckelmann. *Methodologische Schriften/ Studienausgabe, mit einer Einführung besorgt von Johannes Winckelmann.* S. Fischer, 1968.

Wille, Anchrit. *The normalization of the European Commission: Politics and bureaucracy in the EU executive.* OUP Oxford, 2013.

Woodward, Richard. *The organisation for economic co-operation and development* (OECD). Routledge, 2009.

Yin Robert. "Design and methods." *Case study research* 3 (2003).

CHAPTER 4

Legitimacy and Other Reform Drivers

Abstract The increasing relevance of international organizations poses two serious issues linked to their democracy and legitimacy. While input legitimacy has received much consideration, less attention has been devoted to the concept of output legitimacy. Following this perspective, the legitimacy of a political system depends on its capacity to achieve the citizens' goals and solve their problems effectively and efficiently. The extent to which the actions taken by international organizations are legitimized depends on the results of such actions.

Keywords The international organizations in need of legitimacy • Input and output legitimacy

4.1 THE NEW INTERNATIONAL ORGANIZATIONS IN NEED OF LEGITIMACY

The creation of international organizations started right after the Second World War, when national states recognized their interdependence in achieving their political objectives. The setting up of the first international economic institutions, as the General Agreement for Trade and Tariffs (GATT), enabled the states to take advantage of their economic interdependence by opening up borders and enjoying free trade. At the same

© The Author(s) 2020   55
M. Amici, D. Cepiku, *Performance Management in International Organizations*, https://doi.org/10.1007/978-3-030-39472-1_4

time, the states rest firmly embedded within the context of their national political system, able to absorb market inefficiencies (Zürn 2004). This situation resulted in 30 years of stable growth, characterized by the integration of world economies, the prevention of spiralling of protectionism as well as stability and peace among democratic welfare states (Zürn 2004). This success period, defined by Zürn (2004) "embedded liberalism," started to be challenged by its own. The expanding liberalization, accompanied by technological progress, accelerated the globalization process, which started to challenge the capacity of national welfare policies to bring about the desired effects, especially in those areas where the boundaries of transactions enlarged. This, coupled with the rapid increase in direct investments, new and highly sensitive financial markets and new security threats triggered the establishment of "new international organizations" as defined by Zürn (2004: 9). While traditional international organizations were primarily focused on economic issues, the new ones deal with all policy areas, are wider in scope and penetrate deeply into the national systems (Zürn 2004). According to this vision in the *traditional* international organizations (Zürn 2004: 10):

- states were the ultimate and exclusive recipients of regulations;
- such regulations were merely concerned with good transit at the border of states;
- resulting in a high degree of certainty of the effect of such regulations.

Differently, in the *new* international organizations, in the age of globalization (Zürn 2004: 11):

- the ultimate recipients of regulations are societal actors, as consumers and business entrepreneurs;
- regulations affect national borders;
- the new international organizations deal with finding the solution to complex problems whose effects are uncertain.

In this new framework, the new international organizations need to increase and extend their functions and tasks, requiring a higher degree of "supranational and transnational institutional features" (Zürn 2004: 12). On a similar vein, Reinalda and Verbeek (2004) acknowledged the increased relevance of international organizations, according to the following factors. First, the end of the Cold War decreased the competition among the superpowers and allowed for the creation of many international organizations whose status was frozen since the late 1940s. Secondly, the globalization process acted as an incentive for states and other actors to use international organizations to face the increasing number of interdependencies and common global threats. Thirdly, the globalization process also reinforced the role of non-state actors to become active in the international arena by approaching international organizations. Finally, the growth of the legalization of international relations prevented states from ignoring the policies of the relevant international organizations as the European Union (EU), the European Court of Human Rights (ECHR), and the World Trade Organizations (WTO) (Reinalda and Verbeek 2004). Consequently, the new international organizations are much more numerous and intrusive in the citizen's life than the traditional ones, and "the more intrusive these international organizations become, the more justified and intense the demands will be for their democratizations" (Zürn 2004: 29). In fact, as much as international organizations get involved in the exercise of public authority by affecting regulations on the domestic level, as much that authority must be legitimized. This need "grows proportionally to the degree in which international organizations substitute nation-states in their regulative and administrative functions" (Zwanenburg 2005: 61). The international organizations, in fact, now address issues that were previously decided at the national level, and their decisions are increasingly affecting people within states (Woods and Narlikar 2001). In other words, the globalization process transferred the decisions making authority from national governments to international organizations. Consequently, the decision-making at the international level should be accompanied by a democratic process equivalent to these taking place at the nation-state level. Therefore, as much as international decision-making substitute decision making at the national level, as much international organizations are in need to justify their authority in the exercise of power (Mehde 2007). As far as the legitimacy of the decisions taken by international organizations is concerned, the latter has two different aspects, the character, voluntary or binding, and the content (Mehde 2007). The increased binding character of the decisions taken by the international organizations as well as the extended span and scope of their content impact on individuals, firms, or states, thus putting pressure on the justification of their power. The increasing role of international organizations from one side, and the alleged lack of legitimacy from the other, already triggered large-scale tensions (Stutzer and Frey 2005). The protests mainly targeted those international organizations involved in the above-mentioned transformative process, such as the International Monetary Fund (IMF), the World Trade Organization (WTO), the World Bank, and to a lesser extent also the United Nations and the European Union (Stutzer and Frey 2005). Often such international organizations are perceived as undemocratic, favoring "unjust" solutions as well as mostly inefficient, resource waste, and ineffective, as not being able to transform policies into actions (Stutzer and Frey 2005). There are several reasons for this. Although often the media are much more interested in the demonstrations and demonstrators rather than the issues at stake in the international meetings (Stutzer and Frey 2005), democracy and legitimacy concerns seem related to the perception of how efficient and effective an international organization is acting.

4.2   THE DIFFERENT WAYS TO GENERATE LEGITIMACY: INPUT AND OUTPUT LEGITIMACY

The debate over the legitimacy of international organizations is a very complex topic, around which lawyers, political scientists and moral philosophers were confronted for a long time to find answers to the following questions: Are international organizations legitimate? What gives international organizations the right to exercise power? From where they receive their legitimacy? (Schneller 2010). The search for a comprehensive answer triggered an extensive debate among the different epistemic communities of scholars (Zürn 2004; Scharpf 2004; Beetham 1991; Schneller 2010) on the use of different theories and approaches that would be impossible to analytically reconciling here. For our purposes, it would be enough to focus on the most common approaches dealing with the legitimacy of international organizations. The first distinction found is between the normative and the empirical (or descriptive) approach to legitimacy (Beetham 1991). A normative approach is related to the validity of a political order (its elements and rules) in an objective sense (Schneller 2010), while the second one is related to the acceptance of a decision—and the process leading to this—can generate (Zürn 2004). Scharpf (2004) and Weiler (1991) elaborated a similar but more interesting distinction. These latter distinguished between input, social, and output legitimacy. Input legitimacy looks at the way the will of people is represented in decisions taken by the organizations (Mehde 2007). This kind of legitimacy is linked with the formal ties between the electorate and the decision-making system of the organizations. It is concerned with the way the people elect their representatives and how these latter represent them in the context of the international organizations (Mehde 2007). According to Dahl (1989), input legitimacy requires that the following five criteria must be fulfilled: the effective participation of the citizens; voting equality at the decisive stage; an enlightened understanding of the matters to be decided; the citizens' control over the agenda; and the inclusion of all adults subject to the binding collective decisions of the association. Based on the individualism theory, the input legitimacy principle assumes that only the "government by the people" will ensure "government for the people" (Dahl 1989). In other words, only the effective participation of all individuals is the ultimate reference point for the legitimacy of political order (Dahl 1989). In the context of international organizations, increasing input legitimacy would require a more active participation of the citizens in their decision-making process. Stutzer and Frey (2005) proposed, for example, that all citizens of all member states joining an international organization should have the potential possibility to participate in decision making by a random selection. Citizen participation should then take the form of popular initiatives or referendum held in all participating countries for a restricted and casually selected number of citizens (Stutzer and Frey 2005). Despite different attempts, the direct involvement of citizens in the decision-making process of international organizations remains problematic (*see infra*).

Together with input legitimacy, social legitimacy (Weiler 1991) share a similar focus on people but includes those backings which consider the legitimacy of different forms of democratic rule to be dependent in one way or another on the social context in which a political system operates (Schimmelfennig 1996). According to the social legitimacy approach, individuals are not atomistic constituents of society (Schimmelfennig 1996).

These latter are born and socialized into communities from which they acquire their values and normative orientations, developing a collective identity and a sense of belonging (Schimmelfennig 1996). Consequently, democracy is not a form of rule that can be established by whatever association of individuals but only by social groups. It follows that the political order at the level of international organizations must protect the communities (by consensual decision-making) to which the collective identities of the individuals are oriented (Schimmelfennig 1996). Nevertheless, from a practical point of view, input and social legitimacy appear to lack the desirable substance when applied to international organizations, triggering the complex debate over their democratic deficit. Both approaches suggest that the only way to increase legitimacy would be the direct involvement and participation of individuals or groups in the decision-making system (Mehde 2007). This happens through the act of voting, which produces little or no chance of influence the decisions even at the national level (Mehde 2007). As argued by Woods and Narlikar (2001), in fact, accountability and involvement in the decision-making system is tough to achieve through voting as citizens rarely use their votes to sanction officials. They rather use the elections to express their loyalty or favor for a future set of policies. Stokes et al. (1999) also add that voters face relevant problems of information, monitoring, and commitment. At the international level, the situation is worse. There are no direct elections in the context of international organizations[1] and the link between the electorate at the national level and the international decision-making is weak. Contrary, Woods and Narlikar (2001) affirm that the elections are not an effective form of accountability, suggesting for international organizations other most relevant mechanisms of accountability as, for example, strengthening the "horizontal accountability" by increasing transparency, evaluation and monitoring of their activities. In any case, although elections, from a formal point of view, can be considered necessary, they are not a sufficient means for guaranteeing democracy (Mehde 2007). The concept of democracy in the context of international organizations is another highly controversial topic. From one-side gradualists scholars believe that democracy beyond nation-states implies a quasi—identical normative structure at the international level (Bohman 2005). Therefore, the existence of a demos, the idea of citizens and the popular consent are both crucial conditions for the democratic legitimacy at the supranational level. The absence of such elements beyond the nation-states denies such possibility and consequently, international organizations cannot be democratized (Dahl 1999).

On the other side, the transformationalists believe that the concept of democracy implies a transformation beyond the nation-states. For them, the main question is not how to promote democracy as it is now at the national level, but to establish a different type of democracy (Bohman 2010). According to this conception, democracy on a transnational level needs "a transition from a singular to a plural subject, from *demos* to *demoi*" (Bohman 2010: 21). Consequently, an essential element for international organizations to be democratic in this sense is the presence of equal capacities of the different *demoi* to influence and "contest arbitrary exercises of power of international organizations over them" (Bohman 2005: 21). In sum, input legitimacy is mainly focused on the way decisions are made, and according to Scharpf (2004), input legitimacy can only be achieved by the "pre-existence collective identity" with the belief in our "essential sameness." Consequently, the absence of a transnational political community is incongruent with the existence of transnational social spaces (Zürn 2004). Overcoming such incongruence appears particularly difficult. By contrast, output legitimacy focuses on the positive results that any state or administrative entity brings about. According to Scharpf (2004), the output legitimacy is linked with the effective results produced by the respective organization. It does not require a pre-existent collective identity, but only "the perception of a range of common interest that is sufficiently broad and stable to justify international arrangements for collective action" (Scharpf 2004: 12). Consequently, the legitimacy of a political system depends on its capacity to achieve the citizens' goals and solve their problems effectively and efficiently (Schimmelfennig 1996). The higher this capacity, the more legitimate the system (Schimmelfennig 1996). In other words, the degree to which actions taken by international organizations are legitimized depends on the results of such actions. Output legitimacy highlights democracy as "government for the people" in contrast with the input legitimacy perspective of "governing by the people" outlined above. Differently, this approach is not concerned with the structure of the democratic process but on its capacity to deliver the results. It is democratic insofar as the output is in the interest of the citizens. Dahl and Tufte (1973: 135) define "system capacity" as the capacity of a polity "to respond fully to the collective preferences of its citizens." On a similar vein, Buchanan and Keohane (2006: 422) stress "how the justification for having global governance institutions is primarily if not exclusively instrumental: we value them because of the benefits they bring, rather than regarding them as intrinsically valuable." Consequently, "if an institution exhibits a pattern of egregious disparity between its actual performance, on the one hand, and its self-proclaimed procedures or major goals, on the other, its legitimacy is seriously called into question" (Buchanan and Keohane 2006: 422). According to this approach, legitimacy is invariably linked to performance, and improvements in performance lead to an increased legitimacy of the organization as such (Mehde 2007). As stressed by Gutner and Thompson (2010: 228), "for most of the international organizations, performance is the path to legitimacy and our ability to understand performance [...] is crucial". Nevertheless, such perspective poses several practical difficulties and includes ambiguous elements to deal with (Mehde 2007). The difficulty in measuring the results of international organizations as long as there is no direct contacts with citizens or the fact that acceptance refers only to a group of people smaller than the entire population affected are just the most relevant (Mehde 2007). Agreeing on what is considered an effective and accepted output for an international organization could be a quite complex issue. For example, considering the different output legitimacy conceptions developed by Moravcsik (2004), those attached to the libertarian approach will consider a government legitimate if it provides an effective protection of individual liberties against "potentially arbitrary, corrupt and tyrannical power" (Moravcsik, 2004: 339). By contrast, those favoring the social democratic model will consider legitimate an organization bringing about equality and social justice (Moravcsik 2004). On a different level, measuring the results of different organizations imply the adoption of distinct and specific criteria difficult to generalize in analytical terms. But as noted by Gutner and Thompson (2010: 229), in times were international organizations are confronted with new and relevant challenges posed by the globalization process and need to reform, "it is critical that scholars do more than sit passively on the sidelines." Therefore, although such difficulties, the output legitimacy perspective can be a crucial leverage to shift the debate on the alleged democratic deficit of international organizations, from the traditional legalistic and political approach to the management side of international organizations. The output legitimacy perspective is of significant interest as it correlates the performance of international organizations to their legitimacy. From one side, a good performance could reduce the gap between the increased powers acquired by international organizations and the perceived lack of legitimacy, but, on the other side, inadequate performance could question their legitimacy and credibility.

4.3   INTERNATIONAL ORGANIZATIONS AS PRODUCERS OF GLOBAL PUBLIC GOODS

From a management perspective, international organizations, as public, no-profit, and private entities, are considered organizations created to achieve specific objectives, laid down in their founding treaties. They will be achieved by transforming, through processes, the available resources (inputs), mainly provided by the member states, in products or services (outputs), which affect the external environment and produce outcomes (Pollitt and Bouckaert 2004). Thus, the performance of an organization is typically influenced by the way resources are organized, processes for the delivery of products and services (outputs) carried out, as well as how the outputs realized will impact on the organizational environment (outcome). The concept of performance includes contemporaneously the results achieved by an organization, the process carried out for the achievement of such results as well as the different dimensions against which the results achieved are measured. Therefore, each organization requires the following two elements for monitoring and improving performance. First, a constant commitment to modernize their management structures to increase the work efficiency and effectiveness of the different organizational units/functions responsible for services and product delivery. Second, the set-up of a performance management system able to measure the results achieved respect to the ex-ante objectives set, as well as supporting the organization to manage performance information for taking strategic decisions and learning from past results (Pollitt and Bouckaert 2017).

Especially in the public sector, the elements mentioned above are often interrelated, as most of the management reform initiatives implemented in public sector organizations aimed at modernizing their internal administrative structures by introducing performance elements. Reforming the public sector organizations attracted considerable attention over the last 30 years, either by academicians than by politicians and professionals. According to Pollitt and Bouckaert (2017: 31), a "huge amount of public management reforms" mushroomed in many countries' administrations together with comparative studies and analysis (Pollitt and Bouckaert 2004, 2017; Christensen and Lægreid 2001; Ongaro 2009; Verschuere and Barbieri 2009). By contrast, the internal management of international organizations attracted very limited attention and was hardly subject to comprehensive investigations (Balint and Knill 2007). As outlined in the second chapter, the majority of studies and research related to international organizations mainly focused on investigating their role played in the international decision-making context. Until very recently, international organizations were often considered as mere platforms or devices in the hands of the member states governments used for transnational decision-making. They were not perceived as administrative bodies and the research focus was mainly on the political structures (Mehde 2007). In such context, linking management reforms of international organizations to an increase in performance and consequently in organizational legitimacy, was "consistently neglected in the analytical framework of global governance and its alleged democratic deficit" (Mehde 2007: 168). In other words, if administrations as such are not a topic in this context, their reform is even less" (Mehde 2007: 168). Despite this, reforming international organizations should be now a primary concern, considering their recent spectacular growth, in the number, size, and competences, as well as their increasing intrusiveness in the national sphere of member states (Zürn 2004). This rising influence in the lives of many people around the world, in turn, also brings legitimacy problems, which, according to the output legitimacy perspective, could be addressed by enhancing performance. Nevertheless, international organizations also face deep management problems and are generally perceived as inefficient and ineffective in translating ideas and goals into fruitful actions (Dijkzeul and Beigbeder 2003). They suffer about the absence of effective management models and capacities, often leading to the inefficient use of financial resources, have relevant problems of coordination, produce excessive bureaucracy, which in turn results in slow action and failure to fulfill their mandate (Dijkzeul and Beigbeder 2003). Dijkzeul and Beigbeder (2003) define such management problems as pathologies, which, unless correctly addressed, will only worsen in the years to come undermining the globalization progress (Boughton and Bradford 2007). In this scenario, it could be surprising to note that the most active supporters of the modernization in the public sector are important international organizations,[2] which favored with their activism the diffusion of new managerial ideas among public organizations (Hood 1995). As observed by Wright (1997: 8), although public sector reforms are significantly "brought about by the activities of international officials," their "zeal for administrative reforms mysteriously stops short at the door of their organizations." On the same line, Glöckler (2007) stressed how international organizations, while urging member states to carry out structural reforms to use public finances soundly, cannot allow inefficiencies to persist in their organizations. Finally, Balint and Knill (2007: 17) noted how ironic the OECD in 2005, published a report on modernizing public sector employment, to push public sector reforms while "keeping rather old-fashioned structures at home." International organizations, share with national administration many similarities. They exist to satisfy collective needs, to carry out a multifaceted mix of activities, to make use of public money, employ public staff as well as are affected by political short-termism (Yi-Chong and Weller 2008). In other words, while national governments deal with the production of public goods, as much as this latter trespassing the national borders becoming global, the role of producer moves to international organizations (Kaul et al. 1999). Consequently, national governments are progressively confronted with the production of global public goods. They are characterized by strong qualities of publicness, including non-rivalry in consumption and non-excludability, as well as by producing quasi-universal benefits in terms of countries, people, and generations, the state alone are not able to produce (Kaul et al. 1999). The list of global public goods is rapidly growing. It includes, among others, banking crises, internet-based crime and fraud, increased risks of ill-health, practices as drug abuse and smoking, international transport and communication, trade, harmonized taxation, monetary policy, governance, and so forth (Kaul et al. 1999). Examples of international organizations addressing global public goods are copious. The United Nations High Commission for Refugees and the World Health Organization deal with preventing the spread of diseases and providing shelters for refugees, the North Atlantic Treaty Organizations and the United Nations aim at administering and monitoring the peace agreements in different parts of the world. These latter cannot be settled at the domestic level and are now subject to international scrutiny and coordination (Kaul et al. 1999). In doing this, international organizations use largely public money and consequently act according to the principles of transparency, fairness, equity, neutrality, and accountability. Although softened by the relative distance between international organizations and the citizens, such principles are recalled in their founding treaties and guiding principles. They also suffer from legitimacy and trusting problems, as outlined above. Furthermore, the role and functions of international civil servants are very much similar to those of the public officials sitting in national administrations. While holding the nationality of a constituent member state, international civil servants are employed by the international organization, to serve a permanent machinery with a coordinating function and a specific set of values as well as representing collective interests rather than individual states' interest (Yi-Chong and Weller 2008). At the same time, international organizations also enjoy differences from public sector organizations. They are multinational, differ in terms of memberships, have complex structures, as well as exchange in direct contact with citizens. Essential aspects as participation, representation, responsiveness, communication, party-ideological cleavages appeared less pronounced in the international context (Stutzer and Frey 2005). Consequently, as stressed by Bauer (2007: 15), international organizations "are meant to be stable entities, isolated from daily politics of their constituencies and provided with high degree of organizational autonomy as regards the running of their internal affairs." In this context, is much more likely that international organizations refrain from massive internal management changes instead of "increasing reform efforts." (Bauer 2007: 15). This latter could partially explain the reluctance and the delays of the international organizations to modernize their internal structures, as well as the disinterest in a systematic understanding of the specific factors and conditions influencing management reforms in international organizations.

Given that, the need for a further and systematic research in this field is recently increased due to the following reasons:

- the emerging importance of international organizations as relevant and autonomous actors in need of (output) legitimacy. In this context, their internal administrative and management structures are increasingly the target of performance improvements;
- the evidence that many international organizations have recently started modernizing their internal management structures to be more effective and more efficient (Bauer 2007). As also stressed by Baumann et al. (2007: 175), "the trends towards modernization and reform also affect international organizations of which many experienced more or less far-reaching change."

Accordingly, the knowledge of the specific factors influencing management reforms in international organizations should increase. As argued by Bauer (2007), although the interest in public management reforms remained mainly confined to the national level, the differences mentioned above do not prevent us from applying research strategies and hypotheses developed for the public sector, to international organizations (Bauer

2007). Even more, he points out how such differences are "promising theoretical avenues" concerning testing the formulated hypotheses, and studying reforms in international organizations should help to draw a more comprehensive understanding of administrative changes either in public or in international organizations (Bauer 2007: 23). Consequently, the following chapters will aim to deepen our investigation on the specific elements affecting the management reforms in international organizations through studies and research frameworks mainly developed for the public sector organizations.

NOTES

1. Except in the case of the European Union. Since 1979, the citizens of the member states directly elect their representatives to the European Parliament.
2. They include the Organization for Economic and Cooperation Development (OECD), the International Monetary Fund (IMF) and the World Bank WB).

REFERENCES

Balint, Tim, and Christoph Knill. "The limits of legitimacy pressure as a source of organizational change: The reform of human resource management in the OECD." University of Konstanz. Department of Politics and Management. Chair of Comparative Public Policy and Administration. Working Paper n. 1. (2007).

Bauer, Michael W. "Introduction: Management Reform in International Organizations." In *Management Reforms in International Organizations*, eds. Bauer M., Knill C., Nomos, 2007.

Baumann, Soo Mee, Markus Hagel, and Barbara Kobler. "Management in Change-The Reform Broker Concept." In *Management Reforms in International Organizations*, pp. 175–191. Nomos Verlagsgesellschaft mbH & Co. KG, 2007.

Beetham, David. *The Legitimacy of Power.* London: Macmillan Education Ltd, 1991.

Bohman, James. "From demos to demoi: Democracy across borders." *Ratio Juris* 18, no. 3 (2005): 293–314.

———. *Democracy across borders: from Démos to Démoi.* Mit Press, 2010.

Boughton, James M., and Colin I. Bradford Jr. "GLOBAL GOVERNANCE: WHO'S IN CHARGE? Global Governance: New Players, New Rules-Why the 20th-century model needs a makeover." *Finance & Development* 44, no. 4 (2007): 10.

Buchanan, Allen, and Robert O. Keohane. "The legitimacy of global governance institutions." *Ethics & international affairs* 20, no. 4 (2006): 405–437

Christensen, Tom, and Per Lægreid. "New Public Management: The effects of contractualism and devolution on political control." *Public Management Review* 3, no. 1 (2001): 73–94.

Dahl, Robert Alan. *Democracy and its Critics.* Yale University Press, 1989.

Dahl, Robert A., "Can International Organizations Be Democratic? A Skeptic's View", in Ian Shapiro and Casiano Hacker-Cordon (eds), Democracy's Edges, Cambridge: Cambridge University Press, 1999.

Dahl, Robert Alan, and Edward R. Tufte. *Size and democracy.* Vol. 2. Stanford University Press, 1973.

Dijkzeul, Dennis, and Yves Beigbeder. "Introduction. Rethinking International Organizations." *Dijkzeul, Dennis/Beigbeder,* Yves (2003): 1–26.

Glöckler, Gabriel. "From Take-off to Cruising Altitude: Management Reform and Organizational Change of the European Central Bank." In *Management Reforms in International Organizations,* pp. 85–96. Nomos Verlagsgesellschaft mbH & Co. KG, 2007

Gutner, Tamar, and Alexander Thompson. "The politics of IO performance: A framework." The review of international organizations 5, no. 3 (2010): 227–248.

Hood, Christopher. "The "new public management" in the 1980: Variations on a theme." *Accounting, organizations and society* 20, no. 2–3 (1995): 93–109.

Kaul, Inge, Isabelle Grunberg, and Marc A. Stern. "Defining global public goods." *Global public goods: international cooperation in the 21st century* (1999): 2–19.

Mehde, Veith. "Creating a missing link? administrative reforms as a means of improving the legitimacy of international organizations." In *Management reforms in international organizations,* pp. 163–175. Nomos Verlagsgesellschaft mbH & Co. KG, 2007.

Moravcsik, Andrew. "Is there a 'democratic deficit' in world politics? A framework for analysis." *Government and opposition* 39, no. 2 (2004): 336–363.

Ongaro, Edoardo. *Public management reform and modernization: Trajectories of administrative change in Italy, France, Greece, Portugal and Spain.* Edward Elgar Publishing, 2009.

Pollitt, Christopher, and Geert Bouckaert. *Public management reform: A comparative analysis.* Oxford University Press, USA, 2004.

———. *Public management reform: A comparative analysis-into the age of austerity.* Oxford University Press, 2017.

Reinalda, Bob, and Bertjan Verbeek, eds. *Decision making within international organizations.* Vol. 31. Routledge, 2004.

Scharpf, Fritz. W. *Legitimationskonzepte jenseits de Nationalstaats,* Discussion Paper 04/6, Koln, Max Planck Institute for Study of Societies, 2004.

Schimmelfennig, Frank. *Legitimate rule in the European Union.* Center for German and European Studies, University of California at Berkeley, 1996.

Schneller, Lena. "Conceptions of Democratic Legitimate Governance in the Multilateral Realm: The Case of the WTO." *Living Reviews in Democracy* 2 (2010).

Stokes, Susan C., José María Maravall, James A. Stimson, and Jon Elster. *Democracy, accountability, and representation.* 1999.

Stutzer, Alois, and Bruno S. Frey. "Making international organizations more democratic." *Review of law & economics* 1, no. 3 (2005): 305–330.

Verschuere, Bram, and Dario Barbieri. "Investigating the 'NPM-ness' of agencies in Italy and Flanders: the effect of place, age and task." *Public Management Review* 11, no. 3 (2009): 345–373.

Weiler, Joseph HH. "Problems of legitimacy in post 1992 Europe." Aussenwirtschaft 46, no. 3 (1991): 4.

Woods, Ngaire, and Amrita Narlikar. "Governance and the Limits of Accountability: The WTO, the IMF, and the World Bank." *International Social Science Journal* 53, no. 170 (2001): 569–583.

Wright, Vincent. "The Paradoxes of Administrative Reform∗. Teoksessa Public Management and Administrative Reform in Western Europe. Toim. Kickert, JM Walter." (1997): 7–13.

Yi-Chong, Xu, and Patrick Weller. "'To Be, But not to Be Seen': Exploring the Impact of International Civil Servants." *Public Administration* 86, no. 1 (2008): 35–51

Zürn, Michael. "Global governance and legitimacy problems." *Government and Opposition* 39, no. 2 (2004): 260–287.

Zwanenburg, Marten Coenraad. *Accountability of peace support operations.* Vol. 9. Martinus Nijhoff Publishers, 2005.

CHAPTER 5

Management Reforms and International Organizations

Abstract The chapter will focus on how international organizations can improve the results of their actions discussing the possible trajectories of management reforms and how they lead to performance improvements. The management reform content analysis will be grounded on the high-level reform models elaborated in literature to classify the content and the directions of the observed changes in the organizations.

Keywords Management reforms • High level reform models • Trajectories of reform

5.1 The Process of the Management Reform, Reasons and Driving Factors Triggering Management Reforms in the Public and International Organizations

Every reform program is composed of different elements and consequently subject to different levels of analysis. As outlined in the third chapter, we see the management reform as the dependent variable of our research study, whose aim is explaining the reform program by analyzing the most important components, the process and the substance. Processes concern the

© The Author(s) 2020
M. Amici, D. Cepiku, *Performance Management in International Organizations*, https://doi.org/10.1007/978-3-030-39472-1_5

reasons, the driving factors and the actors behind a management reform, whereas the substance includes the content and the intensity of the reform.

Such elements interact in a management reform cycle, as all reform programs:

- aim to achieve some objectives (reasons);
- are influenced by internal and external factors (driving factors);
- follow a trajectory mostly influenced by the most important players (actors);
- include a specific content (the management ideas and ideal paradigms) that can affect the organization with a different intensity.

Finally, the results achieved will depend on the degree of implementation of the formal reform plans, as represented in the conceptual framework "three modes of reality" model described in Chap. 3 (Bouckaert and Halligan 2008; Pollitt and Bouckaert 2004, 2017; Bauer 2007). The same cycle applies to either public administrations or international organizations, despite the existing differences. In the following paragraphs, relying on the literature on public management reforms in national governments, we will highlight the differences and similarities with management reforms in international organizations public.

5.1.1 Explaining the Origin of Management Reforms in International Organizations

As already mentioned, the first part of the reform management cycle concerns the origin or reasons of a reform. Different mechanisms and factors could be at the origin of a management reform program. Scholars from the rational actor behavior approach suggest that organizational changes occur to increase policy delivery or to reach organizational success (Bauer 2007). Public management reforms may also bring symbolic and legitimacy benefits (Pollitt and Bouckaert 2004). Such benefits could be only apparent when politicians limit to announce a management reform process or significant when such reforms have an effect on the level of legitimacy of a given organization. As outlined in the previous chapter, in international organizations, (output) legitimacy is linked to performance, and improvements in performance are generally associated with the implementation of public management reforms. Consequently, different authors

(Mehde 2007; Stutzer and Frey 2005) suggest that management reforms in international organizations originated from their increased importance, as powerful actors in need of legitimacy. In fact, as their level of intrusiveness rises, their role and activities are increasingly contested and put under scrutiny by the national constituents and citizens. Consequently, international organizations should aim at improving their efficiency and effectiveness to increase the level of their output legitimacy ultimately. In other words, the perceived gap between current performance and the low level of output legitimacy could have triggered the management reform processes. The recent evidence of management reforms in international organizations could thus be explained by the perceived need to enhance their output legitimacy perspective. Nevertheless, in literature, other conflicting explanations exist, and management reforms could have different and opposite origins and objectives.

As stressed by Bauer (2007), the modernization process could also be the sign of the organization's weaknesses and a way to survive. In this case, administrative modernization activism will be more likely to happen in those international organizations that feel their role under threat and perceived as inefficient or redundant (Bauer 2007). This is the case of the management reform launched in the OECD in the mid-1990s, as a reaction to the decreasing interest in the organization due to growing competition for policy advice with similar international organizations (Bourgon 2009). Moreover, following life cycle theories, the administrative modernization process could also be explained as a normal step of the administrative life span of an organization (Bauer 2007). Specifically, as the majority of the international organizations have been created several years after the Second World War, they could feel now the need to modernize their administrative structures set up according to obsolete administrative standards (Bauer 2007).

Following the hegemony theory, one could also make the argument that one of the member states generally dominates international organizations. Consequently, the administrative modernization process will follow the pace and substance of the administrative reform of the hegemonic national administration (Bauer 2007). Modernizing the internal management structures could also be originated by the isomorphic tendencies of reforms concepts diffusion (Di Maggio and Powell 1991). In this case, international organizations in search of legitimacy embrace rules, norms, and routines more commonly valued in their organizational environment

(Knill and Bauer 2007). Also, management reforms could be triggered by policy changes linked to new competencies and functions acquired by international organizations (Kerler 2007).

Finally, management reforms could be the result of shocks or crises, intended as unexpected, unpredictable events, which may open "policy windows" for large management reform programs (Kerler 2007). In this case, Examples of this case include the management reform in the European Commission, triggered by the crisis started after the fall of the Santer Commission in 1999, or the reform of the World Bank in 1987, originated by a policy change after the came to office of the new President Barber Conable (Kerler 2007).

Such a list of possible theoretical explanations, although far from being exhaustive, underlines the existence of multiple conditions to engage international organizations in modernizing their administrative structures (Bauer 2007). Consequently, a management reform process could have very different origins across international organizations and a further understanding would require a case-by-case analysis.[1]

Despite the different possible explanations, the reasons for management reform initiatives in international organizations are often related to performance improvements. For example, the declared intent of the managerial reform of the United Nations was "adapting the internal structure, the operational processes and the culture of the United Nations to the expectation of greater efficiency, effectiveness, openness and problem-solving readiness of the constituency" (United Nations 1997: 2). Similarly, the intent of the advocates of the significant reform of the European Commission has been "to equip the Commission to fulfill its role in addressing the challenges facing Europe with maximum effectiveness" (European Commission 2000: 3). More recently, European Commission President Junker, after taking office, committed to "make sure that every action we take delivers maximum performance and value-added" (European Commission 2014: 2). On the same line, the Strategic Compact initiative launched in the World Bank aimed at making "the Bank more effective in delivering its regional program and in achieving its basic mission of reducing poverty" (World Bank 1997: 9). Also the mission statement of the European Central Bank reports that: "we at the European Central Bank are committed to performing all central bank tasks entrusted to us effectively", and the document underlining Strategic Intents and Organizational Principles says that "[...] the Executive Board of the ECB [...] shall manage all resources prudently and shall promote effective and cost-efficient solutions [...]". In 1995, the Annual Ministerial Meeting of the Organization for Economic Cooperation and Development (OECD) requested to "accelerate the process of change with a view to further enhancing the relevance, efficiency and effectiveness of the Organization" (OECD 1995: 12).

Notwithstanding the recognized increased level of intrusiveness of international organizations, the analysis suggests that increasing output legitimacy through better performance could not be the only explanation of management reform in international organizations, although performance is certainly a relevant influencing factor. A common perceived gap between expectations and performance seems to be a necessary initial condition to engage many international organizations in a management reform program (Kerler 2007). Nevertheless, the reasons behind the gap can have quite different origins, as outlined above.

5.1.2   The Driving Factors of Management Reform in International Organizations

A second relevant aspect of the management reform process concerns the driving forces shaping the implementation of management reforms. The mere opportunity or a reason for reform is not sufficient to enable the reform management process.

According to the Pollitt and Bouckaert (2017), the most important driving forces include internal factors, as the elite decision-making and external factors as the socio-economic forces, the political system as well as by chance events, as scandal and disasters. In the government of a nation-state, the elite decision making is generally composed of those responsible for the implementation of the reform, which is generally the minister, together with the top-level officials, also known as mandarins (Pollitt and Bouckaert 2017). The latter, in turn, can be influenced by other actors including more extensive networks, or the same international organizations (Pollitt and Bouckaert 2017).[2] The relations among ministers and mandarins, as well as the degree of politicization of the top civil servants are crucial factors for the success of a management reform initiative.

An additional background factor influencing the direction of a management reform is the administrative culture embedded in the national administration context. The administrative culture is defined by Peters (2008: 118) as a "historically based set of values, structures, and relationships with other institutions that defines the nature of appropriate public administration within society." Among the most important administrative traditions identified one finds, the Anglo-American, Napoleonic (Peters 2008; Ongaro 2009; Kickert 2011), Germanic and Scandinavian (Johnsen and Vakkuri 2006). The administrative traditions have specific features and dimensions regarding the way relations between politics and adminis-tration or between state and society are treated. They also differ: in the conception of the civil service; in the relative importance of management and law in shaping the functioning of the administration; in the degree the principles of equity and accountability matter in the public sector; as well as towards the attitude to performance (Painter and Peters 2010; Peters 2008). Other important aspects influencing the final content of the reform include the dichotomy between the rhetoric and the reality of manage-ment reforms, or according to Pollitt and Bouckaert (2017), the interac-tion between the desirable and the feasible. The latter concerns the perceived gap between the reform objectives desired by the reform advocates and the results achieved. Often politicians tend to announce ambitious reform packages, but these fail to meet the desired results, following the implementation process. The latter is indeed a complex one, as management reforms are increasingly characterized by the interaction of a large number of actors, which deliver the reform programs (Pollitt and Bouckaert 2017).

The effectiveness of the reform is also influenced by the unit level of analysis, as much as the reform will affect all the different layers of the organization, as much it will be effective (Pollitt and Bouckaert 2017). Moreover, individual reforms can also overlap each other with the risk of contradicting or detracting the results previously achieved (Pollitt and Bouckaert 2017). The consequence is that the results of a management reform are difficult to identify as it is their contribution to the declared reform objectives. The specific management reform will emerge by the interplay between all internal and external factors so far discussed (Pollitt and Bouckaert 2017).[3] In the case of international organizations, the decision-making framework influencing a management reform process is quite different and relatively more complex. Compared to national administrations, in the context of international organizations, the number of powerful actors potentially influencing management changes is decisively higher. First, in international organizations, the internal elite decision-making system include also member states representatives from at least three different countries. Secondly, in the wider international context the number and the relevance of the external actors,[4] which could exert a greater influence (positive or negative) in the management reform process, is higher than in the context of national governments (Kerler 2007). As outlined above, although international organizations are set up by member states to pursue their interests, they face relevant information asymmetries. They are often forced to tolerate small deviations of international organizations by their mandate (Plümper 1995). Private actors, namely non—governmental organizations (NGOs)—or according to Bauer's classification, private international organizations of no-profit character—support the member states in monitoring and controlling the work of international organizations. Although not having formal powers, they became an important persuading actor in influencing the management reform processes (Kerler 2007). The other relevant actor in shaping management reform programs is the bureaucratic subsystems of international organizations, which could favor or resist the change. Pollack (2003) points out how the management reform process in international organizations is characterized by the role of informal and formal agenda-setter. The first aims at putting forward a first draft or concept of the reform, while the second one must turn the draft into a formal reform plan and follow its implementation. As stressed by Kelrer (2007), which analyzed the case of the management reform of the World Bank, bureaucracies tend to be rather resistant to management changes as this latter proved to be costly with regards to jobs, income, and competences. Thus Secretariats act very cautiously when dealing with the reform processes (Kerler 2007).

Consequently, in the case of the World Bank, the external actors, namely the member states and private actors, played a more prominent role as informal agenda-setter bringing forward demands for management reform programs (Kerler 2007). On the same line, Bauer (2007) in analyzing the case of the European Commission, acknowledged the crucial role played by the member states as a source of "outside demand" for management reforms, although their influence on the content and trajectory of the reform remained indirect (Bauer 2007). To a lesser extent, there is also evidence of management reforms triggered by the internal bureaucracy demand. It is the case of the management reform of the European Central Bank, where internal factors, as staff demand, cultural factors, and ambitions, were crucial in triggering the reform process (Glöckler 2007). In any case, once the demand for reform is strong enough to enable a management reform process, the latter depends on the role played by the formal agenda-setter, namely the Secretary-General or the President of the international organization. The role of individuals in management reform processes is thus of crucial importance as the success and intensity of a management reform are closely associated with the skills and abilities of those responsible for their implementation. Baumann et al. (2007) studied the role played by the Secretary-General in ten management reform processes in different international organizations.[5] Their conclusions highlight the "immense importance of the Secretary General's qualities for the intensity of the reform, adding that "an organization will achieve reform when its Secretary-General could be identified as a reform broker. In contrast, a Secretary-General who acts as conserver will not be willing to implement change and thus his or her organization will not reform until a reform broker is elected as his or her successors (Baumann et al. 2007). Evidence also shows the crucial role played by the European Central Bank Board, and especially the President and the Vice President, in bringing forward the management reform against the resistance of other stakeholders (Glocker 2007); or the spectacular role played by the Commissioner Kinnock in the successfully implementation of the management reform in the European Commission (Bauer 2007). As outlined above, another relevant aspect influencing the implementation of management reforms is the relation between the responsible, namely the Secretary-General or the President, and the top international civil servants. As observed by Pollitt and Bouckaert (2017), in national administrations, the relations between ministers and senior managers (mandarins) are mainly influenced by the degree of politicization of top civil servants' careers. A high degree of politicization in the career path of top civil servants, leading to a high-level spoil system, could undermine the continuity of a reform (Pollitt and Bouckaert 2017). By contrast, a separate career path of top civil servants, as in the case of the United Kingdom, Canada or New Zealand, can assure the necessary continuity to the reform but could lead to conservatism and resistance to change (Pollitt and Bouckaert 2017).

The international organizations, as mentioned above, are quite stable entities, separated by the political life of their constituencies, so are the careers of the international top civil servants. This results in a low-level spoil system that incentives continuity and favor the "*esprit du corps*" although it could lead to a certain resistance to reform and changes. Beside these driving factors, shaping the implementation of management reforms that, despite the differences, international organizations share with public sector organizations, Bauer and Knill (2007) identified another group of possible driving factors influencing the management reform processes, linked to the specific characteristics of the international organizations.

They include, among others, their size; the level of homogeneity of the functions carried out; the supranational or intergovernmental character of the organization and the attitude of their constituent members towards the management reforms in their respective national administrations (Bauer and Knill 2007). Following this, they analyzed different cases of management reforms in the most important international organizations[6] and classified the influence of the common and the specific driving factors. This led to formulate a series of hypothesis. In brief, according to their study, management reforms in international organizations should be more likely to happen in single-purpose international organizations, of small size, with the presence of a skillful reform leader (Bauer and Knill 2007). The possibilities also increase in case pre-existing performance gaps coincide with a change in the constituency of the organization (Bauer and Knill 2007).

The attitude to management reforms of their constituency and the supranational or intergovernmental character of the organization have no direct impact on the scope and speed of the management reforms (Bauer 2007). This study is a useful framework to assess the role played by the different driving forces in the specific context of international organizations and in predicting the occurrence of a management reform process. Nevertheless, to assess the extent international organizations transformed their internal structures to deliver services more efficiently and effectively, it is necessary to focus on the content of the management reform programs affecting their internal structures and management areas.

5.2   THE CONTENT AND THE PARADIGMS OF MANAGEMENT REFORMS IN PUBLIC AND INTERNATIONAL ORGANIZATIONS

5.2.1   Trajectories of Reform and High-Level Paradigms

According to Pollitt and Bouckaert (2017: 28), a public management reform can be defined as "deliberate changes to the structures and processes of public sector organizations to get them (in some sense) to run better." The reform process includes typically a formulation phase, where decisions on the reform changes are taken, and an implementation phase, where these changes are carried out. More specifically, the formulation phase includes all the decisions concerning "the institutional rules and organizational routines, in the areas of expenditures, planning, and financial management, audit and evaluation, organizations and methods, labor relations and procurement that guide, constrain and motivate the public sector" (Barzelay 2001: 14). The formulation phase ends with an authoritative decision to be executed in the implementation phase. Pollitt and Bouckaert (2017), describe the reform process more dynamically. The reform process is composed of a trajectory and a framework or scenario. It normally includes the substance of the reform and the process of how the reform is implemented (Pollitt and Bouckaert 2017). Trajectories are described as "intentional patterns," leading from a starting point (alpha) to a future desired situation (omega) within the set scenario, including all the three elements (Pollitt and Bouckaert 2017). The future desired destination can be reached with different degrees of reform intensity. This latter refers to the relevance and magnitude of the changes carried out by the reform program on the main functional areas of the organizations. According to Bauer (2007) the management reform intensity can be classified according to the following categories: "no change", "optimization", in case of limited incremental changes, "reform", including different degrees of changes, and "transformation", in case of radical changes as the mission of the organization (Bauer 2007). Similarly, Pollitt and Bouckaert (2004), catalog the reform intensity according to four types: maintain, modernize, marketize, and minimize. Maintain includes strengthening the traditional control mechanisms; modernize involves new structures and processes for government policy-making, thus improving managerial modernization (Pollitt and Bouckaert 2004). Marketize is concerned with the introduction of private sector focus in the public sector organizations (*see infra*) while minimizing refers to privatize functions traditionally in the domain of the public sector (Pollitt and Bouckaert 2004). In addition, changes can address the structures or the process the organizations. As put by Ongaro (2009), reform changes can modify the processes through which public organizations are run, as the way civil servants are recruited or services are delivered, as well as the organizational structures, by the establishment of new agencies. The changes can also differently affect the main management areas of the organizations. These generally include finance, personnel, organization structure, and performance (Pollitt and Bouckaert 2017). Within each management area, reform changes can modify the single management elements. For example, in the finance sector, management reforms can change the budget process, the type of accounting system adopted, or the way the audit process is organized. Similarly, within the personnel policy, changes can affect the recruitment procedures, the appraisal systems, or the remuneration policy. Organizational structure can also be subject to changes. They include the introduction of new coordination mechanisms or the adoption of the centralization or decentralization mechanisms (Pollitt and Bouckaert 2017). Finally, performance can be more or less intensive and extensive, focusing on outputs delivered or outcome and effects produced (Pollitt and Bouckaert 2017). Given that, to classify the content and the directions of the observed changes to explain the general directions and recipes for the public sector reforms, commentators, academicians as well as practitioners elaborated the ideal paradigms or high-level reform models (Pollitt and Bouckaert 2017). Although there are plenty of available reform models, either created ad hoc by governments[7] or by academicians,[8] the most important are generally considered (Pollitt and Bouckaert 2004, 2017; Ongaro 2009), the New Public Management (NPM), the New Public Governance (NPG), the Neo-Weberian State (NWS) and to a lesser extent the Public Value model. Table 5.1 shows the main characteristics of the high-level reform models.

Although such high-level models are a useful classification tool, they are not risk-free. First, the paradigms depict an ideal world, while the real future vision (omega destination) is much more confused and untidier (Pollitt and Bouckaert 2017). Secondly, observed changes in a country management reform could be linked to preset reform paradigms, although the reasons could be elsewhere (Pollitt and Bouckaert 2017). Thirdly, the reform programs often overlap each other, and no chronological waves of reforms are observable. Rather new layers overlie and do not replace or completely wash away the previous layers of reform (Pollitt and Bouckaert 2017). In sum, the reality can be much more complex than following a linear trajectory towards an ideal paradigm, and the relations between decisions and observed changes can be sometimes looser. Also, such high-level models coexist together with specific administrative cultures or traditions as outlined above.[9]

Therefore, the final direction taken by a specific management reform will result in a combination of the management ideas inspired by one of the high-level models and the prevalent administrative tradition of the country, implementing the reform. According to Pollitt and Bouckaert (2017), the administrative tradition could influence the direction of change triggered by the main high-level paradigms of reform, absorbing,

Table 5.1   The main concepts of the ideal paradigms of public management reforms

High-level reform models	Core concepts
Traditional public administration	• Clear distinction between public and private roles • Fixed sphere of competence • Defined hierarchies of offices • Full-time career appointments for officials • Management by application of a developing set of rules, knowledge of which was the special technical competence of the officials concerned
New public management (NPM)	• Greater emphasis on performance (output measurement) • Preference for flat, small and specialized organizations • Use of contracts for hierarchical relations • Injection of market-type mechanisms (MTMs) as performance-related pay or public sector leagues table • Treating service users as customers
New Weberian state (NWS)	• Reaffirmation of the role of the state as the main facilitator of solutions as well as the role of representative democracy • Reaffirmation of the role of administrative law—Suitably modernized—In preserving the basic principles; • Preservation of the idea of a public service with a distinctive status • Shift from an internal orientation towards bureaucratic rules towards an external orientation towards meeting citizens' needs and wishes • Range of devices for consultation with and the direct representation of citizens' views • a greater orientation on the achievement of results rather than merely the correct following of procedure
New public governance (NPG)	• Government more effective and legitimate by including a wider range of social actors • Collaboration with public and private actors through a network approach • Performance focus on the micro (single unit), meso (PA system) and macro level

Source: With adaptations from Pollitt and Bouckaert (2017)

or even defeated them. For example, the attitude towards a law-based civil service that characterizes the French and German administrative cultures cannot easily be changed by a high-level model based on a management culture, as the New Public Management (Pollitt and Bouckaert 2017; Kickert 2011).

5.2.2   The Main Contents of the Three High-Level Reform Models: The NPM, NWS, and NPG

The starting point of all trajectories of management reforms analyzed in literature is commonly identified in reaction to the traditional model of public sector organizations, as it was considered incompatible with the changing economic and social model. As stresses by Osborne and Gaebler (1992: 11), "hierarchical, centralized bureaucracies designed in the 1930s and 1940s simply do not function well in the rapidly-changing information-rich knowledge-intensive society and economy of 1990s." Pollitt and Bouckaert (2017: 72), identify in the traditional model the one "to be replaced by more flexible, fast-moving, performance-oriented forms of modern organizations." This is exactly the aim of the New Public Management (NPM) high-level reform model, which in chronological terms, is the first public management reform movement affecting the public sector organizations. The NPM model was greatly influenced by the perception of inefficient governments unable to sustain effective welfare systems (Pollitt and Bouckaert 2017). It included few but clear objectives as saving money; increase the efficiency to improve organizational performance as well as to respond effectively to citizens' needs. It was also strongly supported by international organizations as the World Bank, the International Monetary Fund and the Public Management Committee of the Organization for Economic and Cooperation Development (OECD 1995), as well as by the neo-liberal governments of Ronald Regan in the United States and Margaret Thatcher in the United Kingdom (Drechsler 2005). The NPM paradigm entailed a different concept of accountability, by moving from process accountability "towards a greater element of accountability in terms of results" (Hood 1995: 94). Such perspective reversed the fundamental doctrine of traditional administration, which accounted for "keeping the public sector distinct from private sector, in terms of continuity, ethos, methods of doing business, organizational design, people, rewards and structures" (Hood 1995: 95). A new emphasis on results was associated to high trust in the market and private business methods as well as low trust in public servants whose activated need to be monitored and evaluated through accounting techniques (Hood 1995), with a consequence of introducing in the public sector, private management styles and techniques. These involved the main organization areas such as personnel, finance, performance measurement through the adoption of new management tools and techniques, including accruals accounting systems, activity-based management systems, performance budgets, performance-based contracts, strategic planning tools. Other common characteristics of NPM management reforms include: the disaggregation of public management organizations into smaller units more easily manageable, a greater focus on competition either between public and private organizations as well as among public sector organizations, explicit and measurable standards of performance, and finally the attempt to evaluate public organizations according to preset output measures (Hood 1995). The possibility to import management practices from the private sector in the public sector organizations also led to a greater emphasis on measuring the satisfaction of public services' users, considered as services "customers". Table 5.2 shows the New Public Management (NPM) reforms oriented in the main sectors and elements of the organization.

This shared feeling of improving the action of governments facilitated the wide-spread of central government reform programs, inspired by the NPM model, in the most advanced OECD countries, mainly of

Table 5.2 The traditional and NPM paradigms' elements of reform

Management sectors/ element	Traditional	New public management
Financial management		
Budgeting	No information on performance	Performance budgeting
Accounting	Cash-based	Accruals accounting
Auditing	Finance and compliance	Performance audit
Personnel management		
Contract policy	Tenured career	Temporary contracts
Promotion and appraisal	Seniority and qualifications	Performance-based/merit principles
Profile senior staff	Expertise and limited responsibility for resources	Management capabilities and responsibility for resources
Personnel authority	Centrally guided	Decentralized
Organization		
Specialization	Multi-purpose, broad scope	Tight focused, specialized
Coordination	Hierarchy	Contract coordination, strategic planning
Decentralization	Centralization	Decentralization
Performance evaluation		
Performance focus	Correctness of procedures	Achievement of results (outputs)

Source: With adaptations from Pollitt and Bouckaert (2017)

Anglo-Saxon administrative tradition, including, among others, the United States, the United Kingdom, Australia, New Zealand, Canada and Sweden, although with variations.[10] However, after implementation of the NPM style reforms in those countries, a strong criticism raised towards the NPM paradigm on a wide range of highly controversial and contested matters. Those against, claim that NPM reforms have been implemented heterogeneously, and posed relevant threats to the traditional core values of the public administration as equity, fairness, and accountability (Moe 1994; Lynn 1996; Terry 1998). On a similar line, Pollitt and Bouckaert (2017) stressed how NPM reforms led to fragmented public sector organizations, each pursuing its own goals and objectives autonomously. Even the OECD, years after the first endorsement of NPM model, started to recognize that reforms produced some unexpected negative results (OECD 2003). Competitive models of government failed to understand that public management arrangements not only deliver public services but also enshrine deeper government values (OECD 2003).

The second high-level reform model, alternative to the NPM, although linked to it, is the recently emerging concept of the *Neo-Weberian State (NWS)*. Firstly, introduced by Pollitt and Bouckaert (2004), it draws on the unsatisfactory results led by the NPM, which neglected the peculiarities of the public sector institutional environment. One of the major critiques addressed to the NPM is considering equal public and private interests. As Drechsler (2005: 18) points out "the use of business techniques within the public sphere confuses the most basic requirements of any state, particularly of a democracy, with a liability: regularity, transparency, and due process are simply much more important than low costs and speed." These are slippery concepts within public sector organizations. The focus on efficiency led by the NPM style reforms need to be put in the appropriate public context, characterized by the conditions outlined above. This is to avoid that the achievement of savings is done neglecting the ultimate goals of the public organization (Drechsler 2005). The NWS model is thus characterized by the presence of both elements of the Weberian (traditional) model of public administration combined with lessons learned from NPM experience. Although the model should not be intended as the mere sum of the traditional elements of the Weberian state plus elements of the NPM (Pollitt and Bouckaert 2017). In other words, the model "preserves the main part of the traditional Weberian model and modernizes it […] which can take various context and country-specific forms" (Drechsler and Kattel 2009: 96). This is in line with Larbi's (1999) argument that selective use of some NPM elements to certain sectors may be beneficial for societies. According to Ongaro (2009), the NWS paradigm is characterized, from one side, by the reaffirmation of the economic role of the state; the supremacy of the legality principle; as well as by the relevance of the specific peculiarities of the public services. From the other, by the tendency to move the focus from the formal correctness of bureaucratic procedures to the results of the administrative action from a citizen perspective; as well as to favoring the managerial aspects of the public servants' activities. Particularly relevant in the NWS model is the new focus on performance, shifting in discourses and practice "from efficiency to effectiveness, i.e., from getting something done cheaply to accomplishing one's goal" (Drechsler 2005: 19). In the NWS model, performance, although framed in a more law-based context, become a major concern. To improve the management of resources, the governments decided to modernize the relevant laws to support a greater orientation on the achievement of results, rather than mere respect of the procedures (Kostakis 2011). In other words, the important traditional concern over processes and procedures aiming to guarantee the legality of the decision is coupled with ex-post concerns about the results of the organization's action (Bouckaert and Halligan 2008). In sum, for Pollitt and Bouckaert (2017: 19), the NWS is a model attempting "to modernize traditional bureaucracy by making more professional, efficient and citizen-friendly." The model was initially intended only "as a summary description, not a theory, not a normative vision or a goal either." (Pollitt and Bouckaert 2017: 19). Then it was conceptually developed by many commentators and included by Pollitt and Bouckaert (2017) as a future vision (an omega in their words) like the other high-level reform models as NPM and NPG. Finally, Pollitt and Bouckaert (2017) acknowledge two different variants of the NWS model. A "Nordic variant" focused on the citizens—as—active customer participation in the state's activities through the co-design and co-production of services and a continental version characterized by a more professional state, citizens as customer-oriented. Thus, according to several authors, the countries followed the NWS reform model, although with different extent and intensity, including Belgium, Italy, Germany, and Sweden. That having been said, when it comes to the identification of the main characteristics of the NWS model in the functional areas outlined above, the picture is not as neat as in the case of the traditional administration and the NPM model. As stressed by Pollitt and Bouckaert (2017), there are cases where managerial trends and innovations could fit in both NPM and NWS reform models.

Thus a more detailed analysis is needed to understand the different rationale behind the adoption of the same kind of reform. For example, budgetary reforms appear as inspired by both paradigms, although the intentions and objectives for their adoption could be different. In the case of organizations following the NPM reform model, the reasons to adopt budgetary innovation is to focus on performance, results, and efficiency, while for NWS followers, the goal is improving their financial control system to better link strategic priorities and resource allocations (Pollitt and Bouckaert 2017). Table 5.3 provides a synthetic representation of the main elements characterizing the NWS model.

The third reform model, the *New Public Governance*, is also partially derived from some unwanted and unpopular effects caused by the NPM led reform programs (Pollitt and Bouckaert 2017). The introduction of mechanisms based on privatization, competition among public sector organizations, and the creation of autonomous public agencies brought to a fragmentation of the public sector system. Moreover, in an increasingly

Table 5.3 The NWS paradigm elements of reform

Management area/element	New Weberian State
Financial management	
Budgeting	Traditional budget with some performance information
Accounting	Full-cash based or a combination of cash/accrual
Auditing	Adding to financial and compliance auditing, investigations of some performance issues
Personnel management	
Contract policy	Tenured and privileged career
Promotion and appraisal	Seniority, qualifications and performance
Profile senior staff	Expertise and management capabilities s
Personnel authority	Centrally guided
Organization	
Specialization	Multi-purpose, broad scope, limited fragmentation
Coordination	Hierarchy with coordination by targets and outputs standards
Decentralization (competitive/internal)	Centralization
Scale	Defending existing structures
Performance evaluation	
Performance focus	Focus on the achievement of satisfaction in service delivery (outcome)

Source: With adaptations from Pollitt and Bouckaert (2017)

plural and interconnected world, the lack of coordination among the different public sector bodies as well as the intra-organizational focus emphasized the need of managing interdependencies among the different authors involved in the public policy implementation and public policy delivery, more effectively (Metcalfe and Richards 1987; Pollitt and Bouckaert 2017). This led towards a shifting in the content of public sector reform paradigms towards more participatory models. In this context, public sector management reforms were increasingly inspired by new management ideas to address better the rising complexity brought by the globalization process. This contributed to the emerging interests on the concept of "governance," "partnerships," as well as "transparency" and "trust" (Pollitt and Bouckaert 2017). The concept of governance in public sector management reforms is closely associated with the growth of the globalization process as well as the development of the network theory. According to Kooiman and Van Vliet (1993), the emerging global issues as the health and environmental protection as well as the technological development, call for designing new and innovative governance approaches to better coordinate the different and interrelated economic systems based on the interaction between government and society, as well as, between public and private sector. The rooted assumption of this new paradigm is that the external environment is a fundamental driver to re-design and implement the organizational development policies as well as the managerial requalification processes in the public sector organizations (Kooiman and Van Vliet 1993). Similarly, Rhodes (1996) argued that new governing structures as networks could be added to hierarchies and market mechanisms. Building on such premises, Osborne (2010) acknowledged that neither the traditional model of public organizations, focused on the political system, nor the NPM paradigm, focused on the internal organization, were hitherto able to capture the complexity of the process leading to the production of the public services of the twenty-first century. He then suggested the introduction of a new paradigm known as New Public Governance (NPG) defined as "a conceptual tool with the potential to assist our understanding of the complexity of these challenges and as a reflection of the reality of the working lives of public managers today" (Osborne 2010: 6). According to the intention of the author, this new paradigm aimed at capturing "the realities of public policy implementation and services delivery within the plural and pluralist complexities of the state in the 21st century" (Osborne 2010: 7). The NPG thus combines in a single paradigm the plural state dimension where different bodies and actors interact to deliver the public services, with the pluralist dimension, where multiple processes characterize the policy-making system (Osborne 2010; Cepiku 2013). Furthermore, from an intellectual perspective, the new paradigm "corrects the theoretical and practical shortcomings of its predecessors, encompassing the contemporary complexities and realities of governing by drawing on organizational sociology and network theory, rather than on political science, or public-choice economic, in order to overcome the fragmentation and uncoordinated character of the twentieth century managerial practice" (Lynn 2010: 124). Consequently, good governance means steering the society through networks and partnerships between governments, business corporations, and civil society (Pollitt and Bouckaert 2017). The main characteristics of this new model, thus, include (Meneguzzo 1995):

- the centrality of the interactions with socio-political actors;
- the government and coordination of complex networks in the social context;
- the external focus towards the socio-political environment.

Bellamy and Palumbo (2010: xi) have proposed a more comprehensive definition of governance paradigm, including the elements mentioned above. According to them, "governance entails a move away from traditional hierarchical forms of organization and the adoption of network forms. It also entails a revision of the relationships between the state and the civil society in a more participatory direction. Governance is finally said to be responsible for shifting the emphasis away from statue law to more flexible forms of regulation and implementation". Cepiku (2005) has also emphasized additional differences between NPM and NPG. While NPM focuses on the internal efficiency of the public sector organizations, the NPG looks at the performance of the whole system of the public sector as well as their interinstitutional networks. While the NPM aims at disaggregating the public organizations and supports the competition between the public and private sectors, the NPG is based on a collaborative approach among public and private entities. Finally, while the NPM is characterized by the dichotomy between politics and administration, the NPG heads towards the overcoming of such dichotomy through a more participatory and collaborative approach. The focus on coordination and networking is particularly relevant for our object of analysis. International organizations should be on the front line in steering and guiding complex networks of actors in delivering global public goods. However, compared to the paradigms mentioned above, the NPG model is the most difficult to operationalize. Despite its clear focus on interdependence, coordination, and networking, the NPG is an extremely broad and ambiguous model (Pollitt and Bouckaert 2017). Although some conceptual schemes exist, it is difficult to decide which elements of the management reforms can be included or not, as few empirical evidence is provided (Pollitt and Bouckaert 2017). Some even started questioning its relevance as a useful comparative paradigm for management reforms. By contrast, others consider the NPG model as a possible candidate to replace NPM as the dominant model, providing a possible inspiration for NPM countries to move towards the NPG model. As put it by Pollitt and Bouckaert (2017: 126) "while the NPG model may at present appear to be rather vague and idealistic, it nevertheless focused on some more contemporary features of politics and society, [...] it may yet be developed into something more theoretically precise and operational". In the waiting for a less vague definition of the content of the NPG paradigm, the following table outlines for each management area, the broad concepts and ideas developed so far (Table 5.4).

In this context of global waves of managerial paradigms of reforms affecting public sector organizations, also fueled by the promotional activities of international organizations, such as the OECD and the World Bank (Hood 1995; Christensen and Lægreid 2002), the influence of such paradigms of reform vis à vis the international organizations was hardly subject to comprehensive investigation (Balint and Knill 2007). Only a few studies deal with changes in management structures of international organizations (Geri 2001; Davies 2002; Dijkzeul 1997; Balint and Knill 2007) if we except the European Commission (Bauer 2005; Egeberg 2006; Levy 2002, 2003, 2004). As outlined in the second chapter, multiple reasons are explaining the limited attention of scholars in the internal functioning of international organizations'. As a consequence, as noted by Balint and Knill (2007: 17), "we have limited knowledge about the extent to which international organizations [...] actually live up with the standard they promote". In their study on the human resources management reform in the OECD, Balint and Knill (2007: 118) suspect that the reason is that "nobody really had any doubts that an organization acting as international reform promoter of NPM at the same time will long have introduced internal reforms along similar lines". However, this

Table 5.4 The NPG paradigm elements of reforms

Management area/ element	*New public governance*
Financial management	
Budgeting	Centralization in accounting practice. Shift towards the whole of
Accounting	government accounting (WGA) approach, bringing all
Auditing	expenditures of the different bodies of organization into a single account.
Personnel management	
Contract policy	Implication for service recruitment, pay and conditions not clear.
Promotion and	Some evidence could be found in civil servants' training
appraisal	programs whether they are focused or not on networking and
Profile senior staff	collaboration.
Personnel authority	
Organization	
Specialization	Not clear trend
Coordination	Network type coordination
Decentralization	Not clear trend
(competitive /	
internal)	
Scale	Not clear trend
Performance evaluation	
Performance focus	Focus on the performance of the network

Source: With adaptations from Pollitt and Bouckaert (2017)

is not the case, as their findings show the opposite, as "OECD still represents a more Weberian bureaucracy type when it comes to issues of human resources management" (Balint and Knill 2007: 118). On the same line, Geri (2001: 453) studying the NPM style reforms in a sample of independent UN agencies found out that "none of these UN specialized agencies is implementing a comprehensive set of NPM reforms" although "all six of the organizations included in the study are under pressure to implement organizational changes intended to improve their efficiency and effectiveness and to improve their relationships with member states and other key stakeholders". According to Geri (2001: 446), the possible reasons lie in the "the complexity of international operations and policy-making, and the multinational nature of international administration," which "act to insulate the administration of IOs from implementing NPM in its totality".

NOTES

1. One of the most comprehensive studies on this topic is Bauer and Knill (2007) "Management Reforms in International Organizations", Nomos.
2. An example includes the administrative reforms adopted by EU member states to meet the Maastricht criteria for joining the European Monetary Union in 1992 (Pollitt and Bouckaert 2017).
3. For a more detailed explanation about the broad forces influencing management reform changes, see the model of public management reform developed by Pollitt and Bouckaert (2017).
4. The external actors can include international non-governmental organizations (NGOs) or multinational corporations as well as subsystems of the organization itself.
5. They include the World Food Program (since 1992), the Food and Agriculture Organizations (FAO) (1976–1994 and since 1994), the International Labor Organization—ILO (since 1999), the United Nations Educational, Scientific and Cultural Organization—UNESCO (1974–198 since 1999),the Council of Europe (since 1999), the European Commission (1985–1995), the World Health Organization – WHO (1988–1998) and the International Monetary Fund—IMF (1987).
6. The list includes, the European Commission, the European Central Bank, the European Parliament, the United Nations, the World Bank, the OECD, the Nordic Council of Baltic Sea States (Bauer 2007).
7. Among them the New Zealand model (Boston 1996), the Belgian Copernicus model (Hondeghem and Depré 2005), the German slim state (Sachverständigenrat 1997),the Canadian model "La Relève" (Bourgon 2009).
8. Among them the Napoleonic model (Ongaro 2009), the French model (Bartoli 2008), the Nordic model (Veggeland 2007).
9. Among them Anglo-Saxon, American, Napoleonic, Germanic and Scandinavian (Painter and Peters 2010).
10. See Hood (1995).

REFERENCES

Balint, Tim, and Christoph Knill. "The limits of legitimacy pressure as a source of organizational change: The reform of human resource management in the OECD." University of Konstanz. Department of Politics and Management. Chair of Comparative Public Policy and Administration. Working Paper n. 1. (2007): 117–131.

Bartoli, Anne. "The study of public management in France : la spécificité du modèle français d'administration", in Kickert, Walter (2008), The study of public management in Europe and the US : a comparative analysis of national distinctiveness, Abingdon, Routledge, 2008.

Barzelay, Michael. *The new public management: Improving research and policy dialogue.* Vol. 3. University of California Press, 2001.

Bauer, Michael W. "The European Commission." *Public Administration and Public Policy* - 113 (2005): 149.

———. "Introduction: Management Reform in International Organizations." In *Management Reforms in International Organizations*, eds. Bauer M., Knill C., Nomos, 2007.

Bauer, Michael W., and Christoph Knill. "Management reforms in international organizations.", Nomos, (2007).

Baumann, Soo Mee, Markus Hagel, and Barbara Kobler. "Management in Change-The Reform Broker Concept." In *Management Reforms in International Organizations*, pp. 175–191. Nomos Verlagsgesellschaft mbH & Co. KG, 2007.

Bellamy, Richard Paul, and Antonino Palumbo, eds. *From government to governance.* Ashgate, 2010.

Boston, Jonathan. The Use of Contracting in the Public Sector—Recent New Zealand Experience. Australian Journal of Public Administration 55 no. 3 (1996): 105–110.

Bouckaert, Geert, and John Halligan. "Comparing performance across public sectors." In *Performance Information in the Public Sector*, pp. 72–93. Palgrave Macmillan, London, 2008.

Bourgon, Jocelyne P. C. International Institutions Reform and Modernization of the OECD. Working Paper No. 42. The Centre for International governance Innovation. (2009).

Cepiku, Denita. "Governance: riferimento concettuale o ambiguità terminologica nei processi di innovazione della PA." *Azienda pubblica* 1 (2005): 84–110.

———. "Unraveling the concept of public governance: A literature review of different traditions." In *Conceptualizing and Researching Governance in Public and Non-Profit Organizations*, pp. 3–32. Emerald Group Publishing Limited, 2013.

Christensen, Tom, and Per Lægreid, eds. *New public management: the transformation of ideas and practice.* Ashgate Pub Limited, 2002.

Davies, Thomas. "*The Administration of International Organizations: Top Down and Bottom up.*" Ashgate, 2002.

Di Maggio, Paul, and Walter W. Powell. "The iron cage revisited: institutional isomorphism and collective rationality studies." *The new institucionalism in organizational analysis*, Chicago: Chicago University Press (a primeira edição em ASQ, 1983 (48): 147–60) (1991).

Dijkzeul, Dennis. "United Nations development co-operation as a form of international public service management." *International journal of public sector management* 10, no. 3 (1997): 165–189.

Drechsler, Wolfgang. "The rise and demise of the new public management." *Post-autistic economics review* 33, no. 14 (2005): 17–28.

Drechsler, Wolfgang, and Rainer Kattel. "Conclusion: Towards the neo-Weberian state? Perhaps, but certainly adieu, NPM." *The NISPAcee Journal of Public Administration and Policy* 1, no. 2 (2009): 95–99.

Egeberg, Morten, ed. *Multilevel union administration: the transformation of executive politics in Europe*. Springer, 2006.

European Commission. *White Paper "Reforming the European Commission"*. 2000.

———. *Communication from the President Mission letter to Commissioner to Competition*. (2014)

Geri, Laurance R. "New public management and the reform of international organizations." *International Review of Administrative Sciences* 67, no. 3 (2001): 445–460.

Glöckler, Gabriel. "From Take-off to Cruising Altitude: Management Reform and Organizational Change of the European Central Bank." In Management Reforms in International Organizations, pp. 85–96. Nomos Verlagsgesellschaft mbH & Co. KG, 2007.

Hondeghem, Annie, and Roger Depré. Inleiding. *Van den Broele*; Brugge, 2005.

Hood, Christopher. "The "new public management" in the 1980: Variations on a theme." *Accounting, organizations and society* 20, no. 2-3 (1995): 93–109.

Johnsen, Åge, and Jarmo Vakkuri. "Is there a Nordic perspective on public sector performance measurement?." *Financial Accountability & Management* 22, no. 3 (2006): 291–308.

Kerler, Michael. "Triggering world bank reform: When member states, NGOs and learning get important." In *Management Reforms in International Organizations*, pp. 133–149. Nomos Verlagsgesellschaft mbH & Co. KG, 2007.

Kickert, Walter. "Distinctiveness of administrative reform in Greece, Italy, Portugal and Spain. Common characteristics of context, administrations and reforms." *Public Administration* 89, no. 3 (2011): 801–818.

Knill, Christoph, and Michael W. Bauer. Theorizing management reforms in International Organizations. Nomos Verlagsgesellschaft mbH & Co. KG, 2007.

Kooiman, Jan, and Martijn Van Vliet. "Governance and public management." *Managing public organizations* (1993): 58–72.

Kostakis, Vasilis. "Commons-based peer production and the neo-Weberian state: synergies and interdependencies." *Administrative Culture* 12, no. 2 (2011): 146–161.

Larbi, George A. "The new public management approach and crisis states." United Nations Research Institute for Social Development (UNRISD), *Discussion Paper* No. 112. (1999).

Levy, Roger. "Modernising EU programme management." *Public Policy and Administration* 17, no. 1 (2002): 72–89.

———. "Critical success factors in public management reform: the case of the European Commission." *International Review of Administrative Sciences* 69, no. 4 (2003): 553–566

————. "Between rhetoric and reality: Implementing management reform in the European Commission." *International Journal of Public Sector Management* 17, no. 2 (2004): 166–177.

Lynn, Laurence E. Public management as art, science, and profession. Chatham House Pub, 1996.

————. "What endures? Public governance and the cycle of reform." In *The New Public Governance?*, pp. 121–140. Routledge, 2010

Mehde, Veith. "Creating a missing link? administrative reforms as a means of improving the legitimacy of international organizations." In *Management reforms in international organizations*, pp. 163–175. Nomos Verlagsgesellschaft mbH & Co. KG, 2007.

Meneguzzo, Marco. "Dal New Public Management alla Public Governance: il pendolo della ricerca sulla amministrazione pubblica." *Azienda pubblica* 8, no. 3 (1995): 491–510.

Metcalfe, Les, and Sue Richards. "The efficiency strategy in central government: an impoverished concept of management." *Public Money & Management* 7, no. 1 (1987): 29–32.

Moe, Ronald C. "The "reinventing government" exercise: Misinterpreting the problem, misjudging the consequences." *Public administration review* 54, no. 2 (1994): 111–122.

OECD. *The Future of the Organization. Paris: Organization for Economic Co-operation and Development.* 1995.

————. *Reform and Modernisation of the OECD. HOD (2003)3.* 2003.

Ongaro, Edoardo. *Public management reform and modernization: Trajectories of administrative change in Italy, France, Greece, Portugal and Spain.* Edward Elgar Publishing, 2009.

Osborne, D. Gaebler, and Ted Gaebler. *"Reinventing Government. How the Entrepreneurial Spirit is Transforming Government*, Reading Mass. Adison Wesley Public Comp. (1992)

————, ed. *The new public governance: Emerging perspectives on the theory and practice of public governance.* Routledge, 2010.

Painter, Martin, and B. Guy Peters. "The analysis of administrative traditions." In *Tradition and public administration*, pp. 3–16. Palgrave Macmillan, London, 2010.

Peters, B. G. "The napoleonic tradition." *International Journal of Public Sector Management* 21, no. 2 (2008): 118–132.

Plümper, Thomas. "Quasi-rationale Akteure und die Funktion internationaler Institutionen." *Zeitschrift für internationale Beziehungen* (1995): 49–77.

Pollack, Mark A. *The engines of European integration: delegation, agency, and agenda setting in the EU.* Oxford University Press, USA, 2003.

Pollitt, Christopher, and Geert Bouckaert. *Public management reform: A comparative analysis.* Oxford University Press, USA, 2004

————. *Public management reform: A comparative analysis-into the age of austerity.* Oxford University Press, 2017.

Rhodes, Roderick Arthur William. "The new governance: governing without government." *Political studies* 44, no. 4 (1996): 652–667.

Sachverständigenrat 'Schlanker Staat' Abschlussbericht. *Sachverständigenrat Schlanker Staat im Bundesministerium des Innern.* 1997

Stutzer, Alois, and Bruno S. Frey. "Making international organizations more democratic." *Review of law & economics* 1, no. 3 (2005): 305–330.

Terry, Larry D. "Administrative leadership, neo-managerialism, and the public management movement." *Public Administration Review* (1998): 194–200.

United Nations. *Renewing the UN: A Program for Reform.* 1997.

Veggeland, Noralv. Paths of public innovation in the global age: Lessons from Scandinavia. Edward Elgar Publishing, 2007.

World Bank. *The World Bank Annual Report 1997.* 1997.

CHAPTER 6

Performance Management: A Theoretical Framework

Abstract This chapter will focus on performance management systems and their reforms by looking at the different literature streams that have contributed to the development of the performance management theory, including public administration, public management, strategic planning and management controls, evidence-based policy, and evaluation. This will lead to define common trends of performance management systems useful to identify the key features when applied to international organizations. The latter are characterized by a strong multilevel governance system where performance is the result of a combination of actions of a large number of actors (governments, subnational entities, NGOs, citizens). Since we consider international organizations very similar to networked structures, we dedicate some space to the specificities of performance management in networks.

Keywords Performance management systems • Performance management of networks • Performance management in international organizations

M. Amici, D. Cepiku, *Performance Management in International Organizations*, https://doi.org/10.1007/978-3-030-39472-1_6

6.1   PERFORMANCE MANAGEMENT: RECENT TRENDS AND SUBSTANCE

The trend towards reforming public sector organizations is closely associated with the increasing orientation of public management towards performances. According to several authors (Pollitt and Bouckaert 2017; Hood 1991; Hood and Peters 2004), performance management is the core of public management. Consequently, public sector reforms included a strong emphasis on adopting performance management systems, to the point that, as put it by Radin (2000: 168), "if there is a single theme that characterizes the public sector in the 1990s, is the demand for performance. A mantra emerged in this decade, heard at all levels of government that calls for documentation of performance and explicit outcome of government action". In this period, performance measurement also became more intensive, extensive, and external (Halachmi and Bouckaert 1996) and "if you can't measure it, you can't manage it" was the popular refrain (Thomas 2003: 1).

Performance is not a unitary concept and encompasses different meanings and levels. As for the concept, in literature, different definitions of performance can be found. Bovaird (1996: 147) formulated a generic description of performance "as a set of information about the achievement of varying significance to different stakeholders." More commonly, performance can be defined as an organization's ability to achieve agreed objectives. Kamensky and Morales (2005) suggest a more detailed definition of differentiating performance and results. The former being a tangible operationalization of results that can be divided into outputs and outcomes, while the latter can be intended as a more generic concept. On the same vein, Gutner and Thompson (2010), stress how performance has two distinct but related meanings as a verb and as a noun. The first concerns the ability to achieve some sort of objectives. The second, as a noun, how the objectives have been achieved. Consequently, assessing organizational performance means analyzing the outcome produced as well as the process leading to the outcome in terms of efficiency, effort, and skills (Gutner and Thompson 2010). The two aspects are closely related. While efficient organizations can complete tasks and achieve goals more effectively, it is also true that "well-functioning internal processes do not necessarily imply that an entity will fulfill its goals" (Gutner and Thompson 2010: 232). On the opposite, "if goals are easy to achieve, an entity might succeed perfectly well even when its performance per se is not very impressive" (Gutner and Thompson 2010: 232). This allows also differentiating between the concept of performance and effectiveness, the latter being the ability to achieve objectives or solve problems, whereas the former is how objectives are achieved (Gutner and Thompson 2010). Different models and metrics are generally employed to measure the performance of organizations according to the extension and intensity of the performance measurement.

The extension of a performance management system can be measured along two different dimensions, span, and depth. Span of performance can be defined as the horizontal expansion of the results and is linked to the mechanistic relationship between inputs, activities, and outputs (Bouckaert and Halligan 2008). The latter is defined as the quantitative and qualitative results in terms of services or products, generated by processing inputs (Bouckaert and Halligan 2008). Normally outputs are never considered an end in themselves, and as much as they are, more easily can be transferred to the private sector (Bouckaert and Halligan 2008). Conversely, the less an output is an end in itself, the more belongs to the public sector (Bouckaert and Halligan 2008). Outputs then leave the organization and enter the society, and their effect is defined as an outcome. This latter should be the primary concern in assessing public sector performance. Therefore, as much as a performance management system is able to measure outcomes as much wider is the span. Although some claimed that also outcomes and effects are not the ultimate aim of public sector organizations, being this latter "guaranteeing a functional level of trust by citizens in all its institutions and organizations" (Pollitt and Bouckaert 2017). Similarly, Gutner and Thompson (2010) proposes a similar metric to measure the different levels of performance achieved by an organization focused on macro outcomes at one end of a continuum and process-based indicators on the other. In this case, the span will be narrow as much as the system will be focused on measuring the internal processes carried out within the organization to achieve the agreed objectives. Conversely, it will be is wider as much as the performance system can measure the ability of the organization to solve problems and enhance welfare (outcomes). Nevertheless, outcomes or effects are generally realized with the contribution of several organizations. Thus, performance management systems should not be just organized at the level of a single organization (micro-level) but at least at the level of policy field (meso-level) or government-wide (macro-level) (Bouckaert and Halligan 2008). This is related to the vertical dimension of performance, which is defined as performance depth.

Also, performance can be conceived at the individual or organizational level (Talbot 2005). Combining span and depth of performance can result in a different focus of performance systems.

The intensity of a performance management system refers to the need for integrating performance information into a performance management cycle. This includes three chronological steps (Bouckaert and Halligan 2008):

- measuring, intended as collecting performance data into information;
- using, intended as integrating performance information into documents, procedures and stakeholder discourses;
- incorporating, intended as using performance information in a strategy for improving decision-making, results, and accountability.

Consequently, as much as performance information produced by the performance system will be used and incorporated into the strategic decision-making system of the organization as much as intense will be the use of performance information.

Considering such a theoretical framework, when it comes to measuring performance, differences also exist about the type of organizations. The metrics outlined so far can be easily applied to business organizations with generally measurable and well-defined objectives, as in the case of corporations, whose final objective is to achieve profit. Conversely, the objectives of public and no-profit organizations are generally more ambiguous and variegated and more difficult is agreeing on what constitutes a goal achievement or a goal outcome (Kay and Jacobson 1983). Furthermore, even if a consensus on the definition of goal achievement is reached, other relevant problems arise when the above-mentioned performance framework is applied to reality. Such difficulties are generally known as disconnections and characterize both dimensions of performance, span, and depth, as well as affect the policy cycle. As for the two dimensions of performance, generally disconnections concern:

- (span) the weak or missing causal link between outputs and the outcome from one side, and between outcome and the level of trust among people, from the other side. This is due to the influence of external factors out of the organizations' reach. Bouckaert and Halligan (2008) define these disconnections as "Grand Canyons."

- (depth) the potential conflicts among the different levels of performance, micro (single organizations), meso (policy area), macro
(government-wide). Single organizations (hospitals) within a policy
area (health) could have conflicting performance objectives (increasing the number of patients) respect to those (decreasing or limiting
the number of patients) set at the policy sector (Health Ministers)
(Bouckaert and Halligan 2008).

The performance management is also subject to a relevant number of
critiques in the literature for the following reasons. An excessive rational-
istic approach (Christensen et al. 2006), the high transaction costs for
maintaining performance systems (Bevan and Hood 2006), as well as the
impossibility to fulfil expectations because of difficulties with delivery and
complexities in the environment (Bouckaert and Halligan 2008). Despite
this, public sector organizations have been for a long-time confronted
with the introduction of performance management systems.

The extent to which national administrative systems have adopted performance management systems can differ sharply, especially as far as span
and depth are concerned. According to Bouckaert and Halligan (2008)[1]
variation in performance management systems are inevitably linked to the
different public administration models.[2] In other words, the more ambitious use of performance information is "less difficult for the public service
culture of the public interest administrative systems to absorb than for
Rechtsstaat system" (Pollitt and Bouckaert 2017: 108). Within this latter,
countries are more used to guide their policies through norms and regulations rather than by results (Pollitt and Bouckaert 2017). Thus, performance management has been less developed in countries as Germany and
France, rather than NPM oriented countries as Australia, New Zealand,
and the United Kingdom (Bouckaert and Halligan 2008).

Inspired by the NPM paradigm, public sector organizations of these
countries recognized a greater emphasis on improving service delivery, on
treating service users as customers as well as on using market type mechanisms. Politicians were thus encouraged to define products or services the
administrative body is expected to achieve, and consequently, this latter
based the relations with providers on performance contracts. Thus, either
more tangible public services (waste collection, postal services, permits
issuing, etc.) or those more intangible (as health care and education),
started to be object of performance measurement through indicator
schemes used for benchmarking and tables of leagues (Pollitt and

Bouckaert 2011). The use of performance indicator schemes was also employed for monitoring the achievement of the objectives set in terms of customer expectations, as well as provided inputs to improve the next services management cycle.

Such an approach, typical of the private sector, aimed to focus the attention towards the efficiency of the government action, by focusing on the productivity intended as the ratio between the inputs employed and outputs produced. Consequently, the span of performance management systems was mainly limited to input and output measures.

The depth of performance was restricted to the level of the single organization. This was due to the NPM orientation towards the decentralization and disaggregation of public organizations. However, this contributed to focus performance evaluation on those objectives more easily to measure, namely the quantity of services or products provided, disregarding those more difficult to measure, which are typically related to the quality of products and services delivered.

Contrary to the NPM, several alternative paradigms, as the Public Value and the Neo Weberian State (NWS) encouraged a different approach to performance, focused on the impact of public sector organizations. In this perspective, performance management systems should include an outcome dimension. This latter should be able to monitor the achievement of much higher order aspirations, compared to the output perspective. They include poverty reduction, national security and public health, among others, reflecting the difference between private value (rubbish is collected) and public value (protect public health) (Aquino 2013).

According to the NWS model, which is based on the increased awareness about the peculiarities of public sector organizations, performance measurement should shift in discourses and practice "from efficiency to effectiveness, i.e. from getting something done cheaply to accomplishing one's goal." (Drechsler 2005: 19). In the NWS model, the attention to norms and regulation and a greater orientation on the achievement of results coexist (Kostakis 2011). In other words, the important traditional concern over processes and procedures aimed at guaranteeing the legality of the decision is coupled with ex-post concerns about the results of the organization's action (Bouckaert and Halligan 2008).

Thus, the emerging relevance of results, in terms of efficiency and economy, is expressed by the introduction of performance management systems focused on the ex-post control approach. Legitimacy will be based on the principle of legality but also on the economy, efficiency, and effectiveness of the functioning of the government and its policies (Bouckaert and Halligan 2008).

In sum, as stressed by Pollitt and Bouckaert (2017: 109), "a modern professional manager in the NWS mold would expect to use performance information, to check that the services the state was delivering were timely and efficient and that they were generating good levels of satisfaction among the citizens who used them". Under the NWS model, the span of the performance system moved from a focus on output to outcome measure, intended as the impact of public action on citizen satisfaction. Depth of performance moved from the micro-level to the level of policy domain.

As traditional public administration is shifting towards Neo-Weberian design models, under the pressure of a focus on performance, at the same time a similar trajectory is also influencing NPM-oriented countries. They moved towards more an integrated governance approach with a focus on the whole of government agendas (Bouckaert and Halligan 2008). This is a reaction to the distortions caused by the use of performance in an excessive fragmented system observed in several NPM oriented countries as Australia and New Zealand. The latter started to reinforce the horizontal relations among departments to counterbalance the strength of the vertical functionally departments through an integrated governance approach, which became the prevailing approach in the mid-2000 (Bouckaert and Halligan 2008).

The governance approach emerged from the search of the new high-level paradigm of the future, which could replace the out fashioned NPM model. In such effort, Osborne (2006) proposed the New Public Governance (NPG) model characterized by the inter-organizational relationships, the governance of processes and service effectiveness and outcomes. The NPG model includes new governance managerial practices and techniques, as networks and the use of ICT, and brings relevant implications for performance measurement and management. This latter becomes an inter-governmental exercise requiring special attention to the role of networks and the capacity to measure their performance (Bouckaert and Halligan 2008). The inter-dependence among organizations can take different forms. It includes the relations between different levels of government, between a combination of governments, at European, national, and subnational levels, forming networks of collaboration (Hooghe 1996; Cepiku 2013) and finally between state and non-state actors, including private and no-profit bodies. At the same time, the span of performance extends to the ultimate results of public action beyond outcome and including citizen's trust in public services as well as impacts (Bouckaert and Halligan 2008). Finally, the contribution of citizens as customers also becomes a crucial aspect of governing performance (Halvorsen 2003). In such a context, measuring performance is a rather challenging undertaking for the following reasons.

First, as stressed by Agranoff (2005: 18), measuring performance of networks is problematic as "the straightforward emphasis on outcome rather than inputs or outputs [...] is not so simple when multiple stakeholders work on policy and programs". Similarly, Bouckaert and Halligan (2008) stress the general understanding that there are many deficits in our capacity to assess performance of this type. The emerging importance of networks requires special attention as the action of public organizations at different levels, as well as non-public organizations, need to be measured separately and in combination with public stakeholders (Bouckaert and Halligan 2008).

Secondly, working through networks implies blurring the traditional organization boundaries, which add complexities to performance management (Bouckaert and Halligan 2008).

Finally, measuring trust and impacts are "inherently more difficult because we must first understand the causal relationships between the measured inputs, outputs and outcomes and the underlying phenomena leading to the observed results" (Flynn and Hodgkinson 2001: 4).

Considering such complexities, Bouckaert and Halligan (2008) suggest different tools and mechanisms to facilitate performance management. They include, among others, integrating initiatives and whole of government approach. The former includes an integrated approach between different levels of governments to strengthen more effectively the control over the different components of the executive branch as well as integrating them with other actors and sectors on national goals and impacts (Bouckaert and Halligan 2008). In this respect, elements of the NPM philosophy, as contract and market mechanisms, coexist with a focus on outcomes and evaluation review (Bouckaert and Halligan 2008). The whole government approach focuses on society as a whole in terms of performance (Bouckaert and Halligan 2008). It attempts to develop national indicators of well-being and seek to link them to the different levels of government and departmental programs (Bouckaert and Halligan 2008).

Examples of the whole of government approach can be found in several countries, including Canada. It developed a comprehensive whole of government planning and reporting framework, with three policy areas and for each five outcomes linked to annual reports on national performance and departmental plans, priorities, and performance (Treasury Board of Canada Secretariat 2006). Finally, another relevant aspect of performance is that decisions and judgments to be fully legitimized need to involve all the stakeholders affected by that decision (Stoker 2006). Knowing whether the final results of public action are delivered requires open consultations with all the relevant stakeholders involved in public sector activities as well as their active engagement. This reinforces the need for linking performance to network management or in other words to managing public sector organizations through networks efficiently and effectively (Stoker 2006), as discussed above. Nevertheless, compared to other paradigms, the role of performance under the NPG paradigm is less clear, considering the difficult question of how measuring the performance of networks (Bouckaert and Halligan 2008).

6.2   ASSESSING PERFORMANCE MANAGEMENT SYSTEMS IN INTERNATIONAL ORGANIZATIONS

As described above, span and depth of performance vary across reform models and public administration frameworks, as shown in several comparative performance studies (Bouckaert and Halligan 2008; Vallotti and Davide 2010). By contrast, the extension and intensity of performance management systems of international organizations attracted little attention in literature. Despite measuring the performance of international organizations is more complex and challenging, compared to national governments, this should not prevent us from dealing with such complexities. As put by Gutner and Thompson (2010: 234), "understanding and explaining the performance of international organizations is uniquely difficult and—uniquely interesting."

International organizations share many complexities with public sector organizations when it comes to defining performance, as they often have multiple goals broadly defined and are influenced by many stakeholders with different degrees of power (Perrow 1986; Moe 1989). Gutner and Thompson (2010) identify three different common obstacles:

- the lofty mandates of international organizations that prevent the possibility of judging performance effectively;

- the "eye of beholder problem" in the performance evaluation, consequently performance can vary significantly depending on the analyst;
- the issue of self-evaluation, as all international organizations evaluate themselves based on performance objectives set and methods of measuring them, preventing objective evaluations and leading to self-serving ones.

Moreover, international organizations are distinct from public sector organizations as they are governed by states and their performance is linked to the ability of governments to cooperate and collectively manage large organizations (Lyne et al. 2006). Member states, moreover, could have sometimes diverging performance objectives. In the same vein, Mehde (2007) notes that international organizations are accountable too many people and to many different governments. Consequently, they need to satisfy a great number of highly diverse actors having very different and sometimes conflicting interests. At the same time, they lack a single public as a point of reference as well as a general election encompassing all the citizens affected by the activities of international organizations, except one case· the European Union. On the one hand, creating satisfactory results is a very ambitious task in this respect; on the other, international organizations need to avoid situations in which they are blamed for poor performance for problems they are not responsible for (Mehde 2007). Additionally, international organizations do not generally engage in service provisions but rather deal with more intangible goods, although with variations. The preservation of environment or cultural heritage can be more tangible than peace or financial stability, but in any case, difficult to measure (Kaul et al. 1999). Nevertheless, as described in the previous paragraph, performance measurement can significantly differ in terms of span and depth, and outcome indicators are not the only performance metric used to monitor organizational performance. According to the performance metric proposed by Gutner and Thompson (2010), with macro outcomes at one end and more process-based indicators at the other, there is a wide range of indicators we can use for measuring international organizations' results. Alongside the outcome perspective, we could focus on the micro-level of the international organization, measuring the efficiency in performing the functions and tasks necessary to achieve higher objectives. In this case the level of analysis is different, the outcome perspective is linked to the international organization's action, that is responsible for achieving the ultimate objectives set in the treaties, whereas the efficiency is generally related to the functioning of the international organization secretariat performing the administrative and management duties (also referred as the international public administration). The two levels are linked, although efficient administrative bodies could have little impact on the achievement of higher objectives (Gutner and Thompson 2010). A third possibility could be looking at an intermediate level between process and outcome, which is defined in public policy literature as "outputs" or "intermediate outputs" (Levy et al. 1974). The latter refers to the intermediate output of the international organization activities, for example, the number of programs financed to reduce illegal migration flows or the number of environmental legislation produced to decrease air pollution. In this case, although the effects of such output on the final problem is not automatic, likely, an organization that performs well in the output production can more easily achieve their objectives in terms of outcome (Gutner and Thompson 2010). Equally, a focus on process indicators is more appropriate in case we are interested in assessing the functioning of the administrative secretariat and understanding whether there is a relation between micro and macro-level performance. The limitation of focusing on process indicators is that good process performance does not necessarily translate into outcome performance (Gutner and Thompson 2010).

Moving to the outcome orientation of international organization performance, helpful insights on how to measure the problem-solving capacity of international organizations can come from regime-effectiveness literature, which explores in more detail the concepts of effectiveness and outcomes and explain their variation (Young 1999; Underdal and Young 2004). According to Underdal (2002: 11), regime effectiveness can be described as whether the regime can "solve the problem that motivated its establishment." In other words, if an environmental regime can objectively increase the physical state of the environment (Gutner and Thompson 2010).

Nevertheless, the regime effectiveness has different limitations when applied to international organizations. The international organization is only one element of the regime—the latter generally includes multiple international organizations and other actors—and consequently, the outcome cannot be associated with a single organization (Gutner and Thompson 2010). However, outcome measures can be difficultly attributed to a single international organization. According to Gutner and Thompson (2010), outcome-based indicators may be appropriate in case international organizations have a predominant role in a given policy area with objectively measurable solutions. Inappropriate in case political factors outside of their control constrained them (Gutner and Thompson 2010). Nevertheless, such a condition, in reality, is extremely difficult to observe. More commonly, international organizations, even if not included in any regime, need to interact with multiple actors and be subject to external factors, to achieve the higher objectives set in the constitutional treaties. In other words, as international organizations are more and more confronted with the production of global public goods, with transnational and diffuse character, these latter will result from a combination of the interactions among different public and private actors at the global level. Consequently, the public policy process at the global level is increasingly seen as "an interaction in which the different actors exchange information about problems, preferences, and means, and trade-off goals and resources" (Kickert et al. 1997: 24). In this respect, a contribution to understanding the role of international organizations as a producer of global public goods can come from the network theory. The policies at the international level are now shaped through organizational networks and their effectiveness depends "on the ability and willingness of a variety of organizational actors, public and private to work together" (Metcalfe 2000: 828).

In this context, the role of international organizations in managing networks is a crucial aspect for increasing the effectiveness of global public production, and consequently to achieve the final objective they have been created. According to network theory, different authors (Agranoff and McGuire 2001; Milward and Provan 2003; Mayntz 1998) recognize in the public sector organizations those entitled to steer and coordinate networks due to their specific peculiarities and strategic coordination mechanisms, as funding, normative regulations and objectives setting (Meneguzzo 2006). *Mutatis mutandis*, it is reasonable to expect that international organizations should play the same strategic role at the international level in the coordination of international policy networks for the production of global public goods.

From a performance management perspective, the focus moves towards network performance, which, as described above, characterizes the New Public Governance reform model. Although the highlighted complexities, the performance management systems of international organizations should be performance network-oriented. In other words, the performance measurement system should support collaborative relations among the network members and evaluate their performance. From an operational point of view, the performance management systems should focus on measuring the outcome (the global public goods). They should include specific indicators for measuring the performance of networks and monitoring the elements useful to detect under which conditions networks are able to perform better (Kenis and Provan 2009). Provan and Milward (2001) consider three performance variables in a network: the outcome produced for the benefit of each partner, the outcome achieved for the community at large as well as the network level outcome. Consequently, performance management in a network is relevant to motivate the network members about the convenience to remain in the network compared to other organizational forms (Provan and Milward 2001). The literature identifies two main components influencing network performance at the three different levels, exogenous elements over which network managers have little control, and endogenous elements that can be instrumentally used by the network manager (Cepiku 2013). The exogenous elements include:

- The type of network, its voluntary nature, and the level of network development (Kenis and Provan 2009). The authors suggest that all network members should firstly share the measurement system of network performance and all external factors influencing such performance should be identified (Kenis and Provan 2009).
- The fact that network objectives should be preliminary set with the agreement of all members (goal consensus) and then subject to periodic evaluation to guarantee that the contribution of each organization is in line with its capacity to deliver it (Voets et al. 2008).
- The form of the network i.e., shared governance, lead organization or network administrative form (Kenis and Provan 2009).
- The type of network relations that can be of collaborative or social type or competitive or market type (Heranz 2010).
- The complementarity of partners, their number and the geographical location as well as their trust and previous collaboration history (Cepiku 2013).

The endogenous elements influencing network performance include the network management processes and the leadership style (Cepiku 2013). The importance of the process variable has been acknowledged by several authors (McGuire and Agranoff 2007; Klijn et al. 2010), which

Table 6.1 Core elements of Performance management area

Areas/functions		Ideal paradigms			
		Traditional	*NWS*	*NPM*	*NPG*
Performance evaluation					
Performance focus		Correctness of procedures	Focus on the achievement of satisfaction in service delivery (outcome)	Achievement of results (outputs)	Focus on the performance of the network
Extension of the performance measurement system	Span of performance	Inputs	Outcome	Outputs	Outcome/impacts
	Depth of performance	Micro	Meso	Micro	Government/governance wide

Source: own elaboration

emphasize the importance of measuring not only the performance network but also the quality of interaction among the network members (Cepiku 2013). Network interaction can be influenced by many factors, including, a wise design, the use of forums, agreements supporting accountability, conflict management, and trust-building activities (Crosby and Bryson 2010).

Table 6.1 shows the research framework adopted to analyze the performance management systems of the selected international organizations based on the core elements of the main ideal paradigms. In particular, the study will include at the following elements:

- the analysis of the baseline for assessing performance, including the way the organization's mission has measured; (Gutner and Thompson 2010)
- the assessment of the indicators used to assess performance, explicitly link these indicators to the baseline identified in the first stage, by explaining how they capture performance results of interest (Gutner and Thompson 2010);
- the identification of the levels of analysis that will be examined, and their interaction;
- the analysis of the sources of good or bad performance and describe the mechanisms by which they shape international organization performance; (Gutner and Thompson 2010)
- the inclusion of network performance elements in the design of the performance management systems.

NOTES

1. Bouckaert and Halligan (2008) undertook a comprehensive assessment of performance management systems of public sector organizations in six industrialized countries. The countries include the United States, United Kingdom, Sweden, The Netherlands, Canada, and Australia.
2. According to Pollitt and Bouckaert (2017), a public administration framework may be essentially Weberian or public management each with its dynamics of development.

REFERENCES

Agranoff, Robert. "Managing collaborative performance: Changing the boundaries of the state?." *Public Performance & Management Review* 29, no. 1 (2005): 18–45.

Agranoff, Robert, and Michael McGuire. "Big questions in public network management research." *Journal of public administration research and theory* 11, no. 3 (2001): 295–326.

Aquino, Simona. ""Aziendalizzazione", nuova governance, e performance delle Amministrazioni Pubbliche: un confronto internazionale." *Economia Aziendale Online* 3, no. 3–4 (2013): 321–348.

Bevan, Gwyn, and Christopher Hood. "What's measured is what matters: targets and gaming in the English public health care system." *Public administration* 84, no. 3 (2006): 517–538.

Bouckaert, Geert, and John Halligan. "Comparing performance across public sectors." In *Performance Information in the Public Sector*, pp. 72–93. Palgrave Macmillan, London, 2008

Bovaird, Tony. "The political economy of performance measurement." *Organizational Performance and Measurement in the Public Sector: Toward Service, Effort and Accomplished Reporting, Quorum Books, Westport* (1996): 145–165.

Cepiku, Denita. "Network performance: toward a dynamic multidimensional model." In *Network Theory in the Public Sector*, pp. 188–204. Routledge, 2013.

Christensen, Tom, Per Lægreid, and Inger Marie Stigen. "Performance management and public sector reform: The Norwegian hospital reform." *International Public Management Journal* 9, no. 2 (2006): 113–139.

Crosby, Barbara C., and John M. Bryson. "Integrative leadership and the creation and maintenance of cross-sector collaborations." *The Leadership Quarterly* 21, no. 2 (2010): 211–230.

Drechsler, Wolfgang. "The rise and demise of the new public management." *Post-autistic economics review* 33, no. 14 (2005): 17–28.

Flynn, Patrice, and Virginia A. Hodgkinson, eds. Measuring the impact of the nonprofit sector. *Springer Science & Business Media*, 2001.

Gutner, Tamar, and Alexander Thompson. "The politics of IO performance: A framework." *The review of international organizations* 5, no. 3 (2010): 227–248.

Halachmi, Arie, and Geert Bouckaert, eds. *Organizational performance and measurement in the public sector: Toward service, effort, and accomplishment reporting*. Greenwood Publishing Group, 1996.

Halvorsen, Kathleen E. "Assessing the effects of public participation." *Public Administration Review* 63, no. 5 (2003): 535–543.

Heranz, Joaquín. "Network performance and coordination: A theoretical review and framework." *Public Performance & Management Review* 33, no. 3 (2010): 311–341.

Hood, Christopher. "A public management for all seasons?." *Public administration* 69, no. 1 (1991): 3–19.

Hood, Christopher, and Guy Peters. "The middle aging of new public management: into the age of paradox?." *Journal of public administration research and theory* 14, no. 3 (2004): 267–282.

Hooghe, Liesbet, ed. *Cohesion policy and European integration: building multilevel governance.* Oxford University Press on Demand, 1996.

Kamensky, John M., and Albert Morales, eds. *Managing for results 2005.* Rowman & Littlefield, 2005.

Kaul, Inge, Isabelle Grunberg, and Marc A. Stern. "Defining global public goods." Global public goods: international cooperation in the 21st century (1999): 2–19.

Kay, D., and H. Jacobson. "Environmental Protection: The International Dimension (Totowa, NJ: Allanheld, Osmun)." (1983).

Kenis, Patrick, and Keith G. Provan. "Towards an exogenous theory of public network performance." *Public Administration* 87, no. 3 (2009): 440–456.

Kickert, Walter JM, Erik-Hans Klijn, and Joop FM Koppenjan, (eds.) Managing Complex Networks, Sage, London. King, L.A. (2003), 'Deliberation, Legitimacy, and Multilateral Democracy', *Governance*, 16(1) (1997): 23–50.

Klijn, Erik-Hans, Jurian Edelenbos, and Bram Steijn. "Trust in governance networks: Its impacts on outcomes." *Administration & Society* 42, no. 2 (2010): 193–221.

Kostakis, Vasilis. "Commons-based peer production and the neo-Weberian state: synergies and interdependencies." *Administrative Culture* 12, no. 2 (2011): 146–161.

Levy, Frank, Arnold J. Meltsner, and Aaron B. Wildavsky. *Urban outcomes: Schools, streets, and libraries.* Univ of California Press, 1974.

Lyne, Mona M., Daniel L. Nielson, and Michael J. Tierney. "Who delegates? Alternative models of principals in development aid." *Delegation and agency in international organizations* 44 (2006).

Mayntz, Renate. "Socialist academies of sciences: the enforced orientation of basic research at user needs." *Research Policy* 27, no. 8 (1998): 781–791.

McGuire, Michael, and Robert Agranoff. "Answering the big questions, asking the bigger questions: Expanding the public network management empirical research agenda." In *9th Public Management Research Conference.* Tucson, AZ. 2007.

Mehde, Veith. "Creating a missing link? administrative reforms as a means of improving the legitimacy of international organizations." In Management reforms in international organizations, pp. 163–175. Nomos Verlagsgesellschaft mbH & Co. KG. 2007.

Meneguzzo, Marco G. "La strategia e la governance delle amministrazioni pubbliche." In L. Hinna, M. Meneguzzo, R. Mussari, & M. Decastri (eds.), *Economia delle aziende pubbliche* (pp. 1–144). Milano: MaGaw-Hill. (2006): 1–144.

Metcalfe, Les. "Reforming the Commission: will organizational efficiency produce effective governance?." *JCMS: Journal of Common Market Studies* 38, no. 5 (2000): 817–841.

Milward, H. Brinton, and Keith G. Provan. "Managing networks effectively." In National Public Management Research Conference, Georgetown University, Washington, DC October. 2003.

Moe, Terry M. "The politics of bureaucratic structure." *Can the government govern* 267 (1989): 285–323.

Osborne, Stephen P. "The new public governance?" *Public Management Review*, Vol. 8 Issue 3 (2006): 377–387.

Perrow, Ch. "1986 Complex organizations; a critical essay, New York: Random House." (1986).

Pollitt, Christopher, and Geert Bouckaert. Continuity and change in public policy and management. Edward Elgar Publishing, 2011.

———. *Public management reform: A comparative analysis-into the age of austerity.* Oxford University Press, 2017.

Provan, Keith G., and H. Brinton Milward. "Do networks really work? A framework for evaluating public-sector organizational networks." *Public administration review* 61, no. 4 (2001): 414–423.

Radin, Beryl A. "The Government Performance and Results Act and the tradition of federal management reform: square pegs in round holes?." *Journal of Public Administration Research and Theory* 10, no. 1 (2000): 111–135.

Stoker, Gerry. "*Why Politics Matters. Making Democracy Work*" Palgrave Macmillan (2006)

Talbot, Colin. "*Performance management.*" In The Oxford handbook of public management. 2005.

Thomas Paul G. "*Accountability Introduction.*" In Handbook of Public Administration, (eds) Peters B.G., Pierre J., Montreal and Kingstone, Sage. 2003.

Treasury Board of Canada Secretariat. Results for Canadians. A Management Framework for the Government of Canada, Ottawa, TBS (2006)

Underdal, Arild. "One question, two answers." Environmental regime effectiveness: Confronting theory with evidence (2002): 3–45.

Underdal, Arild, and Oran R. Young. "Regime consequences." *Methodological Challenges and Research Strategies* (2004).

Vallotti Giovanni, Galli Davide. Research Project "*La misurazione e la valutazione della performance nella PA Centrale.*" Scuola Nazionale Amministrazione, 2010.

van Helden, G. Jan, Åge Johnsen, and Jarmo Vakkuri. "The life-cycle approach to performance management: Implications for public management and evaluation." *Evaluation* 18, no. 2 (2012): 159–175.

Voets, Joris, Wouter Van Dooren, and Filip De Rynck. "A framework for assessing the performance of policy networks." *Public management review* 10, no. 6 (2008): 773–790.

Young, Oran R., ed. *The effectiveness of international environmental regimes: Causal connections and behavioral mechanisms.* MIT Press, 1999.

CHAPTER 7

Analysis and Comparison of the Case Studies: The European Union

Abstract This chapter will seek answers to the following questions: To what extent the European Union measures the results of its action? What are the characteristics of the European Union performance management system compared to the ideal paradigm developed in literature?

The chapter includes a description of the context and history of the European Union, as well as the drivers, the process and contents of the management reforms implemented, and an evaluation of the performance management system.

Keywords European Union • Performance management system in the European Union

7.1 The Organization and Functioning of the European Union

The European Union (EU), within the realm of international organizations, can be classified as a regional organization of general-purpose, although with unique characteristics compared to other traditional regional organizations. The EU encompasses different aspects of both inter-governmentalism and supranationalism, according to the different sectors of competence, as well as a relevant number of functions. These include, normative and rule creation, collecting information and

© The Author(s) 2020   115
M. Amici, D. Cepiku, *Performance Management in International Organizations*, https://doi.org/10.1007/978-3-030-39472-1_7

monitoring trends, mediating role as well as operational functions including allocating resources and providing financial assistance. Such a complexity raised several issues about the nature of the EU. The coexistence of both aspects, as well as its evolutionary process, softened the initial perception of the EU as an international organization.

Comparing to the origins of foundation in 1951, the EU widened its scope significantly through what Haas defined as "functional spillovers" (Haas 1958: 257). The EU thus moved from an economic integration project to a political one with a consequence of deepening the ties with the member states. These delegated parts of their sovereignty in specific fields at the EU level, until the point that today the majority part of the policymaking in the European countries is commonly referred to as EU policy, decided within the EU institutional framework. At the same time, in the most sensitive areas, including internal affairs and security, defense and foreign policy, education policy as well as economic and fiscal policy, the EU acts as a traditional international organization to facilitate intergovernmental bargains.

The functioning of the European Union is regulated by two founding treaties: the Treaty of the European Union (TEU) and the Treaty on the Functioning (TFEU) of the European Union. The first sets out the fundamental principles and norms the EU is based upon, as well as the objectives, the values and organization's competences, whereas the second is focused on setting the rules for the functioning of the European institutions and the decision-making procedures. The treaties spell out the underlying principles for the limits of the EU action and the competences sharing between the EU and the member states. According to article 5 (TEU), the EU can act "only within the limits of the competences conferred upon it by the Member States in the Treaties to attain the objectives set out therein," so all competencies not included in the Treaties remain in the Member States competence. As for the competences conferred to the EU, they can be of exclusive or shared competence. All subjects member states decided to transfer to the EU competence fall under the first category[1], and only the EU can take legislative initiatives, whereas for shared competence subjects, either the EU or the member states can legislate according to the subsidiarity principle. It defines the perimeter of the EU action establishing that "the Union shall act only if and in so far as the objectives of the proposed action cannot be sufficiently achieved by the Member States, either at central level or at regional and local level, but can rather, by reason of the scale or effects of the proposed action, be better achieved at Union level" (art. 5 TFEU).

Also, in some areas of member states' responsibility, the EU can carry out actions to support, coordinate or supplement the actions of the Member States, for example, trough spending programs (art. 6 TFEU). The decisions making system of the EU is based on the following organizational design, including:

- the European Council, which gathers all the EU heads of state or government to provide strategic input for the EU action;
- the Council of Ministers of the European Union made up of national Ministries and mainly dealing with legislative functions;
- the European Parliament, directly elected by the European citizens and involved together with the Council of Minister in the legislative process;
- The European Commission, promoting the general interest of the EU and acting as the executive body of the EU, participating in almost all stages of the EU policy-making, being the administrative body of the EU.

The EU institutional framework also includes the Court of Justice, the European Central Bank, and European Court of Auditors as well as other consultative bodies as the European Committee of the Regions and Economic and Social Committee. Among the EU different institutions, the focus of the analysis will be on the European Commission, considering its strategic relevance in the EU decision-making system. According to article 17 of the Treaty of the European Union, the main objective of the European Commission is to "promote the general interest of the Union and take appropriate initiatives to that end" to achieve the goals laid down in the treaties.[2] In this respect, it is often labeled as the engine of the European integration process or "the conscience of the EU because it is designed to look after the good of the whole" (Ginsberg 2007). To this purpose, the treaties empowered the Commission with a relevant number of roles and functions. These include:

- the initiative role in the EU legislative decision-making process;
- control and monitoring duties on the respect of the treaties by the member states;
- some limited normative functions in the framework of the powers delegated to the Commission by the Council of Ministers to implement their decisions;
- a relevant number of administrative and management duties.

Contrary to a traditional Secretariat dealing with the administrative functions of the international organizations, the European Commission is composed of a political and an administrative level. The political part consists of the President and the College of Commissioners, in office for five years following the electoral cycle of the European Parliament. The President's role range from overseeing the Commission administration to shaping its political agenda by setting the Commission Political Guidelines as well as communicating with the other EU institutions. In doing this, it is assisted by the College of Commissioners composed of a commissioner from each EU member states, working according to the collegiality principle. This means that all commissioners share the responsibility for Commission decisions. These are consequently adopted collectively by the College to safeguard its independence vis à vis the national governments that nominate the Commissioners. This principle poses the College at the very center of the Commission decision making and makes it a unique body in international politics (Nugent and Rhinard 2015).

The administrative part of the Commission is known as "the Services", called Directorate Generals (DGs) and organized according to a specialization logic with most of the DGs covering a policy-issue area (as energy, agriculture, trade, etc.) and few other horizontal issues (budgeting, translations, logistics, etc.). The main DGs responsibilities include drafting of legislative proposals, preparing policy briefs and writing reports, drawing up and manage EU spending programs as well as directly implementing legislation in some restricted policy areas (as in the case of competition) and acting on behalf of the EU in some areas of external policies (as in the case of trade and enlargement policy) (Nugent and Rhinard 2015). The European Commission enjoys a marked degree of autonomy in organizing their internal structures that adopted new working methods based on the different waves of management reforms implemented in the European Commission.

7.2   THE REFORM DRIVERS

Despite the academic interest in the European Commission, the internal management received scholarly attention only after the fall of the Santer Commission in 1999 and the subsequent launch of the Kinnock management reform. At the beginning of 2000, many studies analyzed the management reform and its impact on the internal structures of the Commission as well as on their policy outputs (Bauer 2001, 2002; Bearfield 2004;

Coull and Lewis 2003; Cram 2001; Kassim 2008; Levy 2002, 2003a, 2003b; Metcalfe 2000; Spence 2000; Spence and Stevens 2006; Stevens and Stevens 2006). Before 2000, reforming the internal structure of the Commission was not on the top of the President's agenda.

The first serious reform programs have been launched under Santer Commission and included the *Sound and Effective Management* initiative (SEM2000) aimed to modernize and improve finance and resource management systems as well as to increase coordination between financial controllers in the member states and the European institutions for EU spending programs. A second reform program (MAP 2000) focused on the modernization of staff policy, through decentralization and simplification of staff management procedures. Nevertheless, the results have been rather ambiguous (Bauer 2007). Despite the merit to seriously address the issue of management reform for the first time, the reform programs achieved some positive results in the financial management decentralization although failed to modernize the sensitive human resources management area, due to a conflicts with staff union as well as the lack of a clear leadership from the top (Bauer 2007).

It is not completely striking considering that the European Commission has always been very far from an administration based on a management culture. On the opposite, the European Commission is rather part of the *Rechtstaat* model of public administration characterized by "a combination of Napoleonic and Germanic values" (Levy 2004: 169), which comprises elements as hierarchy, centralization and the strict observance of the legal procedure. Furthermore, elements as its collegial structure, the vertical fragmentation among Directorate General adopting different sub administrative models, the resulting weak horizontal coordination, increased the reluctance of the European Commission towards whatever new management reform.

After the resignation of the Santer Commission in 1999, due to a serious case of mismanagement, Prodi became President of the Commission to draw it away from the deep crisis through a serious and comprehensive re-organization program. The Commissioner Kinnock was appointed for this task. At the beginning of 2000, the White Paper "Reforming the Commission" prompted the broadest management reform of the history of the European Commission. The reform aimed at strengthening the internal management capacities of the Commission to deliver results with maximum effectiveness (European Commission 2001). At the same time, the reform advocates aimed to rebalance the focus of the Commission's task towards its core business, the political guidance, and the legislative initiatives, blurred by the increased relevance of the management tasks. The reform addressed the following areas, strategic planning, human resources, financial management, transparency, and responsiveness.

7.3   THE MAIN REFORM CONTENTS

The content of the management reforms implemented in the European Commission will be analyzed following the research framework described in Chap. 3. We split the reform contents into four management areas (finance, personnel, organization structure, and performance), and for each of them, we identified several management elements (see Table 3.2). The management areas related to the performance management system will be analyzed in detail in the Sect. 7.4.

7.3.1   The Financial Area

7.3.1.1   Budgeting

As for financial management, the most important change in the Kinnock management reform was the introduction of the Activity Based Budgeting (ABB) together with the introduction of the Activity-Based Management (ABM). Both were fundamental elements of the strategic planning and programming cycle (SPP) aiming at connecting the political priorities set at the Commission level, to the objectives defined in terms of output and outcome, to the financial resources needed to achieve them (*see infra*). Specifically, the ABB helped the DGs to link the activities carried out to the financial resources available as well as to performance information. The ABB system was gradually introduced in 2003 and fully applied to the EU budget in 2004. The ABB was combined with a financial double level system, including a central Financial Service acting as a professional support center for ensuring common financial standards for all DGs as well as Finance Units decentralized at the level of the DGs, fully responsible for executing the budget and financial control. This was coupled by the introduction of a new accounting system complying with the standards developed for the public sector by the International Federation of Accountants (IFAC) and helping the Commission to better monitor the concentration of European funds, detecting risk exposure, control pre-financing and monitor payment deadlines as well as managing accounting data on an integrated system, including assets and liability (European Commission 2005).

7.3.1.2 Accounting

In 2000 the European Commission started a transition towards a modern accrual accounting system, fully completed at the beginning of 2005 and within budget (European Commission 2005). As stated in the Report on Commission Reform (2005), this new accounting system complies with the standards developed for the public sector by the International Federation of Accountants (IFAC) helping the Commission to "become a leader in this field", although the requiring efforts in terms of information systems and training. This should also aim at improving the Commission to monitor the concentration of European funds better, detecting risk exposure, control pre-financing and monitor payment deadlines as well as managing accounting data on an integrated system, including assets and liability (European Commission 2005). Nevertheless, the weaknesses of the Commission accounting systems have been lamented by different senior managers and Chief Accounting directors,[3] repeatedly exposing the Commission to public view (Levy 2004).

7.3.1.3 Auditing

Auditing was a major concern in the European Commission. In fact, as stressed in the report of the Committee of Independent Experts (CIE), assessing Commission's procedures in view of the reform, the financial control mechanisms were rather weak. All expenses processed by the managers were sent for prior approval to a separate Financial Service, thus relieving Commission managers of a sense of personal responsibility for the operations they authorize (CIE 1999). This, combined with a weak internal audit functions set within each Directorate, resulted in an insufficient audit system. This latter has been consequently reformed and is currently carried out on three levels. Internally within each DG or Services after decentralizing at the level of General Directors the responsibilities for authorizing payments, centrally by a proper internal audit service (IAS) and externally by the Court of Auditors. The audit reform was supposed to reinforce the new strategic planning and programming cycle (SPP) and the Activity Based Management system, by providing adequate inputs for transforming the Commission in a performance-oriented organization. The internal audit service (IAS) had to contribute to the consolidation of Activity Based Management through its independent appraisals of the management systems of Commission departments, especially concerning the quality of information supplied in the annual reports. Recently the Internal Audit Service also started to carry out a number of audits with a prevailing focus on performance issues within the 2013–2015 Strategic Audit Plan

(European Commission 2014b). Nevertheless, on the IAS website, the last annual audit report for 2014 keeps its traditional audit focus on rules compliance. Similarly, also the Court of Auditors was equipped to carry out performance audits, although the core task is still rooted in the traditional assessment of the reliability of the accounts and the legality and regularity of the transactions made by the Commission. In the same time, as part of the 2000 financial management reform, the European Commission also decided to revise the internal control standards in accordance with the delegation of responsibility for financial management and internal controls to Director Generals. To this purpose, the European Commission adopted a common control framework, including 24 internal control standards (ICS),[4] which were revised in 2007[5] and simplified in 2014.[6] The ICS set out the minimum requirements and tips for assessing control effectiveness, for a number of "building blocks"[7] including Evaluation of Activities, Assessment for Internal Controls and Internal Audit Capability.

In terms of reform models, our review suggests a shift from the traditional models to the NWS model, especially concerning budgeting. The main relevant trend concerns the introduction of performance information in the budget process to improve the financial control system as well as increasing the link between strategic priorities and resource allocations (Table 7.1).

7.3.2   Human Resources Area

7.3.2.1   Recruitment and Contract Policy

In the European Commission the selection procedures were centralized by the setting up of a central personnel selection office (EPSO) in 2002, dealing with all selection procedures of the European Union institutions, with the objective of selecting more motivated and with high quality standards staff, possessing the required specific qualifications (Ban 2010). Furthermore, a new temporary staff category was introduced in order to increase flexibility in staff management through specialist contractual and temporary agent positions. However, the appointment procedures are often unclear. Concerning the appointing of most senior staff, which have been normally subject to specific rules, the reform introduced a new flexible mechanism, which also includes a compulsory mobility scheme and the possibility to establish appointment procedures involving external advertisement even in the presence of an internal candidate (Spence and Stevens 2006). Other changes concern the issue of the nationality principle. It is now required that the immediate subordinate and superior of

Table 7.1 Financial management area

Areas/elements	Ideal paradigms				
	Traditional	*NWS*	*NPM*	*NPG*	*EU*
	Financial management				
Budgeting	No information on performance	Budget with some performance information/format with policy areas instead of functions	Performance budgeting		NWS
Accounting	Cash based	Full cash based or combination of cash/accrual	Accruals accounting	Centralization in accounting practice. Shift towards the Whole of Government Accounting (WGA) approach	NPM
Auditing	Finance and legal compliance	Adding to financial and compliance auditing investigation on some performance issues	Performance audit		Towards NWS

Source: own elaboration

top—officials should be of another nationality than himself/herself (Wille 2007). This reflects the need that policy proposals should not reflect only national positions (Egeberg 2002). Nevertheless, nationality still plays an important role in bringing a number of rigidities to the selection system at the senior level, although it is less important than in the past (Nugent and Rhinard 2015). These include the risk that selections and promotions are based on national balance rather than merit. This also negatively affects the staff morale of those who see their promotion prospects blocked due to their "wrong" nationality (Nugent and Rhinard 2015).

7.3.2.2   Staff Appraisal and Promotion

In reforming the human resources management policy, the European Commission recognized that "a rigorous, objective and fair system for the appraisal of staff performance is essential" (European Commission 2000a: 65). Consequently, the Commission introduced a new performance evaluation system for human resources at middle and lower levels based on individual performance appraisal to increase the link between promotion and merit. The evaluation follows a two-step mechanism, including appraisal and promotion carried out yearly. The appraisal procedure concerns the assessment of the official's performance and abilities by a superior manager. This is based on the job description, tasks assignment, and conducted through extensive dialogues as well as the use of modern methods such as two-way feedback. In the promotion procedure, the Director-General based on the results of the appraisal assessment as well as the official's services to the DG, can award an additional number of points. Promotion follows once that the official reached a set threefold. For senior levels, this mechanism does not apply as appointments and promotions are still influenced by nationalities and political connections (Nugent and Rhinard 2015).

Common trends in the human resource area include: the efforts to link organizational performance and personal accountability through performance appraisal systems based on merit; the introduction of temporary contracts for specialists but in some cases also for senior management; and the rationalization and centralization of recruitment procedures to increase openness and publicity. Nevertheless, the search for a geographical balance among middle and senior staff is still a significant obstacle in promoting performance and merit principle. In terms of reform models, the table shows that most of the changes go in the direction of the NWS ideal model, with some elements closer to NPM, especially concerning the senior management temporary contracts (Table 7.2).

Table 7.2 Human resources management area

Areas/elements		Ideal paradigms			EU
		Traditional	NWS	NPM	
Human resources management					
Recruitment	All levels	Professional experience and national balance	Professional experience and national balance with performance elements	Merit principle	NWS
	Senior staff	Voluntary advertisement and use of standard procedure	Possibilities to external advertisement	Compulsory advertisement and use of standard procedure	NWS
Contract policy	All levels	Expertise and limited responsibility for resources	Expertise and management capabilities	Management capabilities and responsibility for resources	NWS
		Tenured career	Tenured career with limited number of temporary contracts	Temporary contracts	NWS
	Senior staff	Indefinite time contract	Indefinite time with performance evaluation	Temporary contract and related to performance	NWS
Promotion and appraisal	All levels	Seniority and qualifications	Seniority, qualifications and performance	Performance based/merit principles	NWS
	Senior staff	None	For every senior official regularly not based on performance agreements	For every senior official regularly based on performance agreements	Towards NWS

Source: own elaboration

7.3.3   Organization Structure Area

7.3.3.1   Specialization/Decentralization

The debate over specialization and decentralization of the functions in the European Commission was widely present in the White Paper discussing the Commission management reform (European Commission 2000a). The intent of the reform advocates was recapturing the initial role of the European Commission as a mission-oriented organization focused on policy conception and regulatory activities (Schon-Quinlivan 2007). Over time, the Commission has been more and more concerned with administrative aspects, including managing significant budgets and operational programs. As stated in the White Paper (European Commission 2000a: 7), "it is clear that the Commission will continue in the future to engage in all three activities, but the degree of relative emphasis placed on each of them is crucial in determining resources needs, organizational structures and management requirements". In order to refocus the Commission towards its core activities, the management reform set up a framework to allow externalization. The framework specified the typologies and the circumstances for externalization. The three typologies included devolution and decentralization in case of delegation of responsibilities for non-core activities to public service bodies, which can either be part of the Community administrative structures or be part of the national or transnational public bodies, and outsourcing, for delegation of services to private sector bodies (European Commission 2000a). In addition, it is also stated that "the option of externalization will only be chosen if it is a more efficient and effective means of delivering the service or goods concerned". Within such an externalization framework, the European Commission created an extensive network of agencies to which delegate a number of functions. They can be mainly of two types, decentralized agencies, and executive agencies. The decentralized agencies have been created for an indefinite length of time to contribute to the implementation of EU policies. They mainly deal with technical and scientific tasks in different sectors as food security, medicine, transport safety, security etc. However, they are independent bodies with an autonomous administrative and management board composed of representatives of the EU member states and the European Commission or other EU institutions (Spence 2005). Contrary, the European Commission sets up the executive agencies for a limited amount of time, dealing specifically with management tasks related to EU spending programs. These latter are consequently under the direct control of the European Commission, which decides their aims, mandate and structure. Currently, there are six different executive agencies responsible for management tasks related to 2014–2020 European Union funding programs, compared to only four in the previous period (2007–2013), and about thirty-nine decentralized agencies with almost a double increase respect to 2006.[8] Beyond the increasing relevance of the agencies, new departments and services have been created or renamed as well as new competencies and managerial practices have been incorporated in the work of DGs. These include strategic planning and financial management, personnel management and impact assessment (Nugent and Rhinard 2015). Nevertheless, although these new rules and practices devolved more responsibilities to the DGs, the role of the Secretariat General was also reinforced to strengthen the coordination task and improve the supervision of the overall functioning of the Commission. According to Nugent and Rhinard (2015), there has been a simultaneous trajectory over decentralization and centralization of services.

7.3.3.2 Coordination Mechanisms

The European Commission also faces coordination problems at both levels internally, within the different DGs and between the Commission, the Agencies and the other EU institutions. Internally, each department (DG) is generally competent for a specific policy area, but often issues are crosscutting and battles over leadership and resources are frequent. Classical examples include disputes between Environment and Internal Market department (DG) over setting standards in environmental protection as well as between Competition and Regional Policy (DG) for the possibilities of public support to poorer regions (Wishlade 1993). Other specific elements, which further complicate this picture, include the policy fragmentation among DGs (Richardson 1997), as well as the political influence of member states over the division of competences among DGs (Spence 2005). The main mechanisms introduced by the management reforms to improve coordination within the different components of the European Commission include:

- The increased role of the Secretariat General in horizontal coordination, following the management reforms adopted by Prodi and implemented under the Barroso Commission (Nugent and Rhinard 2015).

- The recent introduction of the Corporate Management Board, chaired by the Secretariat General bringing together on a regular basis the Directors-General responsible for budget, human resources and security, and the Director-General of the Legal Service. It provides coordination, oversight, advice and strategic orientations on corporate management issues (European Commission 2018d).
- The improved system for inter-service consultation (CIS-Net) which allows all potentially interested services in an initiative or proposal to be involved and consulted and keep informed about the decision making process.
- The introduction of the Strategic planning and programming cycle (SPP) aiming at identifying, within a multiyear cycle, the main political priorities at the level of the Commission and then translate them at the level of DGs. As noted by Nugent and Rhinard (2015), the planning cycle is a useful practice to avoid short term conflicts among DGs, as these latter can be reminded, generally by the SG, of their previous commitments.
- The setup of Inter-Service groups (IGS) and Inter-Services meetings. These latter are ad hoc and informally organized in policy areas with cross-sectorial implications. As for Inter Service groups, Hardacre (2011) estimates about 250 groups which gather representative of several DGs over a specific cross sectorial subjects. They are generally time-limited as in the case of the ISG on organic farming, set up in 2014 by the DG Agriculture and Rural Development, dealing with EU's core legislation on organic farming and labeling of organic products (Nugent and Rhinard 2015).
- The introduction of a common risk management process at every level of the European Commission[9] as well as a shared project management methodology[10] tailored according to the European Commission's needs.

Within the European Union institutional framework, the European Commission adopted several mechanisms to increase cooperation and coordination with Agencies and the other EU institutions that would be impossible to list here. However, from the strategic planning and programming perspective, the most important fact concerns the increased engagement and contribution of the European Parliament and the Council in the elaboration of the annual Commission Work Program (see below).

As far as the organizational structure is concerned, the analysis shows no clear trends towards specialization of functions and centralization or decentralization mechanisms. Although the externalization activities and the number of agencies and special bodies increased, at the same time, also central control mechanisms have been reinforced. Finally, as for coordination mechanisms, the main common element found is the introduction of the strategic planning process for defining the activities of each department, assigning resources and setting objectives and outputs standards (Table 7.3).

7.4 THE PERFORMANCE MANAGEMENT SYSTEM IN THE EUROPEAN UNION

The first attempt to adopt an integrated performance management system within the European Commission was carried out by the Kinnock management reform program, together with the introduction of the strategic planning and programming cycle for priority setting, allocation and efficient use of resources. Decisions on priorities in the Commission were generally taken separately from the allocation of resources (European Commission 2000a). Also, often the Council and the Parliament empowered the Commission with new tasks without adding additional resources. To further complicate the whole picture, the prevailing management culture in the Commission was much more oriented on controls rather than objectives. All such weaknesses were addressed through the introduction of a rigorous strategic framework (SPP) and new management tools and techniques, the Activity-Based Management (ABM), the Activity Based Budgeting (ABB) as well as a new performance appraisal system for staff. According to the intentions of the reform advocates, all these elements together allowed the Commission to redesign and assess its operative work, setting political priorities, decline these latter into objectives and matching them with resources needed to achieve them. Finally, performance indicators were also introduced to measure the impact of the Commission's action vis à vis the targeted beneficiaries, with the final aim "to equip the Commission to fulfill its role in addressing the challenges facing Europe with maximum effectiveness" (European Commission 2000b: 1). More recently, the President of the Commission Junker has declared that he committed to ensuring that "every action [...] delivers maximum performance and value-added" (European Commission

Table 7.3 Organization structure area

Areas/elements	Ideal paradigms				
	Traditional	NWS	NPM	NPG	EU
Organization structure					
Specialization	Multi-purpose, broad scope, no fragmentation	Multi-purpose, limited fragmentation, scarce number of specialized bodies	Tight focused, specialized bodies, high level of fragmentation	Not clear trend	NWS-
Decentralization of functions	Centralization	Centralization with possibility of externalization in limited cases	Decentralization	Not clear trend	NWS
Coordination	Hierarchy	Hierarchy with coordination by targets and outputs standards (strategic planning)	Contract coordination, market type mechanisms	Network type coordination	NWS

Source: own elaboration

2014a: 3). To monitor whether the European Commission actions deliver the performance or not, an effective performance measurement system is needed first.

In the following paragraphs, the main components of the performance measurement system set up by the European Commission within the European Union framework will be analyzed against the evaluation grid, described in the Chap. 3. The research will include the analysis of the baseline and indicators for assessing performance, as well as the identification of the levels of analysis and their interaction (Gutner and Thompson 2010).

7.4.1   The Strategic Levels of the EU Performance Framework

The EU performance framework, simplified in Fig. 7.1, is composed of three different but interrelated strategic layers, the international layer, the European Union layer and the member states layer.

7.4.1.1   The International Strategic Level

The international strategic level includes strategies elaborated at the international level, above the EU, mainly aiming at producing or preserving the global public goods. Among these, particular attention was given by the EU to the UN 2030 Agenda for Sustainable Development ("UN 2030 Agenda"), adopted by world leaders in 2015, which represents the new global sustainable development framework balancing its three

Fig. 7.1   Performance management levels in the European Union

dimensions, economic, social and environmental. It sets out 17 Sustainable Development Goals (SDGs) to eradicate poverty and achieve sustainable development by 2030 worldwide ensuring that no one is left behind (European Commission 2016b). The Agenda includes 169 underlying targets and an indicator framework composed of 230 indicators agreed at the UN level to monitor the progress towards the achievement of the SDGs. The goals and targets of the UN 2030 Agenda have the following characteristics, are global, universally applicable and interlinked (Table 7.4).

The EU has been committed to sustainable development since the beginning of 2000, setting out its Sustainable Development strategy in 2001. This latter became mainstreamed in key cross-cutting projects and policy initiatives, including, since 2010, also the Europe 2020 strategy (European Commission 2016b). After 2015 the European Commission adopted its approach in implementing the 2030 Agenda and the SDGs[11] based on two work streams (European Commission 2016b). First, the EU decided to fully integrate the SDGs in the European policy framework and current Commission priorities (European Commission 2016b). This was accompanied by a mapping exercise outlining how the different EU policy initiatives contributed to the 17 SDGs. The second aspect concerns the launching of a reflection work on further developing the longer-term vision and the focus of sectoral policies after 2020, preparing for the long-term implementation of the SDGs. As a result of this exercise, the Commission published a reflection paper "Towards a Sustainable Europe

Table 7.4 The UN sustainable development goals (SDGs)

The UN sustainable development goals (SDGs)	
1 No poverty	10 Reducing inequality
2 Zero hunger	11 Sustainable cities and communities
3 Good health and well-being	12 Responsible consumption and production
4 Quality education	13 Climate action
5 Gender equality	14 Life below water
6 Clean water and sanitation	15 Life on land
7 Affordable and clean energy	16 Peace, justice, and strong institutions
8 Decent work and economic growth	17 Partnerships for the goals
9 Industry, innovation, and infrastructure	

Source: UN 2030 Agenda for Sustainable Development

by 2030" at the end of January 2019, outlining three possible scenarios on how to better integrate the UN 2030 Agenda into the post-2020 EU strategic framework.

7.4.1.2 The EU Strategic Level

The EU strategic level is the core of our analysis and includes all the priorities and the objectives set at the EU level and their link with the international strategies. Within the EU strategic level, some performance documents address to all EU institutions and bodies while others are specific for each institution. The following strategic documents belong to the first group:

The Founding Treaties of the EU

Similar to all international organizations, the founding treaties of the EU set the EU limits, competences, and functions as well as the general objectives the EU aims to achieve. These latter are laid down in the art. 3 of the Treaty of the European Union (TEU). Although broadly defined, the capacity to achieve these objectives should justify (or not) the very existence of the organization (Table 7.5).

The EU Ten-Year Strategy

It is a shared strategy between the EU and the member states designed to achieve a shared set of strategic objectives based on those laid down in the art. 3 of the Treaty of the European Union. The EU long term strategy includes priorities, objectives, and targets to focus on EU and member states' actions over ten-years. The first long-term strategy, known as the Lisbon strategy, covered a period of ten years from 2000 to 2010 with a mid-term review in 2005. It was based on three priorities (economy, social protection, and environment) as well as equipped with clear objectives and indicators. At the end of 2010, a new long-term strategy known as Europe 2020 was launched covering the period 2010–2020 and having a similar format. It includes three priorities, five thematic areas, eight targets monitored by nine headline indicators (and sub-indicators) as well as seven flagship initiatives (Table 7.6).

Thematic areas and targets are strictly interlinked, for example, higher educational levels are associated with better employability, which in turn increases employment rates and helps to reduce poverty (Eurostat 2016). Finally, the targets of the Europe 2020 strategy have been also translated into national targets, to reflect the different economic and social

Table 7.5   The general objectives of the European Union

Article 3 (TEU)

1. The Union's aim is to **promote peace**, its values and the well-being of its peoples.

2. The Union shall offer its citizens an **area of freedom, security and justice** without internal frontiers, in which the **free movement of persons** is ensured in conjunction with appropriate measures with respect to external border controls, asylum, immigration and the prevention and combating of crime.

3. The Union shall establish an **internal market**. It shall work for the sustainable development of Europe based on balanced **economic growth and price stability**, a **highly competitive social market economy**, aiming at **full employment and social progress**, and a **high level of protection and improvement of the quality of the environment**. It shall promote scientific and technological advance.

   It shall **combat social exclusion and discrimination**, and shall **promote social justice and protection, equality between women and men**, solidarity between generations and protection of the rights of the child.

   It shall promote **economic, social and territorial cohesion**, and solidarity among Member States.

   It shall **respect its rich cultural and linguistic diversity**, and shall ensure that Europe's cultural heritage is safeguarded and enhanced.

4. The Union shall establish an **economic and monetary union** whose currency is the euro.

5. In its relations with the wider world, the Union shall uphold and **promote its values and interests** and contribute to the protection of its citizens. It shall contribute to peace, security, the sustainable development of the Earth, solidarity and mutual respect among peoples, free and fair trade, eradication of poverty and the protection of human rights, in particular the rights of the child, as well as to the strict observance and the development of international law, including respect for the principles of the United Nations Charter.

6. The Union shall pursue its objectives by appropriate means commensurate with the competences which are conferred upon it in the Treaties

Table 7.6 Priorities of the Europe 2020 strategy

Europe 2020 Strategy (2010–2020)

Priorities	Thematic areas	Targets	Headline indicators	Flagship initiatives
1. Smart growth	1. R&D and innovation	1. Increasing combined public and private investment in R&D to 3% of GDP	1. Gross domestic expenditure on R&D (% of GDP)	1. Innovation union
	2. Education	2. Reducing school drop-out rates to less than 10%	2. Early leavers from education and training, total (3) (% of population aged 18–24)	2. Youth on the move
		3. Increasing the share of the population aged 30–34 having completed tertiary education to at least 40%	3. Tertiary educational attainment, total (3) (% of population aged 30–34)	3. A digital agenda for Europe
2. Sustainable growth	3. Climate change and energy	4. Reducing greenhouse gas emissions by at least 20% compared to 1990 levels	4. Greenhouse gas emissions (2) (Index 1990 = 100)	4. Resource efficient Europe
		5. Increasing the share of renewable energy in final energy consumption to 20%	5. Share of renewable energy in gross final energy consumption (%)	5. An industrial policy for the globalisation era
		6. Moving towards a 20% increase in energy efficiency	6. Primary energy consumption (million tonnes of oil equivalent)	
			7. Final energy consumption (million tonnes of oil equivalent)	
3. Inclusive growth	4. Employment	7. Increasing the employment rate of the population aged 20–64 to at least 75%	8. Employment rate age group 20–64, total (% of population)	6. An agenda for new skills and jobs
	5. Poverty and social exclusion	8. Lifting at least 20 million people out of the risk of poverty and social exclusion	9. People at risk of poverty or social exclusion, EU-28 (million people)	7. European platform against poverty and social exclusion

conditions as well as the level of member states' contribution towards the implementation of the Europe 2020 strategy. The EU ten-year strategy provides a comprehensive and common strategic framework for both the EU and the member states. Its objectives and targets should feed the strategic plans either at the EU institutions level, as well as at the level of the member states. The achievement of Europe 2020 objectives will thus greatly depend on the effective synergy between the EU and the national actions. The monitoring and reporting mechanism assessing the implementation of the Europe 2020 is partly integrated into the economic surveillance framework known as the "EU Semester" related to fiscal and economic policy coordination. Also, progress towards the achievement of Europe 2020 targets can be monitored in the Eurostat web portal[12] allowing each indicator to be tracked at European and national levels.

Strategic Agenda of the European Council

An additional source for strategic inputs at the EU level comes from the European Council, composed by the EU national head of States and governments. According to art. 15 of the Treaty of the European Union (TEU), the European Council "shall provide the Union with the necessary impetus for its development and shall define the general political directions and priorities thereof." In doing this the European Council adopted in June 2014 the "Strategic Agenda for the EU in the times of change", composed of five fields, priorities and actions[13] to guide the EU work for the next five years. Contrary to the Europe 2020 strategy, the strategic agenda adopted by the Council does not include targets or indicators to feed the reporting and monitoring system (Table 7.7).

EU Sectorial Policy Strategies and Objectives

The EU also sets strategies and objectives at the level of the sectorial policies according to the main areas of competence of the EU (see art. 6 TFUE). They include, among others, the EU Energy strategy,[14] the EU Health strategy,[15] the Consumer Policy Strategy,[16] the Strategic Framework for Education and Training 2020,[17] the EU Cohesion policy, the EU Climate action, the Global Strategy for the European Union's Foreign and Security Policy (EUGS), etc. Generally, for each policy strategy, the EU sets medium and long-term objectives, linked to higher strategic documents as the Europe 2020 strategy. For example, the Cohesion policy thematic objectives set for the period 2014–2020 and guiding the

Table 7.7 The Strategic Agenda of the European Council

Strategic Agenda for the EU in a time of change (2014–2020)

Fields	Priorities	Actions
1. Jobs, growth and competitiveness	Fully exploit the potential of the single market in all its dimensions:	Completion of the digital single market by 2015
	Promote a climate of entrepreneurship and job creation,	Improving SME's access to finance and investment
	Invest and prepare our economies for the future:	Improved infrastructure investment
	Reinforce the global attractiveness of the Union	Completion of the negotiations on the Transatlantic Trade and Investment Partnership (TTIP) by 2015
	Make the Economic and Monetary Union a more solid and resilient factor of stability and growth:	Increasing euro area governance and economic policy coordination
2. Empowering and protecting citizens	Help develop skills and unlock talents and life chances for all	Continuing the drive against youth unemployment
	Guarantee fairness	Combatting tax evasion and tax fraud
	Help ensure all our societies have their safety nets in place to accompany change and reverse inequalities	Social protection systems that are efficient, fair and fit for the future
3. Energy and climate policies	Affordable energy	Completion of the EU energy market
	Secure energy	Diversification of EU energy supplies and routes and the development of energy infrastructure
	Green energy	Setting ambitious climate change targets for 2030 and continuing to lead the fight against climate change
4. Freedom, security and justice	Better manage migration in all its aspects	Addressing shortages of specific skills and attracting talent
	Prevent and combat crime and terrorism	Cracking down on organised crime, such as human trafficking, smuggling and cybercrime;
	Improve judicial cooperation among our countries	Building bridges between the different justice systems and traditions

(continued)

Table 7.7   (continued)

Strategic Agenda for the EU in a time of change (2014–2020)

Fields	Priorities	Actions
5. The EU as a strong global actor	Maximise our clout	Ensuring consistency between member states' and EU foreign policy goals
	Be a strong partner in our neighbourhood	Promoting stability, prosperity and democracy in the countries closest to the EU
	Engage our global strategic partners	Engaging global partners on a wide range of issues such as trade, cyber security, human rights and crisis management
	Develop security and defence cooperation	Strengthening the EU's common security and defence policy

implementation of the European Structural and Investment Funds are aligned to the Europe 2020 strategy as shown in Table 7.8.

Similarly, in the case of the climate and energy policy, the objectives[18] of the 2020 climate and energy package adopted by the European Council in 2007 have been included in the Europe 2020 strategy.[19]

The EU Multiannual Financial Framework (MFF)
The Multiannual Financial Framework lays down the maximum annual amount which the EU can spend in the different policy fields for seven years. It is structured around policy areas and defines the maximum annual ceiling for EU expenditure as a whole and per budgetary headings. The current structure of the MFF is the following:

1. Smart and Inclusive Growth
   (a) Competitiveness for growth and jobs
   (b) Economic, social and territorial cohesion
2. Sustainable Growth: natural resources;
3. Security and citizenship;
4. Global Europe

The MFF is adopted after lengthy negotiations by the member states and takes the form of a Council regulation. It is implemented through an

Table 7.8 Europe 2020 strategy and the EU Cohesion Policy objectives (2014–2020)

Europe 2020 strategy (2010–2020)			EU Cohesion Policy (2014–2020)	
Priority	*Objective*	*Target*	*Thematic objectives (TOs)*	*ESI funds*
1. Smart growth	Increase employment	75% of the 20–64 year-olds to be employed	1. Strengthening research, technological development and innovation	ERDF, ESF,EAFRD, EMFF, cohesion fund
	Increase in R&D expenditure	3% of the EU's GDP to be invested in R&D	2. Enhancing access to, and use and quality of information and communication technologies	
			3. Enhancing the competitiveness of small and medium-sized enterprises (SMEs)	
2. Sustainable growth	Climate change and energy sustainability	Greenhouse gas emissions 20% (or even 30%, if the conditions are right) lower than 1990	4. Supporting the shift towards a low-carbon economy in all sectors	
			5. Promoting climate change adaptation, risk prevention and management	
		20% of energy from renewables 20% increase in energy efficiency	6. Preserving and protecting the environment and promoting resource efficiency,	
			7. Promoting sustainable transport and removing bottlenecks in key network infrastructures	
3. Inclusive growth	Education	Reducing the rates of early school leaving below 10% At least 40% of 30–34-year-olds completing third level education	8. Promoting sustainable and quality employment and supporting labour mobility	
	Fighting poverty and social exclusion	At least 20 million fewer people in or at risk of poverty and social exclusion	9. Promoting social inclusion, combating poverty and any discrimination	
			10. Investing in education, training and vocational training for skills and lifelong learning	

interinstitutional agreement between the Council, the Commission and the Parliament[20] and the time length of the MFF should be at least five years. Within this framework, the annual budget is approved following a distinct budgetary procedure, set by the Treaty (TFEU, title II, articles 310–324), which involves the European Parliament and the Council of Ministers[21] (budgetary authorities).

Once the annual budget is approved, the European Commission holds the responsibility for budget implementation,[22] although most of the EU financial resources, around 80%, are allocated and spent by the member states through spending programs managed under the shared management model. Consequently, EU member states are required to collaborate closely with the Commission to assure that the use of the resources follows the principles of sound financial management, as all the actors involved in spending the EU resources are subject to the common rules set by the EU legislator. In the event of unforeseen circumstances, the European Commission can amend the EU budget adopted, by submitting draft amending budgets, following the same budgetary procedure. At the end of each year, the discharge procedure evaluates how the European Commission implemented the EU budget. The verification follows a number of principles including compliance of relevant rules and sound financial management (effectiveness, efficiency and economy) based on several of accountability reports. The main document reporting the results achieved by the EU budget is the Annual Management and Performance Report (AMPR) (June n+1). The AMPR is the key reporting document as includes performance information on the results achieved by the EU budget across all budget headings and policy areas. It shows how the EU's financial programs have contributed to the Union's political priorities and to the strategic objectives of the Europe 2020 strategy (European Commission 2018a). The first section of the document draws on information included in the Program Statements and the Annual Activity Reports produced by all Commission departments (see below). The second section deals with the financial management describing how the EU budget is managed and protected. It is mainly concerned with reporting the achievements of the internal control objectives, the protection of the EU budget and the management assurance of the College of Commissioners.

The EU Spending Programs

The EU budget is a key instrument for achieving the priorities set at different EU levels, and it is implemented by the EU Spending programs linked to the five MFF headings as they run for the same period. Following the ordinary legislative procedure, the EU spending programs are adopted by the Council and the European Parliament through a legal act in the form of a Regulation, which sets the objectives, contents and financial allocations as well as their performance framework. The performance framework includes objectives and indicators to monitor the achievement of the EU spending programs results and demonstrate how these latter are being used to achieve policy goals (European Commission 2018c). The main features of the current monitoring, reporting and evaluation system (also known as MORE) associated to the EU spending programs include:

- a clear linkage with the higher strategic documents. All EU spending programs have been conceived to contribute to the achievement of the Europe 2020 strategy goals, the UN Sustainable Development Goals, and the Commission Political Priorities. In order to make clear such contribution, for the Europe 2020 strategy goals, the European Commission estimated the financial contribution of the single EU spending programs to the three priorities of the Europe 2020 strategy (smart, sustainable and inclusive), based on ex-ante estimation of commitments appropriations.[23] Table 7.9 showing the financial resources included in the draft budget 2019 linked to Europe 2020 priorities and representing 66% of the total of the EU budget for the same year.

Table 7.9 Financial contribution of the EU programs to the Europe 2020 priorities (mil EUR)

	Draft budget 2019		
Europe 2020 Strategy	Smart growth	Sustainable growth	Inclusive growth
Topics	Innovation, education, digital society	Competitiveness, climate, energy and mobility	59 pt
EU spending programs (2014–2020)	21,215.60	65,626.70	19,213.80
Total Europe 2020 strategy			106,056.10
Total budget (Commission—Sect III)			161,500.30
Europe 2020/EU budget			66%

Source: European Commission (2018b)

Whereas for the UN Sustainable Development Goals and the Commission Political Priorities the link with the EU spending programs is less organic, although the Commission recently presented the most relevant spending programs linked to the two strategic frameworks, as shown in the Tables 7.10 and 7.11.

- the presence of objectives and performance indicators to monitor the progress towards the achievement of results for all EU spending programs. Currently, there are almost 60 spending programs linked to the MFF 2014–2020, and their performance frameworks include more than 700 hundreds indicators measuring the performance against 61 general objectives and 228 specific objectives (European Commission 2018b) (Table 7.12);
- the preset of the timing, frequency, actors involved as well as the issues covered by the planning and monitoring reports. Almost all spending programs, based on the MFF timeline, provide performance planning documents and midterm or annual performance-focused report as well as ex-post evaluations. Such details are included in the regulations establishing the EU spending programs and collected for the first time in a single staff working document of the European Commission titled "Overview of the Monitoring, Reporting and Evaluation Frameworks for the MFF 2014–2020 Programmes" and published on June 2014 after the approval of the EU spending programs linked to the MFF 2014–2020.
- the existence of many ways for managing EU spending programs. Specifically, the EU spending programs can be implemented in three different management modes:
  - can be managed directly by the Commission (direct management model);
  - can be managed by the member states with the Commission supervision (shared management model)[24];
  - can be delegated by the Commission to third parts, including agencies of EU member states, partner countries or international organizations (indirect management model).
  As mentioned above, almost 80% of the programs are managed through shared management model, mainly corresponding to the European Structural and Investment funds (ESIF) and the rest

Table 7.10 Contribution of the EU programs to UN Sustainable Development Goals

SDG	EU Programs	SDG	EU Programs
1. End to poverty in all its manifestations, including extreme poverty, over the next 15 years	EFSI, Erasmus+, ESC, ESF, EAGF, EMFF, AFIS, Humanitarian Aid	10. Reducing inequalities between and within countries and in achieving social inclusion and safe migration	Erasmus+, ESC, Customs, ESF, EAGF, AFIS, REC, Humanitarian Aid
2. End hunger and malnutrition, and ensure access to safe, nutritious and sufficient food	EAGF, EMFF, Food&Feed, Humanitarian Aid	11. Enriching the quality of life in cities and communities, in promoting sustainable transport and in alleviating adverse environmental impacts	ITER, EFSI, ESF, EAGF, LIFE,
3. Ensure health and well-being for all	EFSI, Erasmus+, ESC, EMFF, Food&Feed, Health, Humanitarian Aid	12. Decoupling environmental impacts from economic growth, in decreasing its energy consumption and in tackling waste generation and management	Customs, LIFE, Food&Feed, Consumer
4. Ensure access to equitable and quality education through all stages of life	EFSI, Erasmus+, ESF, EAGF, humanitarian Aid	13. Climate mitigation efforts and in establishing climate initiatives. Climate impacts are measured to assess how and to what extent climate change is affecting Europe	LIFE, Humanitarian Aid
5. Ending all forms of discrimination, violence, and any harmful practices against women and girls in the public and private spheres	Erasmus+, EaSI, ESC, ESF, IcSP, Humanitarian Aid	14. Advancing marine conservation, in fostering sustainable fishery and in ensuring healthy oceans	EMFF
6. Ensuring universal access to safe and affordable drinking water, sanitation and hygiene	EAGF, Humanitarian Aid	15. Improving the status of ecosystems, in decelerating land degradation and in preserving biodiversity	EAGF, LIFE,

(continued)

Table 7.10 (continued)

SDG	EU Programs	SDG	EU Programs
7. Progress made in reducing its energy consumption, in securing sustainable energy supply and in improving access to affordable energy	ITER, EFSI, Euratom, EAGF, Consumer	16. Ensuring peace and personal security, in promoting access to justice and in safeguarding effective justice systems	Erasmus+, ESC, ESF, ISF, justice, IPA II, CFSP, EIDHR,
8. Fostering sustainable economic growth, in increasing employment and in providing decent work opportunities	EFSI, COSME, Erasmus+, EaSI, ESC, Customs, ISA2, ESF, EAGF, Creative Europe, IPA II,	17. Progress in strengthening global partnership and in improving the financial governance in the EU	Copernicus, ISA2, CFSP, EIDHR, IcSP,
9. Progress in strengthening R&D and innovation and in promoting sustainable transport	ITER, EFSI, COSME, CEF, ISA2, ESF, EAGF,		

Source: European Commission (2018b)

through direct management mode corresponding to the different sectorial funding programs in the field of research and innovation (ex. Horizon 2020), education (ex. Erasmus Plus), environment protection (ex. LIFE+), judicial cooperation, external relations etc. This implies that the MORE frameworks differ according to the program management model. MORE frameworks under shared management mode are relatively more complex than those under direct management model, due to the number of actors involved in implementing the programs, collecting data and elaborating monitoring reports. Consequently, for programs managed under the shared management mode, more time and resources are needed to aggregate data at the EU level affecting timing and availability of performance information (European Commission 2014b).

Table 7.11 Contribution of the EU programs to Juncker Commission priorities

Ten priorities of the Juncker Commission	*Contribution from EU Programmes*
1. New boost for jobs, growth and investment	H2020, CEF, ITER, EGNOS and GALILEO, Euratom, Erasmus+, EaSI, COSME and ESF, ERDF, CF
2. Connected digital single market	H2020, ERDF, EAFRD, CEF
3. A resilient Energy Union with a forward-looking Climate Change Policy	Euratom, ITER, ERDF, EAFRD, CF, CEF, EAGF, H2020, LIFE Programme + all programmes contributing to the Climate change Policy objectives
4. Deeper and fairer internal market with strengthened industrial base	EAFRD, ERDF, CF, H2020, Egnos and Galileo, Copernicus, COSME
5. A deeper and fairer Economic and Monetary Union	Specific activities in the field of financial reporting and auditing
6. A reasonable and balanced Free Trade Agreement with U.S.	No spending programme involved
7. An area of justice and Fundamental Rights based on Mutual Trust	Justice programme, Rights, Equality and Citizenship Programme, Internal Security Fund
8. Towards a new Policy on Migration	Asylum, Migration and Integration Fund (AMIF), Internal Security Fund (ISF)
9. A stronger Global Actor	All programmes under Heading 4
10. A Union of Democratic Change	No spending programmes involved, but some actions under Europe for Citizens programme

Source: European Commission (2018b)

Table 7.12   Program statements and indicators

Program statements and indicators

Budget heading	No. of programs	No. of programmes for which 100% of indicators are informed	Total number of indicators	Total number of informed indicators	Percentage of informed indicators
1A—Competitiveness for growth and jobs	20 (+2)	12	249	192	74.7%
1B—Economic, social and territorial cohesion	4	2	84	49	58.3%
2—Sustainable growth: Natural resources	5	0	99	83	84.7%
3—Security and citizenship	12	8	176	163	92.6%
4—Global Europe	14 (+1)	12	108	102	94.4%
Special instruments	2	2	2	2	100%
Total	57 (+3)	36	718	591	82.3%

Source: European Commission (2018b)

- the introduction of a performance reserve for the European Structural and Investments funds (ESIf). To increase the result orientation of the EU spending programs under the shared management model, a special reserve ranging from 5 to 7% is available for all operative programs financed by the ESI funds, succeeded in achieving the midterm objectives set in their performance framework. This initiative is part of the efforts carried out by the European Commission to equip the managing authorities of the ESI funds with a clear results-orientation framework. This also includes a clear articulation of the specific objectives for each operative program with indicators, milestone, and targets set in the midterm (2018) and at end of the programming period (2023), a strong intervention logic and ex-ante conditionalities providing the necessary prerequisite for the smooth implementation of the programs (European Commission 2018c).

7.4.1.3 The EU Strategic Level

As mentioned, within the EU strategic level, each EU institution or body, based on the above-mentioned performance framework, designs its own strategic framework. Considering the relevant number of EU institutions and bodies, our analysis will focus on the performance framework of the European Commission being the most relevant institution contributing to the achievement of the EU objectives. The performance framework of the European Commission is thus an integral part of its work and is implemented through the Strategic Planning and Programming cycle (SPP). This latter defines the steps for programming and planning the activities of the European Commission and Directorate Generals (DGs) setting the objectives and allocating the financial and human resources, to contribute to the achievement of the long-term objectives set in the EU wide strategic documents, mentioned above. The cycle can be divided into three main phases, planning, implementing and reporting spread over a multi-annual perspective. The main components of the SPP can be split according to levels (European Commission / Directorate Generals and Services) and stages (planning and reporting) as shown in Table 7.13.

(Planning) The European Commission Political Guidelines
The planning phase of the SPP cycle formally starts with the adoption of the Political Guidelines also known as Commission's priorities, covering the five-years of President of the European Commission' s mandate. The Political Guidelines describe the main priorities and policy areas the European Commission commits to focus for the next five years period. They are elaborated by the President of the Commission with the support of the Secretariat General as well as with inputs from DGs and Services. The Political Guidelines are essentially a political document, generally divided into broad objectives or policy areas aiming at providing a comprehensive picture of the President's view on the most important political

Table 7.13 The main components of the SPP cycle

Stages/Levels	European Commission	DG/Services
Planning	The European Commission Political Guidelines	Strategic plans (SP)
	The State of the Union speech (SU)	Annual Management Plans (MP)
	The Commission Work Program (CWP)	
Reporting	General report on the activities of the European Union	The Annual Activity Report (AAR)

issues of the next five years. Consequently, no specific performance indicators have been set at this level.[25] Nevertheless, stakeholders report that the current Political priorities have high visibility in the Commission and are pivotal in assessing priorities areas and resource re-allocation in the Commission Directorates-General (OECD 2017). These latter are in line with the Europe 2020 strategy, especially the first four priorities, whereas the others reflect the EU's broader international role (Table 7.14).

(Planning) The State of the Union Speech
The second component of the SPP planning phase is the State of the Union speech held in September (n-1), where the President of the European Commission spells out the political priorities for the year to come in the European Parliament plenary session. The State of the Union speech has been recently introduced by the last Treaty reform in 2009 on the image of the USA's State of the Union speech, to make political life of the Union more democratic and transparent. In the Union's speech, the President of the European Commission translates the multiannual political guidelines in annual priorities. These are included in Commission Work Program (CWP), whose adoption is preceded by discussions and negotiations between the European Commission, the European Parliament and the EU Council of Ministers. The state of the Union speech replaced the Annual Policy Strategy (APS) document, which was a key element in the initial planning cycle set up by the Kinnock management reform. The Annual Policy Strategy (APS) "has to become the natural place where strategic decisions on resource orientations are taken, including decisions to adjust the focus of activities and the consequent redeployment of resources—where necessary" (European Commission 2001: 11). The content of the APS was consequently structured around the main policy objectives set in the 5-years political guidelines and for each of the key actions were identified. By contrast, the current state of the Union speech is a less strategic and more political oriented document, loosely structured and focused only on the more pressuring political priorities, without any clear reference to the multiannual Commission guidelines. As an example, in the 2016 state of the Union speech the current President of the Commission affirmed that "whatever work programs or legislative agendas say: the priority today is and must be addressing the refugee crisis" (European Commission 2015b: 2), without providing, at this stage, any detailed action plan.

Table 7.14 The European Commission priorities: an overview

Lisbon Strategy (2000–2010)		Europe 2020 Strategy (2010–2020)		
2000–2004 *Shaping a new Europe* *(Prodi Commission)*	*2005–2009* *A Partnership for* *European Renewal* *(Barroso I Commission)*	*2010–2014* *Political Guidelines (Barroso II* *Commission)*		*2014–2019* *Political Guidelines (Junker Commission)*
Five years objectives: 1. Promoting new forms of governance 2. A stable Europe with a stronger voice in the world 3. A new economic and social agenda 4. A better quality of life	*Five years objectives:* 1. Prosperity 2. Solidarity 3. Security 4. Promoting European values in the world 5. Top priority: growth and jobs	*Five key challenges* 1. Restarting economic growth today and ensuring long-term sustainability and competitiveness for the future 2. Fighting unemployment and reinforcing our social cohesion 3. Turning the challenge of a sustainable Europe to our competitive advantage. 4. Ensuring the security of Europeans. 5. Reinforcing EU citizenship and participation.		*Ten policy areas* 1. A New Boost for Jobs, Growth and Investment 2. A Connected Digital Single Market 3. A Resilient Energy Union 4. A Deeper and Fairer Internal Market 5. A Deeper and Fairer Monetary Union 6. A Reasonable and Balanced FTA with US 7. An Area of Justice and Fundamental Rights 8. Towards a New Policy on Migration 9. A Stronger Global Actor 10. A Union of Democratic Change.

(Planning) The European Commission Work Program (CWP)
The discussions and negotiations among the EU institutions over the State of the Union speech lead to the adoption of the annual European Commission Work Program (CWP). This latter is a key element of the planning cycle translating the political priorities into the concrete actions the European Commission commits to carry out in the year to follow. In 1999, at the beginning of the management reform initiative, the annual European Commission Work Program (CWP) resembled a massive list of legislative and not-legislative proposals, fueled every year by new initiatives added by the different Commissioners to emphasize their dynamism in their portfolio area. The result was a long document focused on a great number of short-term priorities without any information on how and whether the legislative or not—legislative acts would have been adopted. To address these shortcomings, the Kinnock management reform aimed to transform the European Commission Work Program in a more political oriented document presenting the most important initiatives of the European Commission commits to achieve within the year (European Commission 2000a). Despite the intentions, until 2007, little has changed and the European Commission Work Program continued to be a long list of legislative and non-legislative acts with a limited capacity to focus on the most important priorities. In 2007, under the pressure of the Strategic Planning and Programming unit, the number of acts in the CWP has been reduced and all the initiatives classified according to the following different categories (European Commission 2007):

1. *Strategic initiatives*, which include a selected number of legislative or not-legislative proposals of political relevance and advanced stage of preparation, the European Commission commits to adopt within the year;
2. *Priority initiatives* include those legislative or not-legislative proposals to be adopted for 12–18 months;
3. *Simplification initiatives* include those legislative or not-legislative proposals aiming to simplify existing regulations to contribute to the Better Regulation policy (Fig. 7.2).

Currently, the European Commission decided to highlight in the European Commission Work Program the "new initiatives" to be adopted within the year and classified them according to the ten priorities identified in the five years Political Guidelines. It is now clear the connection

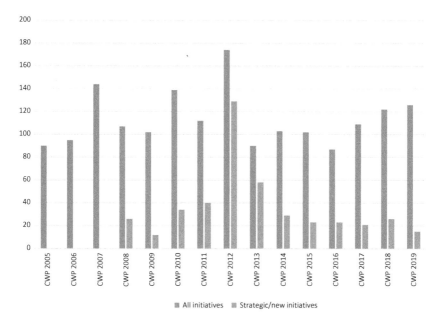

Fig. 7.2 The number of initiatives included in the CWP (2005–2019) (Source: own elaboration based on the CWP 2005–2019)

between the legislative and non-legislative initiatives the European Commission commits to adopt for each political priority identified in the Commission Political Guidelines. Table 7.15 shows the current format of the CWP, in which each legislative or non-legislative initiative is associated with the European Commission's political priorities (marked in green) that contribute to achieve.

In sum, the current CWP now contains a list of all legislative and non-legislative acts the European Commission commits to adopt in the implementation year of the SPP cycle, divided into two parts.

- the first part includes a general description of the main areas and priorities the European Commission will take action;
- the second part (annexes) contains:
  - a list of the "new initiatives" grouped around the main political priorities, and for each a description of the scope and objectives foreseen;

Table 7.15   The template of the 2018 European Commission Work Program (CWP) for the "new initiatives"

The template of the 2018 Commission Work Program (CWP) for the "new initiatives"	
N° Title	Description
A Connected Digital Single Market	
4. Completing the Digital Single Market	Proposal on fairness in platform-to-business relations (legislative, incl. Impact assessment, Art. 114 TFEU, QI 2018); an initiative addressing online platform challenges as regards the spreading of fake information (non-legislative, QI 2018); and a revision of the Commission guidelines on market analysis and assessment of significant market power in the electronic communications sector (non-legislative, Q2 2018)
A Resilient Energy Union with a Forward-Looking Climate Change Policy	
5. Completing the Energy Union	Follow-up to the solidarity aspect or the Energy Union, including a proposal on common rules for gas pipelines entering the European internal gas market (legislative, incl. Impact assessment, Art. 194 TFEU, Q4 2017)
6. Future of EU energy and climate policy (*initiative to be launched with a 2025 perspective*)	Communication on the future of EU energy and climate policy, including the future of the Euratom Treaty (taking account of Declaration No. 54 of five Member States added to the Final Act of the Lisbon Treaty) and on the possible use of Article 192(2), second subparagraph TFEU (non-legislative, Q2 2018)
Deeper and Fairer Internal Market with a Strengthened Industrial Base	
7. Fair taxation in the digital economy	Proposal establishing rules at EU level allowing taxation of profits generated by multinationals through the digital economy (legislative, incl. Impact assessment, Art. 113, 115 TFEU, Q1 2018)
8. Social fairness package	Proposal to establish a European Labour Authority (legislative, Q2 2018); an initiative on access to social protection for atypical self-employed workers (legislative/ non-legislative, Art. 153–155, 352 TFEU, Q2 2018); an initiative on a European Social Security [...]
9. EU food supply chain	Proposal to improve the EU food supply chain (legislative, incl. Impact assessment, Art. 42 and 43 TFEU, QI 2018)

Source: European Commission Working Program 2019

- a list of "simplification initiatives (REFIT)[26]" aiming to decrease the complexity of EU law system and reducing the administrative burdens and costs;
- a list of the priority pending proposals still to be adopted included in the European Commission Work Program of the previous years[27];
- a list of withdrawals or modifications of pending proposals.[28]

The current structure of the CWP is much more oriented to highlight the core initiatives the European Commission committed to achieve in the short term and their link to the long-term priorities.[29] In the same time, it is also an important political, technical and practical document, providing a very transparent representation of the main actions the European Commission is intended to deliver in the next years, allowing all the stakeholders to better monitor the European Commission's activities and to increase their engagement (Hardacre 2011).

(Planning) Strategic Plans and Annual Management Plans
The next documents of the SPP cycle were, until recently, the Management Plans (MPs) elaborated on an annual basis by each DGs and aiming to translate the Commission's political priorities into sectorial operational actions. Since the beginning of the Kinnock management reform, the management plans were the key instrument to measure the contribution of each DG to the overall performance of the Commission. To do this, the MPs tried to integrate priorities, objectives and resources allocation at the operational level with three distinct features (European Commission 2001):

- a common structure Commission-wide;
- a dual-use, enabling the Commission services to organize their internal work by setting clear objectives as well as translate Commission priorities in concrete actions;
- a performance orientation, through the introduction of performance indicators to all objectives set either for the internal or external dimension.

Together with the Management Plans, to strengthen the performance measurement system, the Kinnock management reform introduced a new common framework for setting objectives and indicators through a gradual implementation plan. To design realistic objectives and coherent indicators, the European Commission formulated some basic principles to support the different DGs in designing their performance frameworks. According to the principles laid down in the working documents implementing the management reform, the objectives set in the Management Plans "has to be specific and precise, measurable or verifiable, agreed with many actors, realistic and based on deadlines" (European Commission 2001: 15). Also, "a distinction has to be made between indicators for the immediate output of the activities (e.g. deliverable such as a common market directive), and their overall impact (e.g. such as degree of market integration)" (European Commission 2001: 16).

Despite the efforts and requirements, in 2005, only a limited number of services designed an effective system to measure the impact of their activities through outcome indicators. The difficulty of designing an impact indicator, the short time perspective of the Management Plans, as well as the complexity of the Commission's tasks shared with member states can partially explain the weaknesses in performance measurement. This pushed the Commission to set more policy-oriented objectives, which facilitated the introduction of impact indicators and to elaborate a conceptual map to better define all the typologies of beneficiaries affected by the Commission's action (Fig. 7.3).

After 2007, in the attempt to improve performance orientation, the European Commission continuously instructed their Services to deepen their performance framework through the diffusion of a performance-driven culture throughout the organization and improving the setting of ex-ante objectives and ex-post measurement and reporting of achievements. A decisive step was the incorporation of the performance framework developed for the 2014–2020 funding programs in the structure of the management plans. This allowed, for the first time, the synchronization of the objectives and indicators set at the EU program level with those of the DGs management Plans responsible for the management of the program (or part of it). Yet, while the objectives and targets for EU spending programs level were set for seven-years, the Management Plans time perspective remained limited to one year. Also, the general and specific objectives included in the Management Plans were still not aligned with the political priorities identified in the European Commission Political Guidelines. Furthermore, except in some cases,[30] the link between the "new initiatives" included in the European Commission Work Program 2015 and the activities identified in the Management Plans was rather weak. This led the Juncker Commission to introduce a more effective

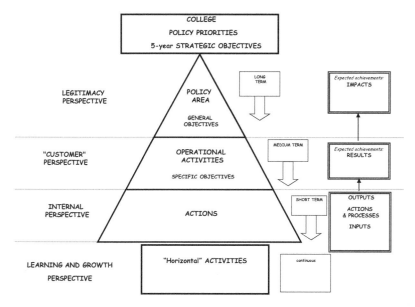

Fig. 7.3 The conceptual map for the identification of DGs beneficiaries. (Source: European Commission, Guidelines on 2007 annual management plans)

solution to better align the DGs strategic documents to the EU performance framework. Starting from 2016, the DGs have to split the content included in the Management Plans in two different documents:

- The first is a five-year Strategic Plan (SP) translating the European Commission Political Guidelines in the long term objectives, impact and results indicators associated with long term targets;
- The second is the new annual Management Plan (MP) focused on the same European Commission Political Guidelines but including only output indicators associated with short-term targets to achieve within the year.

This should result in a more coherent and simplified strategic and operational framework at DG level, strongly aligned with the other SPP cycle documents drafted at the level of the Commission, namely the European Commission Political Guidelines and the Commission Work Program.

The common structure of the Strategic Plan[31] includes the following elements:

The **first part** includes the DG mission statement, the DG vision, principles, and values.

The **second part** describes the operating context in which each DGs carries out its activities. This includes the treaty obligations, the specific DG competences and the financial instruments and programs they are responsible for. This is a relevant aspect for many DGs in charge of managing a relevant number of financial programs with different management modes.

The **third part** concerns with the elaboration of the five year DG strategy to support the delivering of the Commission political priorities as specified in the Commissioner's mission letter, in which the President of the Commission spells out the role and the responsibilities of each DG in delivering the goals of the President agenda. The strategy includes:

- The General objectives, that are the Commission priorities relevant for the DG, and the associated impact indicators
- The Specific objectives, that are the DG policy-related objectives linked to the general objectives and the associated output/results indicator.

In this section, each DG needs to develop its integrated performance framework matching the relevant Commission priorities (general objectives) from one side and specific objectives the DG is responsible for that contribute to the achievement of the general objectives from the other. This need also to be linked to the related priorities of the Europe 2020 strategy as well as the relevant thematic policy strategies and program performance frameworks. The analysis of the strategic plans across the DGs reveals that, although sharing a common structure, each DG elaborated its performance framework with a different level of detail. The table below shows the performance framework of the DG Employment and Social Affairs (DG EMPL) (Table 7.16).

Also, for each Commission general objective, the DG EMPL draws:

- an intervention logic map explaining "how the planned actions carried out by the DG EMPL, or together with the Member States in case of shared management programs, contribute to the delivery of the Commission priorities." (Table 7.17) (European Commission 2016c: 8)

Table 7.16 DG Employment and Social Affairs objectives

DG Employment and Social Affairs objectives

Commission (general objectives)	Empl. (specific objectives)	Contribution through empl. instruments
1. A New Boost for Jobs, Growth and Investment	1.1. Effective support to Member States in their structural reforms in the context of the European Semester 1.2. Stronger social dialogue 1.3. Better functioning labour markets 1.4. Decent and safe working conditions 1.5. A skilled & more entrepreneurial workforce 1.6. Greater social inclusion & effective social protection	Policy guidance, coordination and governance Regulatory process Funded actions to improve the law and policy making process (EaSl-PROGRESS, REC, ERASMUS+, prerogatives) Funding instruments with direct effect on citizens ESF: Employment & labour mobility; social inclusion education, skills & lifelong learning; institutional capacity and effective public administration
2. A Deeper and Fairer Internal Market with a Strengthened Industrial Base	2.1. Improved conditions for geographic and professional mobility whilst tackling risks of distortions and abuses	YEI: Specific support to young people FEAD: Assistance to most deprived EGF: Reintegration into employment
3. A Deeper and Fairer Economic and Monetary Union	3.1. Strengthened social dimension	Easl-MICROFINANCE: Accessibility and availability of microfinance EaSl-EURES: Geographic and professional mobility

Source: Directorate General for Employment and Social Affairs, Strategic Plan (2016–2020)

Table 7.17 Intervention logic map of DG Employment and Social Affairs

Intervention logic map of DG Employment and Social Affairs

General Objective 1. A New Boost for Jobs, Growth and Investment

Need to be addressed	What our policy & regulatory activities Deliver	What our programmes finance	Many expected short/ medium-term results	Expected end outcome
Persistent high unemployment rates in the EU, in particular youth and LTU Low levels of skills, skills mismatches or lack of skills recognition	POLICY – Contribution to the AGS and economic governance package; examination of draft NPB; CSRs – Involvement of social partners in EU social partners and EU governance – Promotion of cross industry and sectorial social dialogue – Mutual learning, exchange of good practices – Further policy guidance with common positions on key priorities and objectives to be pursued	ESF Investment in people through ESF (TO 8–11) and YEI, notably projects in the following areas: – Projects aimed at training people and helping them get work – Projects that help people in difficulty and those from disadvantaged groups to get skills and jobs – Initiatives to improve education and training and ensure young people complete their education and get the skills that make them more competitive on the job market – Support Member States' efforts to improve the quality of public administration and governance	Modernised labour market and sustainable social protection systems Adequate legislative framework ensuring minimum rights in the area of working conditions Participants to programmes: – With increased level of qualification – In training – In employment – Supported through basic assistance or social inclusion measures	– Employment rates have improved – Long term unemployment has decreased – Education participation rates Keep improving – less people are at risk of poverty – Quality and sustainable empl. is fostered
High level of poverty and poor social inclusion Lack of common protection rules at work	LAW – Proposals for legislative measures and to amend/simplify legislative acquis (REFIT) in the fields of working conditions (labour law, OSH) and workers' rights that are in line with better regulation principles – Monitoring transposition and application Funded actions supporting policy and law-making (EaSI PROGRESS, Erasmus+, REC)	FEAD Distribution of food and/or basic goods Participation in social inclusion measures EGF Active labour market policy EaSI MICROFINANCE Support to microfinance and social enterprises		

Source: Directorate General for Employment and Social Affairs, Strategic Plan (2016–2020)

- a performance framework defining "the specific objectives under the first general objective and the corresponding indicators. Their full formulation, definition, milestones and targets are presented in annex 1." (European Commission 2016c: 8) (Fig. 7.4).

Similarly, the Directorate General Regional and Urban Policy associated with each relevant Commission priority (general objective) the financial and non-financial contributions of DG's competence (specific objectives). The financial contributions include the funding programs managed by the DG together with member states and their objectives,[32] whereas non-financial contributions include legislative and non—legislative initiatives, member states support programs, etc. More specifically, as explained in the plan, "the specific objectives capturing REGIO's concrete contributions towards these corporate goals correspond to European Regional Development Fund and Cohesion Fund thematic objectives (TOs)" (European Commission 2015c: 6). These latter are high-level objectives, common to all European Structural and Investment Funds (ESIF), used as a basis for identifying the specific objectives of the DG (European Commission 2015c) as shown in the Table 7.18.

The indicators associated with the general and specific objectives can be found in the performance framework elaborated at the level of the general objective the DG contributes to achieve, as show in Fig. 7.5. This includes impact indicators for the general objective as well as output/result indicator for the specific objectives associated to it. All other elements as the baseline and targets are described in the annex of the strategic plan.

In the strategic plan of the Directorate-General for Agriculture and Rural Development (2016–2020), the DG strategy linking the Commission priorities (general objectives) relevant for the DG with the DG specific responsibilities includes the indicators. The specific objectives and indicators are mainly related to the policy elaboration of the Common Agricultural Policy (CAP) and the management of the funds related to the CAP, i.e. the European Agricultural Guarantee Fund (EAGF) and the European Agricultural Fund for Rural Development (EAFRD). The strategy map is shown in Table 7.19.

In other cases, the representation of the DG's strategy is sometimes less effective, as no tables or maps are included in the description of the strategy. Nevertheless, all DGs and Services defined their specific objectives with indicators, baselines, and targets associated with the Commission

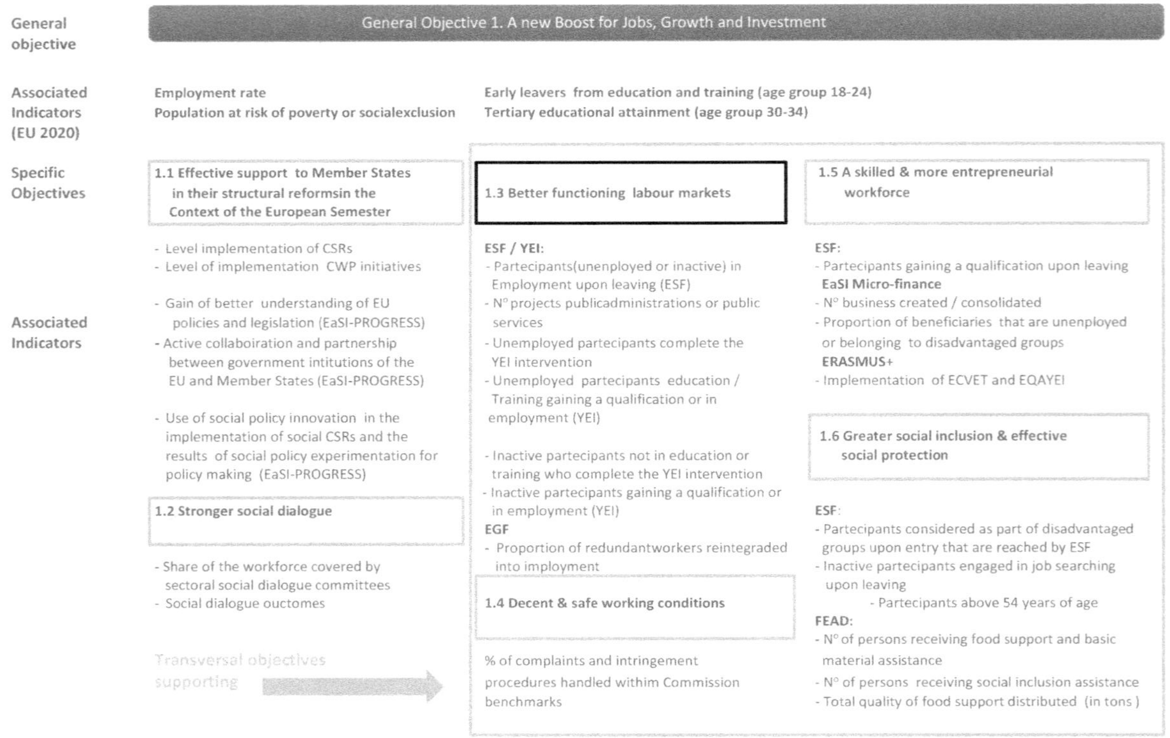

General objective

General Objective 1. A new Boost for Jobs, Growth and Investment

Associated Indicators (EU 2020)

Employment rate
Population at risk of poverty or social exclusion
Early leavers from education and training (age group 18-24)
Tertiary educational attainment (age group 30-34)

Specific Objectives

1.1 Effective support to Member States in their structural reforms in the Context of the European Semester

1.2 Stronger social dialogue

1.3 Better functioning labour markets

1.4 Decent & safe working conditions

1.5 A skilled & more entrepreneurial workforce

1.6 Greater social inclusion & effective social protection

Associated Indicators

- Level implementation of CSRs
- Level of implementation CWP initiatives
- Gain of better understanding of EU policies and legislation (EaSI-PROGRESS)
- Active collaboration and partnership between government intitutions of the EU and Member States (EaSI-PROGRESS)
- Use of social policy innovation in the implementation of social CSRs and the results of social policy experimentation for policy making (EaSI-PROGRESS)

- Share of the workforce covered by sectoral social dialogue committees
- Social dialogue outcomes

ESF / YEI:
- Participants (unemployed or inactive) in Employment upon leaving (ESF)
- N° projects public administrations or public services
- Unemployed participants complete the YEI intervention
- Unemployed participants education / Training gaining a qualification or in employment (YEI)
- Inactive participants not in education or training who complete the YEI intervention
- Inactive participants gaining a qualification or in employment (YEI)
EGF
- Proportion of redundant workers reintegrated into employment

% of complaints and intringement procedures handled within Commission benchmarks

ESF:
- Participants gaining a qualification upon leaving
EaSI Micro-finance
- N° business created / consolidated
- Proportion of beneficiaries that are unemployed or belonging to disadvantaged groups
ERASMUS+
- Implementation of ECVET and EQAVEI

ESF:
- Participants considered as part of disadvantaged groups upon entry that are reached by ESF
- Inactive participants engaged in job searching upon leaving
- Participants above 54 years of age
FEAD:
- N° of persons receiving food support and basic material assistance
- N° of persons receiving social inclusion assistance
- Total quality of food support distributed (in tons)

Transversal objectives supporting

Fig. 7.4 Performance framework of the DG Employment and Social Affairs. Source: Directorate General for Employment and Social Affairs, Strategic Plan (2016–2020)

Table 7.18 Performance framework of the DG Regional and Urban Policy

Performance framework of the DG Regional and Urban Policy

Relevant EC priorities (general objective)	*Contributions through funding (specific objectives)*	*Non-financial contributions (ExAC, CSRs, leveraging public and private investments, ect.)*
1. Jobs, Growth and Investment	T01: RTD and innovation T03: Competitiveness of SMEs T06: Protection of environment, resource efficiency/circular economy T07: Sustainable transport T08: Employment and labour mobility T09: Social inclusion T010: Education, skills and lifelong learning T011: Institutional capacity and effective PA	ExAC on: Research and innovation/ smart specialisation SME/Small Business Act Water, waste and EIA/SEA legislation "Investment Challenges Box"
2. Digital Single Market	T02: Information and communication technologies	ExAC on: Strategic policy framework for digital growth Next generation Network Plans

Source: Directorate General Regional and Urban Policy, Strategic Plan (2016–2020)

priorities. The specific objectives represent an overview of the related performance expectations and constitute the framework for assessing the achievement of DGs policy objectives in the long-term period (European Commission 2016a). The baseline includes either impact indicators to measure the performance expectations set for the general objectives, or results indicators that do the same for the specific objectives. Both are associated with realistic milestones and long-term targets. Also, some DGs also included practical examples of the expected medium-term achievements.[33] The set of indicators included in the strategic plans of the DGs managing the EU spending programs are sometimes analogous to the performance information provided in the Programs statements. As shown in Table 7.20, some of the DGs involved in managing the EU spending programs share the same performance indicators included in the program's performance frameworks, even in the case the programs are managed by the shared management model.

General objective	General Objective 1 A new Boost for Jobs, Growth and investment			
Associated Input Incator(s)	COM (EU 2020)	(1) % of EU GDP invested in R&D (combined public and private investment) (2) Employmentrate population aged 20-64 (3) Tertiary educational attaiment, age group 30-34	(4) Share of early leavers from education and training (5) People at risk of poverty or social exclusion (6) Gross Fixed Capital Formation (GFCF) investments to GDP ratio	
	REGIO-Specific:	(1) Increase in GDP growth (2) Increase in employment	(3) Increase in private investment (4) Dispersion of GDP per capita (all MS)	
Specific Objectives	1.1 Strengthening research, technological development and innovation (TO1)	1.2 Enhancing the competitiveness off small and medium-sized enterprises (TO3)	1.3 Preserving and protecting the environment and promoting resourceefficiency (TO6)	1.4 Promoting sustainable trasportand removing bottlenecks in key network infrastructures (TO7)
Associated output/input Indicators	New researchers in supported entities Enterprises cooperating with research institutions Researchers working in improved improved research infrastucture facilities	Enterprises receving support Employment increase in supported enterprises Increase in expected number of visits to supported sites of cultural and natural heritage and attractions	Additional population served by improved wasterwater treatment Additional waste recycling capacity Additional population served by improved water supply Area of habitats supported to attain a better conservation status	Lenght of reconstructed or upgraded railway line Length of reconstructed or upgraded roads Length of new or improved tram and metro line
	1.5 Promoting sustainable and quality employment and supporting labour mobility (TO8)	1.6 Promoting social inclusion, combating poverty and any discrimination (TO9)	1.7 Investing in education, training and vocational training for skills and lifelong leaning (TO10)	1.8 Enhancing institutional capacity of public authorities and stakeholders and an efficient PA (TO11)
	Employment increase in supported enterprises	Population covered by improved health services Public or commercial buildings built or renovated in urban areas Rheabilitated housing in urban areas	Capacity of supported childcare or education infrastructure	Implementation programme authorities of capacity building measures in agrementwith DG REGIO

Fig. 7.5 Indicators for the general and specific objectives, DG Regional and Urban Policy. Source: Directorate General Regional and Urban Policy, Strategic Plan (2016–2020)

Table 7.19 Indicators for general and specific objectives, DG Agriculture and Rural Development

Indicators associated to the general and specific objectives, DG Agriculture and Rural Development

Commission (general objectives)	Related common CAP objectives (CO)	Impact indicators
1. A New Boost for jobs, Growth and Investment	CAP CO 1: Viable food production CAP CO 2: Sustainable management of natural resources and climate action CAP CO 3: Balanced territorial development	Corporate – Percentage of EU GDP invested in R&D (combined public and private investment) – Employment rate population aged 20–64 CAP-specific – Agricultural factor income – Total factor productivity in agriculture – EU commodity prices compared to world prices – Rural employment rate
2. A Connected Digital Single Market	CAP CO 3: Balanced territorial development	Corporate – Aggregate score in Digital Economy and Society Index (DESI) EU-28 CAP-specific – Percentage of rural population benefiting from new or improved ICT services/ infrastructures
3. A Resilient Energy Union with a Forward-Looking Climate Change Policy	CAP CO 2: Sustainable management of natural resources and climate action	Corporate – Greenhouse gas emissions CAP-specific – Net greenhouse gas emission from agriculture – Nitrate levels in freshwater (water quality) – Minimum share of agricultural land with specific environmental practices/ commitment
6. A Balanced and Progressive Trade Policy to harness Globalisation	CAP CO 1: Viable food production	Corporate – Percentage of EU trade in goods and services as well as investment covered by applied EU preferential trade an investment agreements CAP-specific – Total EU agri-food trade value

Source: Directorate-General for Agriculture and Rural Development (2016–2020)

Table 7.20 The Horizon 2020 indicators included in the DGs strategic plans (2016–2020)

Horizon 2020 performance framework			DGs strategic plans
Pillars	Specific objective	Indicators	2016–2020
Excellent science— European Research Council (ERC)	Strengthening frontier research	Share of publications from ERC-funded projects which are among the top 1% highly cited per field of science	DG RTD (page 49)
Excellent science— Future and Emerging Technologies	Strengthening research in future and emerging technologies	Publications in peer-reviewed high impact journals	DG RTD (page 49)
		Patent applications and patents awarded in Future and Emerging Technologies	DG RTD (page 49)
Excellent science— Marie Sklodowska-Curie actions	Strengthening skills, training and career development	Cross-sector and cross-country circulation of researchers, including PhD candidates (cumulative number)	DG EAC (page 60)
Industrial leadership	Provide dedicated support for research, development and demonstration and, where appropriate, for standardisation and certification, on information and communications technology (ICT)	Patent applications and patents awarded in the different enabling and industrial technologies	DG RTD (page 49), DG GROW (page 15)

Source—own elaboration based on the analysis of the Strategic Plans (2016–2020).

The **fourth** part of the strategic plan consists of a selection of Key Performance Indicators (KPI) monitoring the core aspects of the DGs' policies. They are selected to better represent the ability of the DG to deliver the identified challenges. The KPIs are directly linked to the ten European Commission political objectives and indirectly to the five objectives and targets of the Europe 2020 strategy or relevant objectives set by other EU Regulations or EU spending programs. The following table shows an example of KPIs included in the Strategic Plan (SP) of the DG Regional and Urban Policies (Table 7.21).

The **fifth** and last section of the Management Plans is related to organizational management. This includes the identification of the organizational components necessary for the execution of the DGs strategy plan. For all DGs the main components include (European Commission 2016a):

(a) Human Resource Management
(b) Financial Management and Internal Control and Risk Management

Table 7.21 The Key Performance Indicators (KPI) of the DG Regional and Urban Policy[a]

KPI	Baseline	Milestones	Target	Typology	Political priorities (2014–2019)
Employment increase in supported enterprises	0	338.341 (2019)	423,114 (2023)	Result	1. A new boost for jobs, growth and investment
Number of enterprises receiving support	0	209.200 (2018)	1.101.114 (2023)	Result	1. A new boost for jobs, growth and investment
Additional households with broadband access of at least 30 Mbps	0	3.000.200 (2018)	1.4564.260 (2023)	Result	2. A connected digital single market
Additional capacity of renewable energy production	0	1.800 (2018)	7.669 (2023)	Result	3. A resilient Energy Union
Cumulative residual error rate.			Below the materiality criteria of 2%	Result	

[a]The key performance indicators are included in the Strategic Plan of the DG Regional and Urban Policy (2016–2020), page 27

Source: Directorate General Regional and Urban Policy, Strategic Plan (2016–2020)

(c) Application of Better Regulation principles in decision-making and the management of the DG's acquis
(d) Information management aspects
(e) External Communication activities

For each component, several objectives and output indicators are identified, including the verification source, the baseline, and a long-time perspective target. The objectives set in this section mainly aim at increasing the efficiency of DG's internal processes in the key strategic areas as well to contribute to the policy achievements.

The second document elaborated at the DG level is the new annual **Management Plan (MP)**. This latter describes the actions of the DG for the year, and how these latter contribute to the achievement of the DG's multiannual specific objectives set in the Strategic Plans. The new Management Plans identify the focus areas as well as the main outputs that should be delivered and aim at monitoring the performance expectations (European Commission 2016a). Coherently with the shorter time perspective, the MPs include the identification of outputs to be delivered associated with outputs indicators linked to results and impact indicators set in the strategic plans. The common structure of the new Management Plans include:

- the description of the main outputs to be achieved for the year. In this section, each DG classifies the main actions leading to the outputs to achieve the general and specific objectives set in the strategic plan, as represented in Table 7.22.
- The outputs category includes:
  - the *policy-related outputs* corresponding to the main legislative or non-legislative acts to be adopted according to the Commission Work Program (CWP). All policy related outputs include an indicator (the adoption of the act) and a target (when is supposed to be adopted). The table below shows the link between the legislative or non-legislative initiatives included in the CWP 2019 and the performance framework of the Directorate General for Employment and Social Affairs (Fig. 7.6).
  - the *main expenditure outputs* are those actions related to the management of the EU funding programs. Each action is linked to several output indicators and targets within the year. Some of the DGs involved in the management of EU programs, under the shared management model, specified in their management plans

Table 7.22 Description of the main outputs, DG Agriculture and Rural Development

Description of the main outputs, DG Agriculture and Rural Development		
Commission (general objective) 1. A New Boost for Jobs, Growth and Investment		
CAP common objective: Viable food production		
Specific objective: To improve the competitiveness of the agricultural sector and enhance its value share in the food chain		Related to spending programme: EAGF
Main outputs in 2018:		
All new initiatives and REFIT initiatives the Commission Work Programme		
Output	Indicator	Target
Food chain legislation on basis of CAP competence and depending on the outcomes of an impact assessment currently carried out (PLAN/2017/764; cf. Annex 1 of Commission Work Programme 2018)	Legal rules concerning the governance of the food supply chain so as to improve the position of farmers follow-up to Agricultural Markets Task Force's November 2016 report	First half of 2018

Source: Directorate-General for Agriculture and Rural Development, Annual Management Plan (2018)

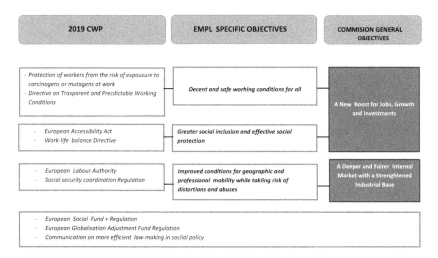

Fig. 7.6 Policy related output of the DG for Employment and Social Affairs. Source: Directorate-General for Employment and Social Affairs, Annual Management Plan (2019)

whether the output is of member states' responsibility or the responsibility is combined between DG and member states. In this latter case, the same target is also as a performance indicator of the member states managing authorities responsible for the program implementation. An example is shown in the Table 7.23.

• The second section corresponds to organizational management outputs for the year, mirroring the same section included in the Strategic Plans with a shorter time perspective. In this case, for each component or function identified in the strategic plan, the main outputs are presented, although the list in the management plan is often not exhaustive. A more detailed annual work program will be elaborated by each responsible unit within the DG through an annual "Unit Management Plan" cascading down the DG-level annual objectives (European Commission 2016a).

Table 7.23   Main expenditure outputs, DG Regional and Urban Policy

Main outputs in 2018: Important items from work programmes/financing decisions/ operational programmes

Output	Indicator	Target
Wide uptake of financial instruments and complementarity with EFSI	Fi-compass assistance delivery in accordance with the 2018 work programme	100% of products agreed for period the delivered
	Amounts of programme contribution invested into final recipients and spent for management costs and fees (**MS responsibility**)	EUR 5 billion by end-2018, baseline EUR 1.5 at end-2017
	Support for the set-up and implementation of financial instruments in member states	100% of announced guidance notes are finalised by the end of March 2018
	Identification of ESIF-EFSI projects (**combined responsibility**)	Approval by EFSI governance/EIB Board of 20 ESIF-EFSI projects by end-2018
	Dissemination of information on identified ESIF-EFSI projects	20 by end-2018 A dedicated initiative is set up with the EIB by end-2018 to enhance the outermost regions' access to EFSI

Source: Directorate-General for Regional and Urban Policy, Annual Management Plan 2018

(Reporting) General Report on the activities of the European Union

The general report on the activities of the European Union is published in February (n + 1) and gives evidence to the main progress towards the European Commission political guidelines.[34] The document is structured around the ten political guidelines and describes the main activities carried out by the Commission in that domain as well as the main achievements. It is an accessible and readable document for the general public and stakeholders.

(Reporting) The Annual Activity Report (AAR)

The *Annual Activity Report (AAR)* is the main document monitoring the performance achievement at the level of the Directorate Generals and Services and is published within June (n + 1). The AAR reports the activities carried out by the DGs as well as the value of the different sets of indicators included in the strategic and in the annual management plans. The current structure of the AAR is the following:

- the first part of the AAR describes the key results and progress towards the achievement of the general and specific objectives of the DG as outlined in their Strategic Plans;
- the second part acknowledges how the achievements described in the previous section were delivered by the DG. It includes the description of the organizational management and internal controls that support management's assurance on the achievement of the financial management and internal control objectives. The last part deals with other components of organizational management: human resources, better regulation principles, information management, and external communication;
- the annexes contain several additional information concerning different management aspects of DGs competence, including the EU programs, the EU decentralized agencies, etc. The last section reports the performance tables showing:
  - the value of the outcome/impact indicators associated with the general and specific objectives of the DGs (included in the strategic plans);
  - the outputs delivered included in the Management plans and related either to general and specific objectives or to organizational management objectives. Table 7.24 shows an example.

Table 7.24   Output delivered by the DG for Regional and Urban Policy

Output delivered by the DG for Regional and Urban Policy			
REGIO indicator/target 2017	Status as of end-Dec '17	Reported results and risks (end-Dec '17)	Propose actions (end-Dec '17)
1. To deliver jobs, growth and investment			
1.1 To support the delivery by Member States of the 2014-2020 programmes' objectives ensuring quality of cohesion policy investment			
REGIO 1. Ensure active support, monitoring and follows up of programme implementation. Target: for all operational programmes (OPs), participation to monitoring committees and review meetings, Annual Implementation Reports (AIRs) and performance assessed and appropriate follow up launched for the programme at risks by end 2017 (detailed reporting to be done via implementation report)	☺	Bottlenecks hindering implementation were discussed in EGESIF in October taking into account analysis of the input received from the Member States The reviewed list of programmes at risk was agreed in the Board in early December. The concerns and the actions planned have been identified for all the 37 programmes currently included in the exercise	02 to continue monitoring of programmes at risk while assisting the geographical units in identifying actions necessary to tackle individual issues hindering implementation of programmes on the list
REGIO 2. 100% of Major Projects submitted by end-September 2017 adopted within 3 months (interrupted time non counted)	☺	DG REGIO received 109 major projects and approved 103 of them within the regulatory 3-months deadline. 5 projects were approved beyond deadline because of interruption and need to re-consult JASPERS. They were anyway approved without undue delay within 100-120 calendar days	
REGIO 3. 100% of Partnership Agreements (PAs)/OP modifications adopted on time (interrupted time non counted)	☺	The number of delayed processes has been steadily decreasing, falling seven percentage points from 43% to less than 34% since the end of September. Since the last reporting, 117 programme amendment processes have been completed, of which 82% were complet5etd within the regulatory deadline	
	☺	For OP amendments that were processed in WAVE, the average duration of an amendment is 79 calendar days, which is below the regulatory deadline of three months, 73% of these amendments have been processed within the deadline.	02 to continue monitoring the OPA processes and highlighting any issues to the responsible director
		Since the introduction of the simplified internal process (mid May 2017), 162 programme amendments have been received and processed in WAVE, 127 programme amendments were adopted, out of which 83% (105) within the three months regulatory deadline	

Source: Directorate-General for Regional and Urban Policy, Annual Activity Report 2018

7.4.1.4   The Member States Level

The third strategic layer is at the level of the EU Member States and includes the national strategies and the related performance frameworks. Currently, there are two shared performance frameworks between the EU and the member states. The first is the Europe 2020 strategy strategic framework and the second is linked to the management of the EU structural funds. As for the Europe 2020 strategy, its success heavily depends on member states coordinating their efforts with the EU. To facilitate such coordination, the targets of the Europe 2020 have been translated at the national level in a way that EU-level goals will be achieved only if all member states will reach their national targets.[35] This allows us to consider the initial situation of each member states to better define their level of ambition (Table 7.25).

Europe 2020 targets should then guide the priorities set and resource allocation also at the national level to complement EU actions towards the achievement of the Europe 2020 goals. For this purpose, different mechanisms to increase the coordination of planning and programming exercise among member states and the EU institutions have been recently adopted. Among them, the Commission set up the annual cycle of EU-level policy coordination, also known as European Semester, to increase coordination of economic, social and budgetary priorities at the EU and national level to ensure progress towards the Europe 2020 targets (Eurostat 2016). This mechanism requests the member states to submit each year April (n-1) a National Reform Program, which illustrates the way the countries' policies sustain the social and economic growth to achieve the Europe 2020 targets. In other words, each member state needs to describe the concrete actions and the main reforms carried out in the next year to contribute to the achievement of the Europe 2020 targets set at the national and the EU level. Following the submission of the National Reform Programs, the European Commission can provide country-specific recommendations (CSRs) to each member state. The CSRs "address the implementation of the Europe 2020 strategy and other economic challenges on the national level and provide a timeframe for member states to respond accordingly and implement the policy advice in their annual economic policy and budget cycle" (Eurostat 2016: 18). In the next National Reform Program, the member states need to give evidence of the corrective actions taken to address the country-specific recommendations. A second shared performance framework is linked to the management of the EU structural funds. The EU Member states manage a large part of the EU budget through the shared management model of the EU spending programs, which account for approximately 80% of the EU budget. The bulk of these programs corresponds to the European Structural Investments funds (ESIF),[36] for which the Commission and the member states are jointly responsible for their implementation. Also, the use of structural funds is based on the principle of complementarity and requires the co-financing of the operative programs from the member states. As described above, to increase the results orientation of the ESI funds, the Commission, together with the

Table 7.25 National targets of the Europe 2020 strategy. Source: European Commission (2010)

EU/Member State	Employment rate	Gross domestic expenditure on research and development	Greenhouse gas emissions	Share of renewable energy	Energy efficiency	Early leavers from education and training	Tertiary educational attainment	Poverty and social exclusion
EU-28	Increasing the employment rate of the population aged 20–64 to at least 75%	Increasing combined public and private investment in R&D to 3% of GDP	Reducing greenhouse gas emissions by at least 20% compared to 1990 levels	Increasing the share of renewable energy in final energy consumption to 20%	Moving towards a 20% increase in energy efficiency (equalling a reduction to 1483 Mtoe of primary energy consumption)	Reducing school drop-out rates to less than 10% (of the population aged 18–24)	Increasing the share of the population aged 30–34 having completed tertiary education to at least 40%	Lifting at least 20 million people out of the risk of poverty and social exclusion (compared to 2008)
Belgium	73.2%	3%	-15%	13%	43.7	9.5%	47%	-380,000 persons
Bulgaria	76%	1.5%	+20%	16%	16.9	11%	36%	Reduce by 260,000 the number of persons living in monetary poverty
Czech Republic	75%	1% (public sector only)	+9%	13%	39.6	5.5%	32%	-100,000 persons
Denmark	80%	3%	-20%	30%	17.8	10%	>40%	Reduce by 22,000 the number of persons living in households with very low work intensity
Germany	77%	3%	-14%	18%	276.6	<10%	42% (ISCED 2011 level 4–8)	Reduce by 20% the number of long-term unemployed (unemployed for more than one year) compared to 2008. (equalling to a reduction of 320,000 longterm unemployed persons)

Estonia	76%	3%	+11%	25%	6.5	9.5%	40%	Reduce to a rate of 15% the number of persons living at risk of poverty after social transfers (compared to 17.5% in 2010)
Ireland	69–71%	2.5% of GNP (Approximately 2% of GDP)	−20%	16%	13.9	8%	60%	Reduce by a minimum of 200,000 the population in combined poverty (either consistent poverty, at-risk-of-poverty or basic deprivation).

member states, adopted a shared performance framework for monitoring, reporting and evaluate the use of the ESI funds. Consequently, all managing authorities share the same common objectives (OTs) set for all ESI funds and need to define their indicators and targets to account for how the resources managed are directed towards the common objectives. To support the managing authorities, the Commission published guidance for member states intended to ensure that the programs deliver what has been planned. The guide encourages the member states to define a strong performance framework for each priority of the operative programs managed, including a set of indicators, milestones, and targets as well as a shared monitoring and reporting system.

7.4.2   Discussion

The strategic framework of the EU appears as a rather complex performance system with multiple strategic frameworks in place at different levels of the organization and outside. In this case, it is fundamental that they are well-coordinated and mutually supportive (OECD 2017). Relying on the research framework developed in Chap. 2, the EU performance management system will be mainly assessed according to two dimensions of a performance management system, span and depth.

(span) Assessing the span of the performance management of the EU means analyzing the horizontal expansion of the results linked to the mechanistic relationship between inputs, activities outputs and outcomes. As much as the performance management system can measure outcomes as much wider is the span (Bouckaert and Halligan 2008). The first step in this direction is looking at the coherence of the performance chain represented in the strategic documents analyzed above. The first group of documents setting the priorities at the EU level includes:

- the Europe 2020 strategy, which is *de facto* the reference strategy for setting the performance objectives at a lower levels of the organization. This, although Europe 2020 strategy does not encompass the totality of the EU competencies and expenditures. It is also the strategic reference framework for the EU member states and it is equipped with shared targets, indicators, and an integrated monitoring system.
- The Council strategic agenda recalls some of the priorities included in the Europe 2020 strategy but without a clear linkage. Few refer-

ences can be found in other strategic documents of the organization and there is a lack of targets, indicators, and monitoring systems.

- The multiannual financial framework (MFF) which is both an expression of the political priorities—as it sets the areas of EU spending over a seven year period—as well as a budgetary planning tool. The current MFF structure is aligned to deliver the Europe 2020 priorities, although the MFF includes also other EU competencies and expenditures not represented in the Europe 2020 strategy. For example, almost 40% of the EU budget is devoted to agriculture, rural development, and fisheries which is only indirectly represented in the Europe 2020 targets.
- The EU spending programs which contain robust performance frameworks are integrated with the current MFF system and linked to the Europe 2020 strategy. Nevertheless, the high number of performance reports on the single EU programs (Programs Statements) while are impressive and comprehensive of budgetary and performance information, are difficult for anyone person to come to terms with (OECD 2017).

The second group of documents is set at the European Commission level, which is the main contributor to the EU objectives. The main document is the European Commission Political Guidelines which is a fundamental tool for planning the European Commission activities to answer the EU challenges including those linked to the Europe 2020 strategy. It is the key document for allocating resources within the Commission and its services through the annual Strategic and Planning Cycle. The review of the strategic planning and programming cycle of the European Commission highlighted the progress towards improving the coherence and the effectiveness of the performance measurement system within an extremely complex operating framework. The changes in the SPP cycle introduced in 2014 and 2016 strengthened the coherence of the performance measurement system and will bring full benefits in the years to come. Among the changes, the most beneficial include:

- The incorporation of the indicators associated to the EU funding programs in the Strategic and Management Plans of the DG and Services

- The introduction of the multiannual Strategic Plans at the level of the DGs strengthens the link between the DGs action and the Commission Political Priorities. Also, the multiannual perspective allows the Strategic Plans to focus on setting and monitoring impact and results, while the Management Plans focuses on the short-term outputs needed to achieve the long-term objectives.
- The current Commission Work Program is also better aligned with the Commission Political Priorities, highlighting the contribution of the new legislative and non-legislative initiatives planned to the different Commission Political Priorities.
- The uniform adoption by all DGs of a common set of the indicators measuring impact, results, and outputs according to general, specific and operational objectives.

The coherence of the performance chain is also reinforced by the elaboration of a common conceptual background shared at the Commission level, allowing all the DGs to be aligned on a common framework linking impact, results and output indicators to the different perspectives and beneficiaries of the EU action. Following this, the general objectives are direct to measure the extent to which the EU action is effectively addressing the main challenges of the EU society—composed of citizens, markets and territories (legitimacy perspective). The general objectives are identified in the Commission Political Guidelines coherently with the main political and strategic documents at the EU level or above, as the UN Agenda 2030, the Europe 2020 strategy or the EU sectorial policy strategies. The general objectives of the European Commission are not directly associated with indicators. These are identified in the DG Strategic Plans and associated to the specific objectives measuring the DG contribution towards the achievement of the European Commission general objectives. On average, each Strategic Plan (2016–2020) contains 4.56 impact indicators, 22.52 results indicators and 0.72 output indicators[37] associated to the specific objectives. The DGs with a higher number of impact indicators in their Strategic Plans are generally those entrusted with higher responsibilities in managing the main EU spending programs.[38] Moreover, most of the impact indicators included in the Strategic Plans are the same included in the EU spending programs performance frameworks, as shown in Table 7.18.

The results indicators associated to the specific objectives measure the direct and immediate effect of DG intervention and can be evaluated on a shorter time perspective (milestones). They should be able to measure the effect of the EU action towards the selected target population, which can be a group of companies or citizens, or the governments of the member states (*customer perspective*). Finally, the *internal perspective* is addressed by the Annual Management Plans and concerns the activities carried out by the DGs to achieve both the general and specific objectives set in the strategic documents. The indicators in this case will be input/output-oriented aiming to evaluate the processes efficiency implemented by the DGs.

To visually represent their common conceptual background, each DG elaborates the *intervention logic map* to identify the specific causal links between needs, objectives set, actions, resources and results Although the quality of the documents shows high degree of variability, Fig. 7.7 shows one of the most exhaustive example.

Nevertheless, despite the progress towards a more coherent and effective performance chain, several disconnections between documents set at different levels and with different perspectives time still prevent the EU performance management system to be more effective.

The first disconnection is that the time-perspective of the different EU strategic documents is not aligned. In fact:

- the long term EU strategies, as the Europe 2020 strategy, has a time of ten years (from 2010 to 2020);
- the Multiannual Financial Framework (MFF) and the EU spending programs have formally a time of seven years (currently from 2014 to 2020). Although the actual length is over 13 years, considering that the proposals are first made two years before (n-2) and the spending programs have an eligibility period of three years after (n+3) the end of the programming period;
- the strategic agenda of the European Council has a time of five years (currently 2014–2019);
- the Commission mandate linked to the Commission's political guidelines is set for five years following the electoral cycle of the European Parliament (currently from 2014–2019).

The result is represented in Fig. 7.8. The time of the current Europe 2020 strategy is not aligned with the Multiannual Financial Framework and the EU spending programs in turns are not synchronized with the Commission political guidelines which are set for five years following the

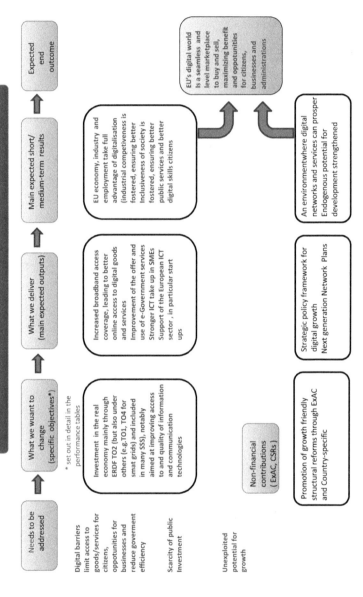

Fig. 7.7   The intervention logic of DG Regional and Urban Policy (2016–2020). Source: European Commission (2016a)

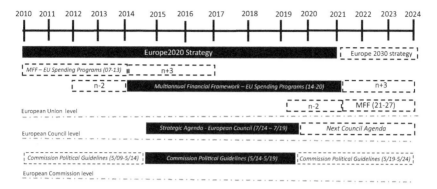

Fig. 7.8 The time-perspective of the different EU strategic documents. Source: own elaboration

electoral cycle of the European Parliament. Also, the previous EU spending programs (n+3) overlap with the current programming period.

The consequence is that the current period of the strategic documents prevents the achievement of the strategic goals through implementing policy more effectively and efficiently (European Parliament 2017). The debate over the duration of the strategic documents and, in particular, of the multiannual financial framework, did not attract much interest either in academia or among the member states (European Parliament 2017). These latter seem quite accustomed to the seven-years MFF and only interested in estimating their net position vis à vis the EU budget and the amount of funds received (European Parliament 2017). The European institutions either did not deal with the duration of the MFF in a detailed way, only a few documents refer to the optimal duration of the MFF (European Parliament 2017).

The second possible shortcoming is linked to the presence of multiple and overlapping strategic frameworks within the same organization. This can impede clarity and transparency in the performance chain, affecting the coherence between the higher-level strategic goals and more intermediate and operational objectives as well as the accountability framework (OECD 2017). The clarity of the EU strategic framework will depend on the level of complementarity of such documents as the different frameworks cover different kinds of areas. For example, the main documents setting the EU strategic frameworks, the Europe 2020 strategy, the UN Agenda, and the Council Agenda have different time perspectives, include different objectives or sometimes the objectives are similar but measured with different indicators or as in the case of the Council agenda, the indicators are missing. Also, the monitoring and reporting mechanisms are diverse, while the Europe 2020 strategy is fully integrated in the EU semester for policy coordination with the EU member states, the Commission deals with monitoring, reporting and reviewing progress towards the Sustainable Development Goals in the EU context (European Commission 2016a).

Europe 2020 and the MFF cover different areas of competence. Although some relevant shifts have been made in the current MFF (2014–2020) to better align it with the EU strategic objectives, the current expenditures structure still reflects the traditional division, with almost 70% of expenditures related to agriculture and cohesion policy (European Parliament 2017). Whereas in the Europe 2020 strategy, little space is dedicated to both areas. The relation between the MFF and the EU spending programs is more linear, as all EU spending programs are split into the different budget chapters grouped within the budget headings, which corresponds to a policy area. Nevertheless, each spending program has its performance framework, and no single performance frameworks exist at the level of the MFF headings or policy area. This can make it difficult for stakeholders to understand, for example, what the budget as a whole, or the single budget headings, are trying to accomplish (OECD 2017). The new reporting mechanism elaborated by the Commission, which integrates information on financial expenditures and program performance in a single document (the Annual Management and Performance Report) is definitively more accurate and informative than in the past. Nevertheless, for the general public is still very complex to come to terms with it. For this reason, the communication on performance should be further improved. To this regard, the OECD in a recent assessment report on Budgeting and Performance in the European Union suggests the EU to adopt a single document including the goals and objectives that the EU Budget intends to achieve. It should "be structured by reference to the existing EU budget headings, drawing together the various goals and objectives that are already articulated in various other policy domains such as Europe 2020 and specifying, in each policy area, a limited number of headline targets to be pursued during the course of the budget year" (OECD 2017: 15).

(depth) The above—mentioned focus on measuring impact and results of the EU's actions should be connected to a deeper performance management system, as the outcome is generally realized by the contribution of a range of organizations. In the case of the EU, the performance management is deeper as much as the performance levels (international, European and national) are linked and integrated. In other words, as much as the objectives and targets are shared and commonly used across the different strategic levels, as much as deep is the performance management system. Considering the relation between the international and the European level, the most visible strategic link is the UN 2030 Agenda for Sustainable Development and the achievement of the Sustainability Development Goals (SDGs). Currently, a recent Commission staff working paper[39] mapped how European policies contribute to the different SDGs showing that EU policies address all 17 goals. The SDGs are thus being pursued by the EU policy instruments and integrated in all the Commission ten priorities (European Commission 2016b), although at the moment, the SDGs and the Europe 2020 strategy remain two different strategic documents each with its objectives, targets, and indicators. Nevertheless, as mentioned above, the European Commission envisaged different possible scenarios to better integrate the SDGs into the post-2020 growth strategy of the EU, including the adoption of the United Nations 2030 Agenda as the next strategic framework of the EU and the member states (European Commission 2019). If this were the case, the performance link with the international strategic level would be highly reinforced, thus providing a strong performance alignment at the international level. The other fundamental link for a deep performance management system is the relation to the national level. The outcome planned at the EU level can be achieved only in collaboration with member states' contribution, as these latter hold relevant responsibilities either in managing EU spending programs (indirect and shared management model) as well as in adopting legislative and non-legislative initiatives in their areas of competence. Their action is thus crucial for the achievement of the objectives set by the EU level; consequently, the depth of the performance management system adopted will depend on the degree of integration with the performance management system of the member states. In other words, as much as the objectives and indicators set at the European level will be integrated into the national performance management systems, as much as deeper will be the whole EU performance system. The Commission is deeply aware of the crucial role of the member states in achieving the

objectives set and vice versa; member states believe in achieving the objectives more effectively at the European level. Said that performance
accountability requires mutual trust and effective cooperation, indispensable for setting up a rational, shared and deeper performance system
(Stiglitz 2003). In this respect, some initiatives have been carried out to
increase the coordination of performance systems.

As described above, the EU and the member states currently share two
performance frameworks, the Europe 2020 strategy and the performance
framework for the ESI funds. As for the Europe 2020 strategy, the
European Commission and member states set together with the main
important priorities and targets as well as those of the main EU policy
areas.[40] Consequently, common objectives and indicators are set at different levels, including the policy areas (meso-level) as well as at the level of
the single organization (micro-level). All member states formally committed to achieve the objectives set at the European level and different monitoring and evaluation mechanisms have been introduced to this purpose,
as described above. Nevertheless, the mechanisms for monitoring member
states' compliance are rather weak, as the whole performance mechanism
is still prevalently based on mutual collaboration and policy coordination,
especially in the policy areas of member states' competence, typical of the
network approach. As stressed by Metcalfe (1996, 2000), all different
configurations of policy governance at the EU level are all network-based
and managed through organizational networks.[41] Such networks need to
be managed effectively by the European Commission to achieve the
desired and planned objectives. Despite this, the Commission "has never
been comfortable with the task of building and strengthening networks of
close working relationships with national administrations, […] maintaining an arms-length relationship and an attitude of watchfulness, if not
mistrust towards them" (Metcalfe 1996). This attitude also influences the
coordination of performance. Instead of strengthening the collaboration
with member states towards a common performance objective, the
European Commission often perceives the national administration as an
external factor threatening the achievement of performance objectives.
For example, in the EU programs management field, the role of member
states administration is included in the section of the Strategic Plans dedicated to the "main external factors influencing the achievement of the
intended results", together with economic and financial crises.[42]
Consequently, also the performance of the network is not adequately
assessed, despite its relevance. As outlined above, the performance

measurement systems should support the collaborative relations among the network members and evaluate their performance, including specific indicators for measuring the performance of networks. This includes measuring conflict resolution and reconciliation abilities, quality and frequency of interactions, inclusiveness of decision making, stability and flexibility of rules etc. (Cepiku 2013). From the case-study analysis, there is no evidence of specific indicators assessing the quality of the network management strategy.

The depth of the European Commission management system seems very much dependent by the willingness of member states to incorporate priorities, targets, and indicators in their national performance system. The poor attitude of the European Commission towards the network approach and the weak coordination mechanism could hamper this process. At the same time, the current structure of the European Commission performance system is more coherent with a deeper level of performance measurement system and with a higher level of integration of their components.

In terms of reform models, the outlined features of the performance measurement system of the European Commission mainly fit with the characteristics of the Neo-Weberian State model. As for the extension of the performance measurement system, the span is wider respect to the traditional model and NPM, due to the increased attempt to go beyond outputs and measuring the effects of the European Commission actions towards the different categories of beneficiaries identified in the common conceptual background. As for the performance depth, the analysis reports ambiguous findings yet. Although the direction is towards a deeper performance system by setting objectives and targets at the level of EU policy areas, still weaknesses remain. The difficulty to integrate member states' actions at the EU level, the complex decision-making system as well as the poor attitude of the European Commission towards network management still prevent the full exploitation of the extended performance measurement system. In line with the NWS model and far from the NPM principles, different efforts have been made to decrease the fragmentation within the different DGs of the European Commission through the introduction of common strategic plans and cross-organizational tools, frameworks and policies. Increased integration also targeted major EU spending programs and projects. As for the general focus on performance is concerned, this latter moved towards the outcome measurement, while the attention to performance network is increasing.

Table 7.26 Performance management area

Areas/functions		*Ideal paradigms*				
		Traditional	*NWS*	*NPM*	*NPG*	*EU*
		Performance evaluation				
Performance focus		Correctness of procedures	Focus on the achievement of satisfaction in service delivery (outcome)	Achievement of results (outputs)	Focus on the performance of the network	NWS
Extension of the performance measurement system	Span of performance	Inputs	Outcome	Outputs	Outcome/impacts	NWS
	Depth of performance	Micro	Meso	Micro	Government/ governance wide	Towards NWS

Source: own elaboration

Nevertheless, the extent to which the Commission will be able to measure the effectiveness of its actions will also greatly depends by a change in the organizational culture, which is still attached to the importance of the correctness of the procedures, the respect of the codes of conduct, typical of the traditional model. As outlined above, the prevailing administrative culture in the Commission is a conflicting topic. Some consider positively the effect of the management reform, whose performance system was a relevant component, on the organizational culture. According to Nugent and Rhinard (2015), most of the outside observers acknowledged a significant improvement in the functioning of the European Commission, which improved transparency, increased effectiveness of the resources used, and allowed for a more predictable policy processes (Wille 2013). By contrast, many Commission staff, consider the Commission after the reform, a more bureaucratized and rule-bound organization, losing much of its dynamism and policy entrepreneurship as well as flexibility and informality, indispensable to play its unique supranational role (Nugent and Rhinard 2015). This vision highlights the tensions and critics over the excessive mechanistic and rational approach of the performance management system. Doubtless, this latter contributed to standardize the day-to-day work of the Commission staff, and increase the "bureaucratization" of the Commission, as argued by some, but also improving the Commission functioning, as recognized by others. This is the typical trade-off when introducing new managerial innovations, and finding the right equilibrium is (often) a never-ending story (Table 7.26).

NOTES

1. According to art. 3 (TFEU) the following subjects are of exclusive EU competence: customs union, the establishing of the competition rules necessary for the functioning of the internal market; the monetary policy for the Member States whose currency is the euro, the conservation of marine biological resources under the common fisheries policy; and the common commercial policy (art. 3 TFEU).
2. See art. 3 TUE.
3. The author refers to the case of the appointment and then suspension in 2002 of Marta Andersen as official responsible for overseeing the Commission's accounts and payments. Once appointed she expressed her concerns on the current Commission accounting system (Sincom), considered vulnerable to frauds (Spence 2005).

4. As reported in the European Commission web site dedicated to control systems "the Commission's framework was developed specifically for its environment. It is based on international good practice and inspired by the COSO framework". http://ec.europa.eu/budget/biblio/documents/control/control_en.cfm#fn1

5. Communication of the Commission "Revision of the Internal Control Standards and Underlying Framework", SEC (2007)1341.

6. European Commission "Simplified & Reduced Internal Control Requirements", Ares (2014) 1329924-28/04/2014.

7. The building blocks included in the "Simplified & Reduced Internal Control Requirements" document are: Mission, Ethical and Organizational Values, Staff Allocation and Mobility, Staff Appraisal and Development, Objectives and Performance Indicators, Risk Management Process, operational Structure, processes and Procedures, Management Supervision, Business Continuity, Document Management, information and Communication, accounting and Financial Reporting, evaluation of Activities, assessment of Internal Control Systems, Internal Audit Capability.

8. Data published on the web site http://europa.eu/about-eu/agencies/index_en.htm compared with data reported by Spence (2005). Decentralized agencies also include Agencies under Common Security and Defense Policy and EURATOM agencies and bodies.

9. See Communication SEC (2005) 1327 "Towards an effective and coherent risk management in the Commission Services."

10. The PM^2 is the project management methodology designed by the European Commission to facilitate the managing of projects within the organization and beyond. The PM^2 methodology has been adopted also by the European Council, the EU External Action Services, the Committee of the Regions, the European Central Bank and over 20 EU Agencies located all over the EU Member States. The free version of PM2 methodology (OpenPM²) is available for all organizations.

11. See Communication COM (2016) 739final "Next Steps for a Sustainable European Future."

12. See https://ec.europa.eu/eurostat/web/europe-2020-indicators

13. The five priorities are 1. Jobs, growth and competitiveness, 2. Empowering and protecting citizens, 3. Energy and climate policies, 4. Freedom, security and justice, 5. The EU as a strong global actor.

14. See https://ec.europa.eu/energy/en/topics/energy-strategy

15. See http://ec.europa.eu/health/strategy/objectives/index_en.htm

16. See http://ec.europa.eu/consumers/eu_consumer_policy/our-strategy/index_en.htm

17. See http://ec.europa.eu/education/policy/strategic-framework/index_en.htm

18. The objectives include a cut of 20% in the greenhouse gas emissions (from 1990 levels), an increase of 20% of the EU energy from renewables and an improvement of 20% in energy efficiency.

19. The positive scoring of the EU in the achievement of these targets prompted the European Council to adopt in 2014 the 2030 climate and energy framework, covering the period 2021–2030 increasing the level of the targets set by the former framework. Finally, in November 2018, the European Commission presented the 2050 long-term strategy aiming at transforming the EU economy in a climate-neutral economy by 2050.

20. Since 1998 have been adopted the following MFFs: "Paquet Delors" (1988–1992), "Paquet Delors II" (1993–1999), "Agenda 2000" (2000–2006), "MFF (2007–2013) and MFF (2014–2020).

21. The budget procedure is established by art. 314 of the Treaty on the functioning of the European Union and lasts from the 1st of September to 31 of December of the year before the budget is executed.

22. Art. 317 of the TFUE makes clear that the Commission holds the ultimate responsibility for the implementation of the whole EU budget.

23. The estimation is made considering the complexities of such calculation, due to the multi-dimensional character of the initiatives funded within the single programs as well as the multi-level governance-based approach of such initiatives involving diverse stakeholders (EU member states, local authorities etc.) (European Commission 2018b).

24. Under the shared management mode, the co-legislator fixes the legal framework and determines the allocations by MS and category of region. The Commission adopts the programs. As regards implementation, the Commission cooperates with Member States' administrations (at the national, regional and local levels), who are in charge of the operational implementation (European Commission 2016a).

25. Although the Political Guidelines do not include indicators, these latter are identified in the Strategic Plans of the DGs and Services for each Commission priority. These statistical indicators are high-level context indicators designed to track the longer-term and indirect impacts of EU action.

26. REFIT is the European Commission's Regulatory Fitness and Performance program to make EU law simpler and to reduce regulatory costs without compromising policy objectives. REFIT thus contributes to a clear, stable and predictable regulatory framework supporting growth and jobs (European Commission 2015d).

27. The Annex III of the CWP 2019 includes 84 pending proposals still to be adopted in 2019.

28. The Annex IV of the CWP 2019 includes 10 proposals subject to modifications or withdrawals.

29. Together with the Work Program (CWP), the Commission also publishes the "list of planned Commission Initiatives", listing the CWP initiatives that are yet to be adopted as well as the foreseen initiatives that derive from the various agendas, including Communications, International Agreements, delegated and implemented acts, and other legislative and non-legislative initiatives that are not foreseen in the CWP.

30. Among the MPs 2015 analysed specific references to the "new initiatives" included in the CWP 2015 have been found in the DG EMPL MP 2015 (page 8, 27, 30, 38), DG EAC MP 2015 (page 9), DG CONNECT 2015 MP (page 62), DG DEVCO MP 2015 (page 36, 96). In the 2015 MP of DG EMPL, the "Degree of implementation of EMPL's initiatives of the CWP" has been included in the Key Performance Indicators.

31. Considering that the Junker Commission term of office ends on 2019, there is a disclaimer on the documenting saying that "the current Commission's term of office runs until 31 October 2019. New political orientations provided by the incoming Commission for the subsequent period will be appropriately reflected in the strategic planning process".

32. The DG Regio is responsible for managing part of the Cohesion policy together with DG Employment and DG Agriculture. The main Cohesion Policy fund managed by the DG Regio is the European Regional Development Fund, funds programs, which contribute to the achievement of the 11 thematic objectives (TOs) together with to all other Cohesion policy funds (European Social Fund, European agricultural fund for rural development, European maritime and fisheries fund and Cohesion fund).

33. In the Strategic Plan (2016–2020), DG REGIO included several examples of medium-term achievements for selected thematic areas. Among else, for Research and Innovation "Around 130,000 firms will receive R&I support and almost 72,000 researchers will benefit from improved ERDF-supported research facilities", for Direct job creation "Interventions financed by DG Regional and Urban policy will support the direct creation of 423,100 new jobs, 29,500 of which will correspond to new researchers employed under ERDF research measures. Many more jobs will be created indirectly" etc.

34. The report is published following art. 249(2) of the Treaty on the Functioning of the European Union.

35. In a few cases Member States have not set up national targets or cumulatively the national targets are not ambitious enough to reach the EU-level goal. For example, the fulfillment of all national targets in the area of employment would bring the overall EU-28 employment rate up to 74%, which would still be one percentage point below the Europe 2020 target of 75%. (Eurostat 2016).

36. The European Structural and Investments funds include the following funds: the European Regional Development Fund (ERDF), the European Social Fund (ESF), the Cohesion Fund (CF), the European Agricultural Fund for Rural Development (EAFRD), the European Maritime and Fisheries Fund (EMFF).
37. The classification of the indicators is based on the common framework used by all DGs for the elaboration of the indicators. The framework requires to use impact indicators for measuring the outcome of the intervention beyond the immediate effects, result indicators to measure the direct and immediate effect of the intervention, and output indicators to measure activities directly realized by interventions (European Commission 2015a).
38. The DG GROW, responsible for part of the Horizon 2020, set 12 impact indicators, the DG EAC, responsible for Erasmus + and part of Horizon 2020 set 12 impact indicators, the DG REGIO responsible for the ERDF, the Cohesion Fund and IPA instrument set 10 impact indicators, the DG RTD responsible for part of the Horizon 2020 and DG EMP for ESF fund set 7 impact indicators.
39. See European Commission (2016b).
40. See for example the Strategic Framework on Education and Training (ET 2020). http://ec.europa.eu/education/policy/strategic-framework/index_en.htm
41. Metcalfe (2000) identifies the following governance models in the EU decision-making system, the Community method (ex. Agricultural Policy), the EU Regulatory Model (ex. Internal Market and Competition Policy), the Multilevel Governance (ex. Cohesion policy Policy), the Coordination and Benchmarking (ex. Research and Development, Environment, Employment) and Intensive Inter-governmentalism (ex. Foreign Policy Justice).
42. See for example the Strategic Plan 2016–2020 of the Directorate General for Regional and Urban Policy (European Commission 2016a), page 26.

References

Ban, Carolyn. "Reforming the staffing process in the European Union institutions: Moving the sacred cow out of the road." *International Review of Administrative Sciences* 76, no. 1 (2010): 5–24.

Bauer, Michael W. *A Creeping Transformation?*. Vol. 6. Springer Science & Business Media, 2001.

———. *Reforming the European Commission: a (missed?) academic opportunity.* ECSA-Austria, 2002.

———. "Introduction: Management Reform in International Organizations." In *Management Reforms in International Organizations*, eds. Bauer M., Knill C., Nomos, 2007.

Bearfield, Nicholas David. "Reforming the European Commission: driving reform from the grassroots." *Public Policy and Administration* 19, no. 3 (2004): 13–24.

Bouckaert, Geert, and John Halligan. "Comparing performance across public sectors." In *Performance Information in the Public Sector*, pp. 72–93. Palgrave Macmillan, London, 2008.

Cepiku, Denita. "Network performance: toward a dynamic multidimensional model." In *Network Theory in the Public Sector*, pp. 188–204. Routledge, 2013.

Committee of Independent Experts. *First Report on Allegations regarding Fraud, Mismanagement and Nepotism in the European Commission*. 1999

Coull, Janet, and Charlie Lewis. "The impact reform of the staff regulations in making the Commission a more modern and efficient organization: an insider's perspective." *EPIAScope 2003*, no. 3 (2003): 2–9.

Cram, Laura. "Whither the Commission? Reform, renewal and the issue-attention cycle." *Journal of European Public Policy* 8, no. 5 (2001): 770–786.

Egeberg, Morten. *An organizational approach to European integration-What organizations tells us about system transformation, committee governance and Commission decision making*. No. 19. ARENA, 2002.

European Commission. *White Paper "Reforming the European Commission"*. 2000a.

———. *Press Release "The Commission approves its Reform Strategy"*. 2000b.

———. *Communication from the President in agreement with Mr. Kinnock and Mrs. Schreyer to the Commission, "Implementing Activity Based Management in the Commission"*. 2001.

———. *Communication from the Commission to the European Parliament and the Council, Progress Report on the Commission Reform Beyond the Reform Mandate*. 2005.

———. *Communication from the Commission to the European Parliament and the Council, the European Economic and Social Committee of the Regions, Commission Legislative and Work Program 2007*. 2007.

———. *Communication from the Commission: Europe 2020 – A Strategy for Smart, Sustainable and Inclusive Growth*. 2010.

———. *Communication from the President Mission letter to Commissioner to Competition*. 2014a.

———. *Report from the Commission to the European Parliament, the Council and the Court of Auditors, Synthesis of the Commission Management Activities in 2013*. 2014b.

———. *the Council and the Court of Auditors, Synthesis of the Commission's management achievements in 2014*. 2015a.

———. *State of the Union speech 2015, Time for Honesty, Unity and Solidarity*. 2015b.

———. *Directorate General for Regional and Urban Policy, Annual Management Plan*. 2015c.

———. *Directorate General for Agriculture and Rural Development, Annual Management Plan*. 2015d.

———. *Directorate General for Regional and Urban Policy, Strategic Plan 2016 – 2020*. 2016a.

———. *Communication from the Commission to the European Parliament, the Council, the European Economic and Social Committee and the Committee of the Regions: Next steps for a sustainable European future*. 2016b.

———. *Directorate General for Employment and Social Affairs and Inclusion, Strategic Plan 2016–2020*. 2016c.

———. *Report on the follow-up to the discharge for the financial year 2016*. 2018a.

———. *Draft General Budget of the European Union for the financial year 2019*. 2018b.

———. *Guidance for Member States on Performance framework, review and reserve*. 2018c.

———. *Governance in the European Commission*. 2018d.

———. *Reflection Paper Towards a Sustainable Europe by 2030*. 2019.

Eurostat. *Smarter, greener, more inclusive? Indicators to support the Europe 2020 Strategy*. 2016

European Parliament. *Policy Department for Budgetary Affairs: The next Multiannual Financial Framework (MFF) and its Duration*. 2017.

Ginsberg, Roy H. *Demystifying the European Union: The enduring logic of regional integration*. Rowman & Littlefield, 2007.

Gutner, Tamar, and Alexander Thompson. "The politics of IO performance: A framework." *The review of international organizations* 5, no. 3 (2010): 227–248.

Haas, Ernst B. *The Uniting of Europe*, Stanford: Stanford University Press. 1958.

Hardacre, Alan. The European Commission. In Hardacre, Alan, and Erik Akse, eds. *How the EU Institutions Work and… how to Work with the EU Institutions*. John Harper Publishing, 2011.

Kassim, Hussein. "'Mission impossible', but mission accomplished: the Kinnock reforms and the European Commission." *Journal of European Public Policy* 15, no. 5 (2008): 648–668.

Levy, Roger. "Modernising EU programme management." *Public Policy and Administration* 17, no. 1 (2002): 72–89.

———. "Critical success factors in public management reform: the case of the European Commission." *International Review of Administrative Sciences* 69, no. 4 (2003a): 553–566

———. "Confused expectations: Decentralizing the management of EU programmes." *Public Money & Management* 23, no. 2 (2003b): 83–92.

———. "Between rhetoric and reality: Implementing management reform in the European Commission." *International Journal of Public Sector Management* 17, no. 2 (2004): 166–177.

Metcalfe, Les. "The European commission as a network organization." *Publius: The Journal of Federalism* 26, no. 4 (1996): 43–62.

———. "Reforming the Commission: will organizational efficiency produce effective governance?." *JCMS: Journal of Common Market Studies* 38, no. 5 (2000): 817–841.

Nugent, Neill, and Mark Rhinard. *The European Commission*. Macmillan International Higher Education, 2015.

OECD. *Public Governance Directorate Budgeting and Performance in the European Union. A review in the context of EU Budget Focused on Results*. 2017.

Richardson, Tim. "The trans-European transport network: environmental policy integration in the European Union." *European Urban and Regional Studies* 4, no. 4 (1997): 333–346.

Schön-Quinlivan, Emmanuelle. "Administrative reform in the European Commission: from rhetoric to relegitimization." In *Management Reforms in International Organizations*, pp. 25–37. Nomos Verlagsgesellschaft mbH & Co. KG, 2007.

Spence, David, "Plus ca change, plus c'est la meme chose? Attempting to reform the European Commission." *Journal of European Public Policy* 7, no. 1 (2000): 1–25.

———. *The European Commission*. John Harper Publishing, London. 2005.

Spence, David, and Anne Stevens. "Staff and personnel policy in the Commission." *The European Commission* 3 (2006): 173–208.

Stevens, Anne and H. Stevens. "*The internal reform of the European Commission*", in The European Commission, ed. Spence D., John Harper Publishing, London. 2006.

Stiglitz, Joseph E. "Democratizing the International Monetary Fund and the World Bank: governance and accountability." *Governance* 16, no. 1 (2003): 111–139.

Wille, Anchrit. "Senior officials in a reforming European Commission: Transforming the top?." In *Management Reforms in International Organizations*, pp. 37–51. Nomos Verlagsgesellschaft mbH & Co. KG, 2007.

———. *The normalization of the European Commission: Politics and bureaucracy in the EU executive*. OUP Oxford, 2013.

Wishlade, Fiona G. "Competition policy, cohesion and the co-ordination of regional aids in the European community." *European Competition Law Review* 14 (1993): 143–143.

CHAPTER 8

Analysis and Comparison of the Case Studies: The Organisation for Economic Cooperation and Development

Abstract This chapter will seek answers to the following questions: To what extent the OECD measure the results of its action? What are the characteristics of the OECD performance management systems compared to the ideal paradigm developed in literature?

The chapter includes the context and history of the OECD, the management reforms assessment, including the evaluation of the OECD performance management system.

Keywords OECD • Performance management system in the OECD

8.1 Organization and Functioning of the OECD

The OECD was created in 1947 as the Organisation for European Economic Cooperation (OEEC) to manage American and Canadian aid under the Marshall Plan to help rebuild Europe, liberalize trade, develop a European Payments Union, and eventually construct the foundations of the European Common Market. By 1960 the task of reconstruction was completed, and the OEEC converted into an organization that no longer focused solely on Europe but also aimed to contribute to the growth of the global economy and the development of the Third World. It is now considered to be the "rich countries club" (Pal 2012). Since 1961 membership has expanded from nineteen to over thirty, encompassing members from all but the African continent (Woodward 2007).

© The Author(s) 2020   193
M. Amici, D. Cepiku, *Performance Management in International Organizations*, https://doi.org/10.1007/978-3-030-39472-1_8

To achieve its aims, the OECD has, over the years, extended its activities to almost every conceivable field of government policy, except culture and defense. It does so at the request of the member countries and usually works based on multidisciplinary and comparative policy research (AIV 2007; Bourgon 2009).

Its mission is to promote policies that will improve the economic and social well-being of people around the world. The OECD, based in Paris, works with governments to understand what drives economic, social and environmental change, measures productivity and global flows of trade and investment. It analyses and compares data to predict future trends, sets international standards on a wide range of sectors, from agriculture and tax to the safety of chemicals. "The elasticity of its mission has unquestionably contributed to its durability as a mechanism of global governance. It perpetually refurbishes its portfolio of responsibilities to meet the exigencies of both its members and its fellow institutions of global governance. Equally, the absence of a specific purpose is a major source of vulnerability for the OECD because its functions can be appropriated or replicated by other institutions" (Woodward 2007).

In the near future, the OECD will focus on five priorities: measuring and promoting well-being, sustainability and inclusiveness; renewing the social contract; harnessing productivity and competitiveness; preparing for the digital transformation; leveling the playing field (cf. the 2018 secretary general's Strategic Orientations and the 21 × 21 Agenda).

It has been noted that the OECD policymaking lacks a coherent long-term vision; such absence makes it harder to decide which issues should be prioritized and which ones can be left off the agenda and to streamline the structure of the secretariat (AIV 2007). It is seen to wander between academic studies, which are usually influential and can also be produced because member countries provide data to which private research bodies have little or no access, and preparatory and advisory policy research in the context of globalization (AIV 2007).

The organizational design is rather basic and comprises the council, the committees, and the secretariat (Fig. 8.1).

The council, the highest body of the OECD and ultimately responsible for decision making, is made up of member state representatives. It is chaired by the secretary-general and oversees the OECD's work and broad agenda. Through the yearly ministerial meeting, it sets the broad direction for the future of the organization. It has three plenary standing committees, such as the budget, the executive, and the external relations committees.

Council
Oversight and strategic direction
Representatives of member countries
and of the European Commission
Decisions taken by consensus

Committees
Review, discussion and
implementation
Representatives of member
and observer countries

Secretariat
Research and analysis
Secretary-General
Deputy Secretaries-General
Directorates

Fig. 8.1 The OECD macrostructure. Source: with adaptations from www. oecd.org

In particular, the budget committee assists the council in preparing the budget priorities and the biennial Programme of Work and Budget (PWB). It monitors the implementation of the agreed budget and assists the council on the Integrated Management Cycle (IMC). Although, in council, decisions by mutual agreement are the rule, since 2006, there have been a number of exceptions involving majority voting.

A hierarchical system of specialized committees—populated by senior officials from national administrations—is in charge of advancing ideas and reviewing progress in specific policy areas. Through its committee structure, the OECD's substantive policy agenda and outputs respond directly to the needs of and are closely monitored by senior policy officials from capitals in a way that is unique among international organizations. It is these committees that produce the outputs of the OECD, the policy advice, guidelines, principles ("soft law"), and best practices. The working methods of the committees are one of the institution's hallmarks, the source of its added value, and the support it enjoys in capitals.

The OECD Secretariat, in charge of administrative and management duties, supports both the council and the committees. It consists of the secretary-general and some 2500 permanent staff, the core of whom are policy experts in the diverse fields within which the OECD is involved.

Thus, the OECD is a hybrid organization, unusual among international organizations, in that it is half diplomatic and half think-tank (Pal 2012). The OECD Secretariat collects and analyses data, after which committees discuss policy regarding this information, the council makes decisions, and then governments implement recommendations. The final outputs are generated by its committees, which work through some 228 working groups and subgroups, task groups (some of them ad hoc). Every year the OECD publishes more than 250 books and 40 databases and is widely seen as an authoritative source of independent data (Salzman 1999; Woodward 2007), also essential to the work of other international bodies (Woodward 2006).

The range of methods and instruments that the OECD has developed during its half-century of existence are not based on the threat of sanctions, but rather on voluntary compliance with agreements, cooperation, persuasion, proposal of alternative views and the systematic comparison of strengths and weaknesses (Fig. 8.2; AIV 2007).

Information sharing and data collection

Synthesis of country practice

Comparative analysis

Discussion, decisions and implementation

Best practices

Peer reviews

Recommendations and multilateral surveillance

Fig. 8.2 OECD's way of working. Source: with adaptations from the OECD website

One of the tools worth mentioning is peer review: mutual examination by governments, multilateral surveillance, and a process through which the performance of individual countries is monitored by their peers, all carried out at committee-level, are at the heart of its effectiveness.

Discussions at the OECD committee-level sometimes evolve into negotiations where OECD countries agree on rules of the game for international co-operation. They can culminate in formal agreements by countries, for example, on combating bribery, on arrangements for export credits, or the treatment of capital movements. They may produce standards and models, for example, in the application of bilateral treaties on taxation or recommendations. They may also result in guidelines, for example, on corporate governance or environmental practices.

Ougaard (2010) shows a rapid increase in the number of formal instruments in force by the OECD. These include negotiated treaties and major policy statements that stipulate multi-lateral commitments. Examples are "decisions" that are binding on countries approving them; "recommendations" with which countries can voluntarily comply or not regardless of if they voted or not; and "agreements" that are legally binding on all members (Hunter 2013).

The OECD budget consists of part I including member country contributions to the base budget, according to a formula consisting of a portion related to the relative size of the national economy and a portion shared equally. Part II is for special-purpose bodies and specific projects, funded by contributions. Both part I (representing around two-thirds of part I expenditure) and part II budgets can contain "voluntary contributions" for specific projects. These are frequently solicited at the director or departmental level within a directorate and contribute to the further decentralization of the OECD as an organization (Pal 2012). The part I budget for 2017 is EUR 200.1 million. The consolidated part II budgets for 2017 amount to EUR 97.7 million. The overall consolidated OECD budget for 2017 comes to EUR 374 million. The US and Japan are leading contributors.

Some characterizing features of the Organisation, which influence the reform drivers and contents, are worth noting. The most frequently mentioned is its working methods, such as soft law, benchmarking, standards, peer review, and peer pressure, which are, to some extent, corollaries of the member countries' like-mindedness (Marcussen 2004; AIV 2007). Differently from the European Union or the United Nations, it relies on informal mechanisms to ensure compliance, including the loss of reputation for those departing from the agreed standards (Bourgon 2009). Carroll and Kellow (2011) call it "social attitude." The OECD has socialized bureaucrats in member and non-member states into a culture of identifying and learning from best practice and has facilitated the creation of international networks in different policy domains, to form an international élite. The level of compliance is probably high due to the sunshine effect: the effect of publicity drawing attention to non-compliance. The ownership of the OECD by its member countries is what makes its work of much higher value and strengthens the engagement and awareness of members. Governments cannot easily criticize the OECD analyses and decisions because they are based on input provided by senior civil servants working in member states (insider knowledge), and oppositions can, at the same time, use them to criticize the performance of governments (Carroll and Kellow 2011; Pal 2012). The complicated and nuanced process behind the research effort is critical to the OECD's influence and makes soft law authoritative altogether (Pal 2012; AIV 2007). At the same time, the consensus-based decision-making process for all major issues makes fundamental change extremely difficult (AIV 2007).

Moreover, unlike other international organizations, the OECD is not accorded an exclusive or leading role in any policy domain (Woodward 2007). It is a remarkably lean organization, compared to the United Nations or the European Union, and does not have major operational responsibilities like the International Monetary Fund, the World Trade Organization, and the World Bank.

Another attribute that sets the OECD apart from other international organizations is its limited and selective membership (Bourgon 2009).

Finally, voluntary contributions play a key role in the presence of funding problems. While they provide more leeway when it comes to funding and make donors more committed to and interested in the results, they also encourage short-term policy, lead to fragmentation of activities and create inappropriate incentives for those whose jobs depend on such contributions (AIV 2007).

8.2   Reform Drivers

Four main forces—two external and two internal—could be identified as the drivers of OECD reforms. First of all, the end of the Cold War brought the risk of losing the central political imperative at the global level, declining economic weight and, consequently, *weakened representativeness and influence* (Bourgon 2009; Woodward 2009). The Organisation effectively engaged in a cooperation and accession process with some Eastern European countries and Russia. However, China, India, Brazil, and other developing countries grew and became more integrated into the global economy, making this driver persistent. Policy decisions of the emerging economic players were having a greater impact on member countries, most notably in the areas of investment, intellectual property, energy, environment, and development assistance, threatening the Organisation's ability to set international norms and guidelines (Bourgon 2009). The OECD member countries account for 60% of world GNP, and this percentage is falling rapidly (AIV 2007). The OECD's long-term dependence on the West has now become an obstacle to its efforts to adapt to the rise of non-Western powers. Also, the historic domination of the OECD staff by the three post-war allies is striking; these three countries remain very heavily represented (Clifton and Díaz-Fuentes 2011).

The second driver was intensified institutional competition and overlap, especially with the European Union, leading to declining interest by some of its larger members and most important financial contributors (Woodward 2007; OECD 1997, 2003a). When asked what the major challenge facing the OECD is, Gurría responded: "Relevance, relevance, relevance" (Pal 2012).

The *identity crisis* that followed was a third driver and was addressed through an increase in the number of topics and membership enlargement rather than strategic prioritizing. Carroll and Kellow (2011) argue that financial constraints were also imposed because the OECD lacked a sense of strategic priorities and was wasting resources.

Finally, the Organisation was faced with expenditure cuts that gave way to *high financial pressures*. These started in the mid-90s and were enduring. The 1995 Ministerial Meeting asked the OECD to "accelerate the process of change to further enhancing the relevance, efficiency, and effectiveness of the Organisation" (OECD 1995). The new secretary-general, Donald Johnston, was asked to reduce expenditures by 10% over three years. These financial pressures initially urged by the US, UK, and Australia, continued for a decade (Bourgon 2009). Between 1996 and 1999, the OECD budget was reduced by approximately 18%.

Part I contributions came under severe strain in the early 2000s relative to the overall budget, and so the OECD and its committees began to search more assiduously for "voluntary contributions." The OECD budget was stretched to bursting point conceding, and it "has come to rely heavily on voluntary contributions to accomplish its work program" (OECD 2003c: 7).

In 2007, the Ministers agreed "to provide a strong and sustainable financial foundation for the Organisation, both now and in the long term, that will allow it to maintain at least the quality and volume of outputs [...] and the real level of part I budget resources taking into account the rate of inflation" (OECD Council 2008).

This financial commitment was subject to a number of conditions, the three main ones being: (i) strict prioritization; (ii) budget transparency; (iii) efficiency savings. Regarding the latter, the secretary-general attempted planning productivity gains, which attainment is, however, difficult to assess, given the lack of genuine cost accounting (OECD Council 2008).

Later on, Johnston noted: "Members did not deliver the budget stability they promised would follow the reductions. Instead, the staff had to deal with further cuts and repeated job uncertainty at the end of each year. In addition to the upheaval of the move and adapting to new ways of working" (Pal 2012: 77).

In 2010–2011, the distinction between "permanent" and "project" staff eroded almost completely—partly because more and more staff with longer tenure spend a significant portion of their time working on projects (Pal 2012). The OECD's PWB for 2011–2012, which encompassed the celebrations for the 50th anniversary of the Organisation, was based on zero real growth, with nominal increases of 0.7% in 2011 and 1.5% in 2012, following a decision of OECD ministers in 2008. The secretary-general noted that, within this constrained budget, significant reallocations were made to adjust to new priorities.

The external and internal reform drivers did not act in isolation but rather combined, increasing the pressure to change. Moreover, reforms had mixed financial repercussions: efforts to improve relevance through membership enlargement increase the financial burden putting further stress on an already tight budgetary situation (Woodward 2007), while management for results reforms attempt to improve efficiency.

The great increase in the number of topics covered by the Organisation, the membership enlargement and its limited funding, pointed to the need to adopt managerial instruments to review and plan the goals and activities. Before reforming its management systems, the OECD lacked effective means to set priorities and evaluate the work of the secretariat (Bourgon 2009). Managerial reforms resulted in the OECD's IMC, among others.

8.3 THE MAIN REFORM CONTENTS

The OECD reacted to the aforementioned drivers by implementing several reforms, pursuing the aims of relevance and effectiveness, and accountability and efficiency.

The reforms, implemented since the mid-90s, had an initial internal focus followed by a second cycle addressing the need to open up the Organisation. These could be grouped under four categories (Woodward 2007, 2009; Bourgon 2009; Pal 2012):

- Structural reforms (1996–1997): these included consolidating organizational structures, reviewing committees, introducing clusters for addressing cross-cutting interdisciplinary issues, the creation of key central committees. All support services were regrouped under a new Executive Directorate to improve services and reduce costs. The Centre for Co-operation with non-Members was created to improve coherence and coordination of rapidly expanding outreach relations. The Directorate for Public Affairs and Communications was established to raise the OECD's visibility and enhance its engagement with civil societies.
- Management reforms: human resources management reforms (in 1995 and 2008), strategic prioritizing through the Strategic Management Framework, and results-based budgeting and control through the Integrated Management Cycle (2002).
- Financial reforms: financial management reforms (2001), the introduction of across-the-board cuts through the Priorities and Resource Allocation System (PRAS; 2001–2002), zero-based budgeting and budget reform through the Budget and Financial Management Programme (BFMP 2008), reallocation of the burden among member countries.
- Governance reforms: revised decision-making mode (shifting from consensus to qualified majority voting) and membership enlargement and enhancement of outreach activities aimed at making the Organisation more transparent, inclusive, and influential.

These reforms were carried out under the leadership of the secretary-general Donald J. Johnston (1996–2006) and continued by his successor Angel Gurrìa, who has refined and accelerated the process of change

(Woodward 2009). Reform directions came from the annual Ministerial Meetings (especially in 1995 and in 2007), the Vinde exercise, reviews undertaken by special advisors such as Nicholson (2003), Julin (2003), and Noburn (2004) and by the Heads of Delegations. All proposed greater resort to evaluation (selective evaluation of activities, rolling reviews of committees and their mandates, some based on the profile of delegates participating at the meetings, among others).[1]

OECD reforms are ranking high also in the "21 for 21" agenda of Angel Gurría: the eighth and last goal refers to "ensuring effective and efficient financial, administrative, communications and management practices within the Organisation". In the words of the secretary-general: "Unlike other institutions which have embarked in long and protracted internal reform processes, I believe the OECD requires 'evolution' rather than 'revolution'."

The focus here is on management reforms, which are the most neglected by the academic literature that considers such reforms minor.[2] The attempt to introduce a focus on results aimed to sharpen accountability at all levels; to reassure member countries that the resources they entrust to the OECD are managed efficiently and used for the purposes for which they were intended; and to ensure both that OECD outputs respond to the most important policy concerns of governments, and that the results produced are those that are expected to have an impact on policy-making in capitals (OECD 2017).

The main contents of management reforms implemented in the OECD in the last years will be analysed below, following the research framework described in Chap. 3. We split the reform contents into four management areas (finance, personnel, organization structure, and performance), and for each of them, we identified several management elements (see Table 3.2). The management area related to the performance management system will be analysed in detail in Sect. 8.4.

8.3.1   Financial Area

8.3.1.1 Budgeting
In the OECD, as argued by Davies (2017: 337), the budget, in the past, "has been seen as an exercise in manipulating numbers rather than an opportunity to analyze expenditure patterns, [...] with little use of productivity or efficiency indicators to measure the effectiveness of its programs

and weak linkages between the budget, expenditures and management information systems". In this framework, the OECD started major reform changes in the budget process, introduced since 1996 under Secretary-General Donald J. Johnson, whose mandate focused on modernizing the OECD to respond effectively to the changing needs of the globalized economy (OECD 2001). He began to modernize the Secretariat and its working methods by revising the Financial Regulations and adopting a new management system, the Program and Work Budget (PWB), as the "basic charter of the organization's activities, staffing and financing" (OECD 2001: 97). The reform process, as far as the budget process is concerned, including a shift towards a two year-budget system instead of one year in 2003 and, since 2004–2005, the full adoption of the results-based budgeting (RBB). This latter was linked to a common framework of strategic objectives and output areas, set at the organization level, and is also used for planning, monitoring, and evaluating projects (OECD 2004). The RBB, in the words of the reform advocates, provided for member states a more strategic approach to resources allocation, supporting the prioritisation of outputs needed to achieve the expected outcome and for OECD managers, a clear understanding of what is expected to be achieved by the budget (OECD 2003b). The budget reforms of 2008 and the implementation of the BFMP mean that from 2009, financial management will be based on outputs and their cost rather than inputs.

8.3.1.2 Accounting
As far as the accounting systems are concerned, the OECD is certainly the first and the most cutting-edge in adopting new accounting procedures. In fact, in the framework of the above-mentioned reform programs, in 2000 the OECD claimed to be "the first organization in the world to prepare and publish its financial statements following the International Public Sector Accounting Standards (IPSAS), certified by independent auditors" (OECD 2002: 9). The first financial report based on the accrual method was published in 2001, although in addition to the traditional financial report documents. Since then, the new accounting system has been consolidated through several reform initiatives as the Budget and Financial Management Program in 2007 to align better financial and accounting processes and systems with the output based—framework. The accrual accounting system seems currently fully embedded within the organization. In the last financial statement available for 2014, it is reported that "the financial statements have been prepared following the

International Public Sector Accounting Standards (Ipsass) issued by the International Public Sector Accounting Standards Board (IPSASB) [...]" (OECD 2014: 104). Moreover, external auditors chosen among the Supreme Audit Institutions of the OECD member countries, check the regularity and the respect of international accounting standards in the OECD financial statements.

8.3.1.3 Auditing

Audit and evaluation have been both issues at the top of the OECD reform agenda. Currently, the Directorate of Internal Audit and Evaluation located within the Secretariat supervises both internal audit and evaluation functions, while external audit is delegated to an external audit institution, which since 2008, is the Supreme Audit Institution of France. The audit system also includes an Audit Committee at the level of the Council. According to the OECD Audit Architecture, "internal audits provide the Secretary-General an independent and objective assurance and advisory activity designed to add value and improve OECD's operations. It helps the organization achieve its objectives by bringing a systematic, disciplined approach to evaluate and improve the effectiveness of risk management, control and governance processes" (OECD 2008: 13). Compared to the audit, the evaluation function is more concerned with performance assessment. An in-depth evaluation has been fully integrated into the OECD management cycle (PWB) to assess whether the organization achieved efficiently and effectively the objectives set. More specifically, the objectives are twofold. From one side, the in-depth evaluation provides a systematic assessment of the relevance, effectiveness, and efficiency of OECD's substantive committees. From the other side, the in-depth evaluation identifies the main strengths and weaknesses of the Committees' action, and it is used as a basis for learning exercise to improve future performance.

The number of the initiatives outlined witness the efforts of OECD in reforming the financial management sector to increase budget efficiency, link performance information on the way money is spent, and increasing transparency and accountability. At the same time, the divide between the rhetoric and the substance of the reform initiatives is still wide, blurring the intended results of the reform. As stressed by Davies (2017), the chronic problem common to many international organizations to relate budgets and expenditure plans to accounting records could have largely contributed to this. The cost accounting systems tended to be very weak in international organizations preventing the possibility of developing

Table 8.1   Financial Management area

	Ideal Paradigms				
	Traditional	NWS	NPM	NPG	OECD
Areas/ elements	Financial management				
Budgeting	No information on performance	Budget with some performance information/ format with policy areas instead of functions	Performance budgeting	Centralization in accounting practice. Shift towards the Whole of Government Accounting (WGA) approach	Towards NWS
Accounting	Cash based	Full cash based or combination of cash/accrual	Accruals accounting		NPM
Auditing	Finance and legal compliance	Adding to financial and compliance auditing investigation on some performance issues	Performance audit		NWS

Source: own elaboration

effective analytical cost accounting systems (Davies 2017). In terms of reform models, our review suggests OECD is shifting from the traditional model to the NWS model. The main relevant trend concerns the introduction of performance information in the budget process to improve the financial control system as well as increasing the link between strategic priorities and resource allocations (Table 8.1).

8.3.2   Human Resources Area

8.3.2.1   Recruitment and Contract Policy
Selection procedures in the OECD are open and competitive except for project staff that could be appointed without the open publication of the vacancy and with a temporary contract (Balint and Knill 2007). For the

recruitment of senior officials, the major innovation concern the new policy applied to Directors and General Directors, which include only fixed-term contracts. This also applies to internal staff promoted to top senior-level positions, that once appointed, need to leave the indefinite contract (Balint and Knill 2007). According to Carroll and Kellow (2011), this leads the middle-ranking and senior staff to mainly focusing on current issues and tasks, with little or no time to examine other than current and recent records for the lessons they might contain. Finally, as for the profile, both technical and management skills are requested, especially after the introduction of the result based management (RBM) system, although there is no specific regulation on this topic (Balint and Knill 2007).

8.3.2.2 Staff Appraisal and Promotion

As for the career structure and staff appraisal, the OECD Secretariat worked since 1999 to strengthen the performance management framework of staff given the adoption of the result based management system (RBM). According to documents, OECD designed and introduced a performance management system able to translate organizational objectives to individual objectives for those who perform the work to achieve organizational objectives (OECD 2004). The system should allow on an annual basis to set performance objectives, conducting performance reviews and coaching as well as evaluating performance and supporting staff development (OECD 2004). The system should also be the basis for staff advancement. It is also foreseen the extension of the current appraisal system to senior levels (Deputy Secretary Generals and Deputy Directors), by the adoption of performance agreements (OECD 2004). However, some argue (Balint and Knill 2007) that seniority is still a quite important factor for career progression. No sophisticated catalogs of criteria for linking performance and promotion exist, and performance-related pay system has not been implemented (Balint and Knill 2007). Although, the OECD carried out in 2004 a study to compare best practices in linking performance and financial rewards in OECD governments to open the debate for an eventual adoption (OECD 2004). The application of staff performance objectives and assessments linked to the results-based framework began across the Organisation in 2008.

Management reforms in the human resources domain are generally the most complex to carry out, and international organizations do not make any exception. In this context, the introduction of reform initiatives in the selected international organizations, have been further complicated by the lack of a clear and accepted management culture of their own (Davies 2017). As outlined above, the co-existence of diverse administrative culture brings different attitudes towards public service as well as towards management practices. Some become more accepted than others, and those centrally adopted can find difficulty to be homogeneously adopted through the whole organization. Nevertheless, some evidence shows that despite the difficult management environment and the privileges enjoyed by international staff, innovative elements in the human resources management have been introduced in the OECD. These include the efforts to link organizational performance and personal accountability through performance appraisal systems based on merit; the introduction of temporary contracts for specialists but in some cases also for senior management; as well as the rationalization and centralization of recruitment procedures to increase openness and publicity. Nevertheless, the results of staff appraisals are insufficiently used for decisions about promotions or prolongation of contracts. In terms of reform models, the table shows that most of the changes go in the direction of the NWS ideal model, with some elements closer to NPM, especially concerning the senior management temporary contracts (Table 8.2).

8.3.3 Organization Structure

8.3.3.1 Specialization/Decentralization

The basic structure of the OECD, which includes the Secretariat, the Council, and the Committees system, has mainly remained unchanged since its establishment, retaining its basic hierarchical configuration (Carroll and Kellow 2011). This latter was designed to support member states to assert effective control over the organizations as well as to participate in its work (Carroll and Kellow 2011). However, although the basic structure remains unchanged, the number of organizational units within the Secretariat, as well as the number of committees, sharply increased over time. As noted by Carroll a Kellow (2011), while in 1971, within the Secretariat, there were nine directorates, in 2010, there were twelve excluding the executive units under the supervision of the Secretary-General. Currently, the number of thematic directorates is twelve plus the Executive Directorate dealing with Human Resources and Procurement and the Public Affairs and Communications Directorate. In 1996, the newly appointed Secretary-General Johnson to improve quality and reduce costs, as well as increasing

Table 8.2   Human resources management area

Areas/elements		*Ideal paradigms*			
		Traditional	*NWS*	*NPM*	*OECD*
		Human resources management			
Recruitment	All levels	Professional experience and national balance	Professional experience and national balance with performance elements	Merit principle	NWS
	Senior staff	Voluntary advertisement and use of standard procedure	Possibilities to external advertisement	Compulsory advertisement and use of standard procedure	NWS
		Expertise and limited responsibility for resources	Expertise and management capabilities s	Management capabilities and responsibility for resources	Towards NPM
Contract policy	All levels	Tenured career	Tenured career with limited number of temporary contracts	Temporary contracts	NWS
	Senior staff	Indefinite time contract	Indefinite time with performance evaluation	Temporary contract and related to performance	Towards NPM
Promotion and appraisal	All levels	Seniority and qualifications	Seniority, qualifications and performance	Performance based/merit principles	NWS
	Senior staff	None	For every senior official regularly not based on performance agreements	For every senior official regularly based on performance agreements	NWS

Source: own elaboration

OECD visibility and communication created these two new departments for grouping all support services (Bourgon 2009). On the same line, in 2003, some support services and functions were outsourced (OECD 2003d). In addition, there are also six special bodies,[3] which mainly act as specializing agencies or forums within the OECD on specific thematic policy areas as development, nuclear energy, transportation etc. The Committee structure also remained quite stable, although their slow increased in number over time due to the changing interest of member states towards policy areas, triggered different but unsuccessful attempts to rationalize the overall system (Carroll and Kellow 2011). The OECD database[4] currently contains 150 committees including sub-committees, working parties, groups of experts, ad hoc groups. In sum, compared to the initial configuration, there is no clear decentralization or centralization trend. Despite the relative increase in the number of Committees and the setting up of specialized bodies over time, the bulk of the work is still heavily in the hands of the Secretariat members through the hierarchical system of supervision of each Directorate (Carroll and Kellow 2011).

8.3.3.2 Coordination Mechanisms

The main coordination mechanism adopted in the OECD is the implementation at all organizational levels of the integrated strategic management framework, the Program and Work Budget (PWB), combined with the creation of "clusters." The first links process, resources, and activities of the Directorates, Special bodies and all Committees to the objectives set at the organizational level by the Council and the Secretary-General over a biannual time span. The second addresses the issue of the complex public policy issues, which overcome the defined bureaucratic boundaries and requires a higher level of coordination among the administrative bodies involved. To this aim, the OECD introduced the concept of "clusters", grouping all OECD Committees and subsidiary bodies around six clusters,[5] which also represented the six strategic objectives of the organizations embedded in the PWB cycle. Furthermore, within the Secretariat management structure, each Deputy Secretary-General was held responsible for dealing with one of the set clusters, thus often defined as "managers of clusters" (OECD 2003d).

As far as the organizational structure is concerned, our review shows no clear trends towards specialization and centralization or decentralization mechanisms in the OECD. Although the externalization activities and the number of agencies and special bodies increased both, at the same time, also central control mechanisms have been reinforced. Finally, as for coordination mechanisms, the main common element found in all organizations is the introduction of a strategic planning process for defining the activities of each department, assigning resources, and setting objectives and outputs standards (Table 8.3).

Table 8.3 Organization structure

Areas/elements	Ideal paradigms				
	Traditional	*NWS*	*NPM*	*NPG*	*OECD*
Organization					
Specialization	Multi-purpose, broad scope, no fragmentation	Multi-purpose, limited fragmentation, scarce number of specialized bodies	Tight focused, specialized bodies, high level of fragmentation	Not clear trend	Towards NWS
Decentralization of functions	Centralization	Centralization with possibility of externalization in limited cases	Decentralization	Not clear trend	Traditional
Coordination	Hierarchy	Hierarchy with coordination by targets and outputs standards (strategic planning)	Contract coordination, market type mechanisms	Network type coordination	NWS

Source: own elaboration

8.4 THE PERFORMANCE MANAGEMENT SYSTEM IN THE ORGANIZATION FOR ECONOMIC COOPERATION AND DEVELOPMENT

An external consultant (Peter Nicholson) was engaged in 2002 to consider ways in which to enhance the influence of the OECD on policy outcomes in capitals. Part of his mandate covered a thorough review of committees, as well as a survey conducted in late 2002 of members' medium-term priorities.

These piecemeal reforms preceded a report by a Heads of Delegations working group in 2002 that recommended to adopt "a comprehensive, integrated program of reform to improve decision-making on the OECD's priorities and PWB and to implement results-based budgeting and management" in order to "shift the culture of the Organisation away from a focus on activities, processes and budgeting by institutions to one focused on strategic objectives and outcomes, performance indicators and achieving value for money".

The implementation of the IMC, described in the next paragraph, started immediately after. The first step in implementing the IMC was the adoption of a PWB for 2003–2004, partially using outputs rather than activities (fully for 2005–2006).

8.4.1 The Integrated Management Framework

The IMC (Fig. 8.3) is the sequence of planning, budgeting, and monitoring/reporting aimed at underpinning effective performance. Planning is focused on the MTO Survey; budgeting on the PWB; and monitoring/reporting on the Programme Implementation Reporting (PIR) and the In-Depth Evaluation (IDE). It is aimed at introducing a coherent set of strategic planning and priority-setting; at establishing a work programme and the related allocation of resources, and at introducing standardized monitoring and evaluation (OECD 2009a).

The IMC is intended to provide a systematic linkage between:

- Strategic planning or medium-term priority setting at the council level providing a medium-term planning focus (3–6 years);
- Biennial committee planning and prioritization;
- Biennial resource reallocation decisions by council;
- Programme of work and budget;

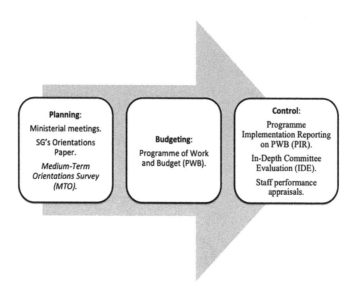

Fig. 8.3   The Integrated Management Cycle at the OECD

- Annual performance reporting (PIR); and
- In-depth, rolling evaluations within a medium-term cycle.

The implementation of the IMC started with a survey of members' medium-term priorities conducted, in late 2002, in the framework of the Nicholson review. This review served as a prototype for the subsequent MTO Survey. The second step was the PWB, which evolved.

8.4.2   Planning

Since 2002, the OECD has had in place a Strategic Management Framework based on six strategic objectives (or clusters) that reflect the OECD Convention:

1. Promote sustainable economic growth, financial stability, and structural adjustment;
2. Provide employment opportunities for all, improve human capital and social cohesion and promote a sustainable environment;

3. Contribute to shaping globalization for the benefits of all through the expansion of trade and investment;
4. Enhance public and private sector governance;
5. Contribute to the development of non-member economies;
6. Provide effective and efficient corporate management.

These strategic objectives "cascade" down to output groups and, at a lower level, to output areas. The Strategic Management Framework provides the basis for council decisions on resource allocations; and for committee planning, budgeting, and reporting. Since 2007–2008, this framework has encompassed part II programmes.

The MTO Survey is an exercise aimed at gaining input from capital-based delegates to ensure that the committees' policy objectives are well aligned with the needs of policy-makers. As such, it addresses the aim of strengthening the Organisation's relevance.

The aims of the MTO are to (i) influence the strategic directions and resource allocations for the next PWB and possibly subsequent biennium (ii) better integrate medium-term policy and resource planning frameworks and decisions; and (iii) have a medium-term strategic view as part of the budget planning and resource reallocation framework.

Members are requested to complete the two sections of the survey: in the first section, members are asked—concerning each of the output areas included in the survey—whether they believe that OECD resources should be increased; maintained at about a constant level; decreased; or exited. Responses need to be based on an assumption of zero real resource growth. In the second section, members are requested to rank in priority order the secretary-general's strategic priorities. In the words of the secretary-general: "the identification of what to stop doing has always been the Achilles' heel" of such exercises.[6]

The results of the surveys feed into the process of developing the PWB.

An example of the MTO survey 2007–2008 is provided in Tables 8.4 and 8.5.

The first round of the MTO survey had a number of significant limitations and provided only indicative guidance on desired shifts in priorities and budgets for 2005–2006. The main limitations were: a partial coverage of activities; a disequilibrium between the proposals to increase priorities and to decrease priorities, as some of the areas identified for cuts involved relatively small budgets; some members, including one major budget contributor did not respond to the questionnaire; some responses focused on

Table 8.4   The Medium-Term Orientations Survey: section I

Medium-Term Orientations Survey (2007–2008)

Output area	2005					Desired direction (2007–2008)			
	Part I base budget	*Share of part I base budget*	*VC estimates*	*Share of VC to part I base budget*		*Increase*	*About constant*	*Decrease*	*Exit*
⋮	⋮ KEUR	⋮ %	⋮ KEUR	⋮ %					
4.3.1. Governance and management of public institutions and resources	2986	3.5%	6409	214.6%					
4.3.2. Support for Improvement in Governance and Management (SIGMA)	127	0.1%	4606	3626.8%					
4.3.3. Tax administration	535	0.6%	1053	196.7%					
4.3.4. Territorial development policies	1734	2.0%	2761	159.2%					
⋮	⋮	⋮	⋮	⋮					

Table 8.5 The Medium-Term Orientations Survey: section II

Medium-Term Orientations (2007–2008)

Secretary-general's priorities	*Expected impacts*	*Member ranking 1–10 [1=highest priority 10=lowest priority]*
1. Climate change	Identify efficient policies to adapt to the impacts of an urgent global problem.	
2. Demographics	Raise awareness of the challenges associated with on-going demographic changes and the costs and benefits of alternative policies to tackle them.	
3. Health	Strengthen the moves to improve health system performance; increase the capacity to seize new opportunities and combat threats.	
4. Health costs of environment	Stimulate political action by contributing to a better understanding of health costs of environmental degradation; identify the most effective policy interventions—whether upstream (by reducing environmental degradation) or down-stream (by financing the associated health costs).	
5. Financial management of large-scale disasters	Prepare governments, the insurance industry and financial markets for effective mitigation and response.	
6. Bio-economy	Address regulatory and social bottlenecks.	
7. Security	Improve social and economic security.	
8. Global infrastructure	Awareness of need for global infrastructure: Transport, energy, water, communications.	
9. Outreach—India programme	Improved mutual understanding of the growing interaction between OECD economies and India. Support reform-oriented policy makers in India.	
10. Teachers	Identify policies to improve the quality of teachers and leadership in schools.	

committees and their subsidiaries rather than Output Areas. Some member countries suggested that the exercise was akin to the unsuccessful former PRAS exercises and questioned the merit of the approach. Also, some delegations expressed reservations about using such data in making judgments on priorities and the PWB.

8.4.3   Linking Resources to Budget

The PWB was the first element of the IMC linking planning, prioritization, budgeting, reporting, and evaluation to be implemented. It is the expression of the OECD's priorities and the result of a mixed top-down and bottom-up process, formal and informal, involving members and the secretary-general.

Top-down priority-setting consists of members influencing priorities when they discuss issues in council, in the executive committee in special session, as well as in sectoral ministerial and other high-level meetings. A major opportunity for members to establish and comment on priorities is the annual ministerial council meetings, which are preceded by preparation by the secretary-general of a strategic orientation paper. Chronologically, the PWB preparatory process begins with the MTO survey.

Bottom-up priority-setting refers to the prioritization of all OECD outputs and resources, mainly carried out at the committee level, engaging all members. Output results are reviewed, prioritized, adjusted, or terminated in the early part of the PWB preparations. This process takes into account expected resources: each output result is costed based on these likely resources.

The programme of work sets out the strategic objectives, output groups, output areas, and output results.

Strategic objectives are defined by the OECD convention and represent the long-term policy goals of member governments that guide the Organisation's strategic planning, priority-setting, budgeting, and resource allocation.

Within output areas, the OECD output results are organized, and through them, accountabilities are attributed. An output group includes two or more output areas that contribute to the achievement of the same strategic objective. The output group is the basic level for resource allocation and decision making in the PWB. In institutional terms, output groups, in most cases, correspond to directorates.

The OECD delivers eight types of output results: data/models/indicators, statistical reports; analytical/outlook reports; good practice reports; peer reviews or surveys; policy recommendations; soft law, guidelines and declarations; hard law: conventions and legal agreements; evaluations.

The output area costs refer to total resources (part I or part II budget allocations and voluntary contributions) to be used to produce the output results in a given output area.

The first round of PWB for 2003–2004 saw an unprecedented shift of resources towards high priority areas, including work on supporting the Doha Round of WTO negotiations, corporate governance, anti-corruption, taxation, steel, shipbuilding, and competition (OECD 2003b: 2). Since the PWB for 2005–2006, committees have had the opportunity to be engaged from the outset. In particular, to articulate the expected outcomes they wanted to achieve, and to specify the output results they assessed would be most likely to have the desired policy impacts in member and non-member economies over the biennium.

The improved outcome and output specification in the 2005–2006 PWB included three levels of impact identified for expected outcomes; the introduction of output result categories in the PWB to facilitate benchmarking and comparative evaluations of outputs; and the phasing-in of council and committee templates.

In the OECD glossary, outcomes are impacts on end-users deriving from applying the output results. Outcomes describe what the OECD member governments want to achieve in funding OECD output results and explain why those output results are undertaken. Outcomes help define committee mandates and are essential for subsequent evaluation of impacts. The OECD identifies three broad levels of outcomes: (i) increased awareness/understanding of OECD output results; (ii) actual application of output results by members (e.g. a policy change); (iii) the effects of the use of output results and their contribution to achieving the strategic objectives. The higher the level of outcome, the more difficult it is to measure and, usually, the longer the timeframe for it becomes evident.

The review of the PWB process and the effectiveness of the priority-setting mechanism in 2003 concluded that the new system worked better than its predecessors, resulting in a record shift in corporate priorities across the organization and a more strategic, coherent budget planning and communications tool (OECD 2003a).

8.4.4   Performance Controls

The progressive introduction, since 2002, of results-based planning and budgeting created the enabling conditions for adopting control and evaluation mechanisms such as the Programme Implementation Report (PIR) and the In-Depth Evaluation (IDE).

The PIR is undertaken shortly after the end of a biennium—to get feedback from members while the completed output results are relatively new (and familiar)—and covers that period. In the IDE process, each committee is reviewed on a six-yearly cycle.

The PIR responds to members and management need to know whether the approved PWB was delivered and how well this was done; the IDE to the need to know how well individual committees are planning, organizing, and delivering their work, and the extent to which it is being used and having an impact over a longer timeframe. Moreover, the IDE fulfils the need to understand why a committee is performing well or otherwise and what actions can be taken to improve its performance when this is shown to be necessary.

Five indicators of performance are applied in the framework of the PIR at the corporate level: *quantity, timeliness,* and *cost* for the monitoring of performance; *quality* and *impact*/potential impact for the evaluation of performance. IDE focuses on assessing committees about the evaluation criteria of *relevance, efficiency,* and *effectiveness.* The results of successive PIR exercises provide an important input into IDE.

Both processes involve looking at the past to improve future performance, but the respective time-frames are quite different. The PIR looks at the expected impact and actual impact in the short-term. The IDE process looks at actual impact over the longer term. Both involve surveys in capitals, but the scope of the surveys differs. The PIR survey covers the breadth of part I results, whereas the focus of the IDE is a committee and the output areas for which it is accountable.

The council agreed to establish the PIR in January 2004; it was conducted later that year, covering 2003 completed output results. It was the first systematic and comprehensive reporting (across part I) undertaken in the OECD's history. The mechanism was reviewed in 2006 and revised, inter alia, to include non-member economies.

The main purposes of the PIR are:

- Corporate reporting and evaluation: showing members how the OECD performs overall each year;
- Committee effectiveness: informing each committee how it might improve its performance through adjusting its priorities or choices of outputs; and
- Organizational effectiveness and learning: revealing ways to increase or improve the impact of the OECD and its outputs.
- Transparency and accountability within the Organization.

As the key aim of the PIR is to improve committee performance, it is not intended to be self-evaluation by committees, which are not directly engaged in the survey before it has been completed. While the PIR is not intended to be applied to draw conclusions regarding priorities across committees or output areas, the survey results should be used by committees to consider how best to allocate their resources in future PWBs.

It covers the Organisation's PWB, looking at quantity, as well as the quality and timeliness policy of output results and spending against budget (at output area level).

The PIR consists of two parts: (i) a survey collecting ratings for quality and impact/potential impact from users in capitals; (ii) and output and budget reporting, prepared by the secretariat and submitted to directors, committee chairs, and senior management of the Organisation. The reporting refers to the performance dimensions of timeliness, cost, and quantity.

An example of the PIR survey is provided in Table 8.6.

The survey screen lists the output results included in terms of their presentation in the PWB for 2005–2006 as follows: strategic objective;

Table 8.6 The Programme Implementation Report: survey screen

Survey of OECD 2007 Output Results for quality and Impact / Potential Impact							
Strategic Objective:							
Output Group:							
Output Area:							
Committee Accountability							
Expected Outcomes							
Rating scale:							
Please give a rating of 5 to 1 under Quality and a rating of 5 to 1 under Impact / Potential Impact for each Output Result							
Quality & Impact / Potential Impact:	5 very high	4 high	3 medium	2 low	1 very low	NA1 Unaware of output result	NA2 cannot assess due to non-participation	NA3 choose to make no response
2007 Output Results	Quality			Impact / Potential Impact				
	Rating	Comments		Rating	Comments			

output group; output area; committee accountability; and expected outcomes (important information for completing the impact/potential impact rating).

The assessment of the impact and potential impact is intended to reflect the respondent's view of the potential or actual impact of an output result—regardless of its quality—in relation to that anticipated at the time members agreed that the OECD should help to address the policy issue. The following criteria guide judgments:

- Actual or potential contribution to expected outcomes and the significance of those expected outcomes.
- Level of policy relevance and usefulness of an OECD output result to a member government, and the actual or potential impact on policy-making in terms of: public debate; national policy reform/ formulation; visibility and credibility of the OECD; strengthening international co-operation/policy networks; development of international standards or guidelines; implementation of international standards or guidelines.

If an assessment cannot be made, respondents should select one of the three "No Assessment" (NA) options: unaware of the output result; they cannot assess due to non-participation; choose to make no response.

Indicative quality criteria to aid respondents in evaluating the quality of output results include the following:

- Purpose: the aims are clearly stated; questions to be answered or issues to be addressed are established.
- Analytical soundness: any assumptions that are made are clear and explicit; arguments are logical, objective, and supported by analysis, facts, and evidence.
- Accuracy/reliability: any data and facts provided are accurate; forecasts are robust; sources are attributed and opinions disclosed; all essential material facts are included, and the degree of uncertainty or risk noted.
- Completeness: where appropriate, an adequate range of options is presented. The costs, benefits, and risks of these to the intended client(s) are analysed together with suggestions as to how risks can be minimized and benefits maximized.

- Participation and consultation: the participants are those needed to produce the result being sought; key stakeholders, including non-members, are identified and consulted.
- Practicality and relevance: the result responds to ministerial/senior official policy information needs. For some results, timeliness is crucial, while for others (e.g. guidelines or recommendations), the expected continued relevance (durability) may be important. Generally, the output result takes account of current economic, political, and social realities and consistency with other policies/actions.
- Presentation and conciseness: the main policy messages are clear, concise, and can be readily understood.

While participation rates have improved significantly, the number of non-responses, as well as the number of no assessments, is an issue that merits particular and careful assessment by committees. They may sometimes be since the member countries in question take no interest in particular output results. A high number of "NA/NR" may also be an indication for a committee that it should focus and reduce its outputs or improve communication and dissemination.

An in-depth evaluation of OECD Committees was introduced in September 2005, and as such, is the final element of the IMC to become operational. Nine committees are evaluated per biennium, which means that each committee is evaluated once every six years.

The evaluations, financed from the part I budget, are conducted under the responsibility of the evaluation committee, which is composed of six ambassadors. It reports the results of individual evaluations to the executive committee and provides an annual report on its work to the council.

The IDE focuses on the relevance of a committee's work programme and mandate, the effectiveness of its output results in terms of their impact and the achievement of objectives, and the efficiency with which it functions. Based on this assessment, it provides a set of recommendations that are monitored for their implementation.

Evaluations are primarily retrospective, using both quantitative and qualitative data as basis for assessing the: (i) relevance of a committee's work programme and mandate objectives; (ii) extent to which it is effective in achieving impacts that are in line with its objectives; (iii) efficiency with which it functions.

The process involves a considerable effort of data collection through the conducting of surveys and interviews, as well as drawing on in-house data sources from both within and beyond the IMC.

The questionnaire survey, which is used to collect data from policymakers in Member countries, refers to the performance dimensions summarized in Table 8.7 (OECD 2009b).

Relevance aims at checking whether the objectives correspond, and will continue to correspond in the future, with the needs, problems, and issues faced by the beneficiaries of OECD activities. It draws on the results of the MTO surveys, which have the highest weight. A low rating in respect to the criterion of relevance does not necessarily call into question the importance of a particular policy area to the OECD as an organization (it is the MTO exercise that performs this function) but raises issues about what a committee's work in the policy area is aiming to achieve.

The evaluation of effectiveness relates to the extent to which a committee's work has had policy impacts and their long-lasting nature. It is defined as whether output results are being widely used and if they are bringing about widespread policy development impacts [and if they are] contributing towards long-lasting changes in member governments' and the European Commission's policy. The assessment draws mainly on data generated by the questionnaire survey and the PIR exercise and follows a logical chain of reasoning: for policy development impacts to occur, output results have to be used by policymakers, and for them to be used, policymakers must at the very least be aware that they exist.

The evaluation criterion of efficiency is defined as whether a committee is optimizing the relation between its financial and human resource inputs and the quality of its output results, with a particular emphasis on its orientation and functioning as key factors.

The criterion of sustainability checks whether the activities give rise to long-lasting changes, whether impacts address or are likely to address, policy needs, issues, and problems in a durable fashion.

Finally, in order to capture a wider range of impacts than those explicitly sought and formalised as expected outcomes and mandated objectives, a fifth criterion—unexpected impacts—reflects the need to highlight instances of positive repercussions of the activities of committees over and beyond those intended, and any negative repercussions that may be occurring as a result of their actions.

Evaluation results are used to reinforce transparency and accountability, to inform council decisions on mandate renewals, and to help improve future committee performance. Against this backdrop, the formal objectives of the IDE process are to:

Table 8.7 In-depth evaluation areas

Criterion	Evaluation questions	Data sources (primary in italics)
Relevance	Are the mandated objectives and the Expected Outcomes of the Committee relevant to policy needs, problems and issues of its clients, and other stakeholders, and will they continue to be so in the medium term?	*Clients and other stakeholders.* Committee mandates. PIRs. MTOs.
Effectiveness	To what extent are clients and other stakeholders aware of the Committee's output results? When the visibility of outputs is low, how can this be explained? To what extent are the Committee's output results being (or are likely to be) used as an input into the policy-making processes of clients and other stakeholders? If output results are used, in which cases are they used and how? If the output results had not been available, how would policy-making processes have differed? If output results are not used, why is this the case? How significant is the (real or likely) influence of the Committee's output results used in the policymaking processes of clients and other stakeholders?	*Clients and other stakeholders.* PIRs
Efficiency	How well does the committee function? Does the work of the committee progress without significant problems and delays, and if not, why not? Does coordination within the OECD occur as planned and what are its consequences? Does coordination with external bodies occur as planned and what are its consequences? To what extent are the Committee's output results viewed by committee members, clients and other stakeholders as being timely, relevant, reliable and sufficient? When the quality of output results is viewed as low, how can this be explained?	*OECD officials. Committee members. Clients and other stakeholders.* PIRs
Sustainability	To what extent are the policies of clients and other stakeholders being (or likely to be) aligned durably with the OECD's strategic objectives? How much is this due to the use and influence of the Committee's output results in policy-making processes?	*Clients and other stakeholders.*
Unexpected/ unplanned impacts	Are unexpected/unplanned impacts occurring as a result of the Committee's work? If they are positive, do they correspond with the policy needs, issues and problems of clients and other stakeholders? If they are negative, why have they occurred and what are their consequences?	*Clients and other stakeholders.*

- Ensure an effective committee structure, appropriate mandates, and good committee working practices;
- Improve organizational effectiveness;
- Establish best practices.

8.5   Discussion

Summing up, the OECD performance management framework is the main part of the managerial reforms implemented at the OECD and refers to both the short and the longer term. It goes from the activities and functioning of its committees to the quality, quantity, and impact of the outputs they produce (Fig. 8.4).

Reforms regarding how performance is planned, measured, and managed at the OECD have a clear neo-Weberian nature. Structure prevails over strategy (output groups correspond to directorates rather than strategic priorities). The prevailing human resources management mechanism is merit and individual assessments of performance are scarcely used for decisions over carrier or promotions.

Performance management mechanisms have permeated the upper level of political and strategic decision making while are scarcely used at the operational level (depth). The span of performance management covers several dimensions from relevance to output quality, quantity, and timeliness, efficiency and effectiveness (Fig. 8.5, Table 8.8).

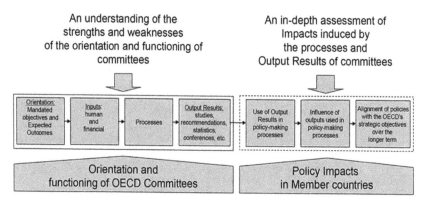

Fig. 8.4   The cause-effect chain of performance management at the OECD

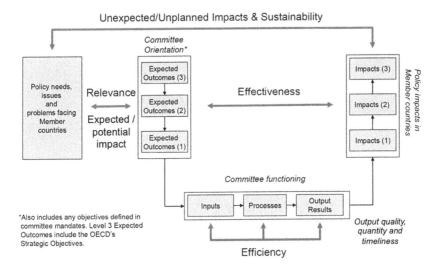

Fig. 8.5 Performance management dimensions at the OECD

OECD reform results should be assessed against the main objectives: first, enhanced accountability towards member countries in terms of efficiency and effectiveness and, second, relevance of outputs compared to the most important policy concerns of governments and impact on policy-making in capitals. A third aim was to assist the OECD council in identifying priorities and allocating resources.

There has been no formal evaluation of the reform results, although the IMC tools have been periodically reviewed (for example, the PWB in 2003, the PIR in 2006, and the MTO in 2007). Some elements are to be found in Bourgon (2009).

Reforms led member states to be more involved in setting priorities and allocating resources.

By 2003, operating costs were reduced by 20% through internal management and administrative simplification, efficiency gains in support services and outsourcing (OECD 2003b). Such savings were more a result of budget cuts than efficiency gains. The main result of structural reforms was to build momentum towards successive reforms.

The creation of clusters did not noticeably improve the ability to address cross-cutting issues (Bourgon 2009).

Also, the committee review was the most costly and least successful reform.

Table 8.8 Performance management area

Areas/functions		Ideal paradigms				
		Traditional	*NWS*	*NPM*	*NPG*	*OECD*
Performance evaluation						
Performance focus		Correctness of procedures	Focus on the achievement of satisfaction in service delivery (outcome)	Achievement of results (outputs)	Focus on the performance of the network	Towards NWS
Extension of the performance measurement system	Span of performance	Inputs	Outcome	Outputs	Outcome/impacts	Towards NWS
	Depth of performance	Micro	Meso	Micro	Government/ governance wide	NWS

Source: own elaboration

Managerial reforms displayed some political and methodological weaknesses, although the adoption of a two-year budget cycle (the PWB) is considered to have had a positive impact.

According to the secretary-general, in introducing the "21 for 21 agenda", management tools and regulations in the areas of finance, communications, human resources, and operations have been upgraded and, most importantly, a culture of value for money has been established that is now delivering results.

In conclusion, the OECD case study analysis illustrates how clear and present problems such as financial pressures or political indifference or declining influence can be effective catalysts for change (Bourgon 2009).

The reform results include a reduction of operating costs of 20 percent by 2003, by simplifying internal management and administrative processes, improving the efficiency of support services and outsourcing some functions (OECD 2003b). These efficiency gains and savings, however, were more a consequence of reduced budgets than organizational realignment.

Structural reforms served to build momentum towards further reform and demonstrated that reforming international organizations is possible and necessary to sustain the support of member countries and ensure a well-functioning multilateral system.

On the other hand, the PIR and the MTO exhibit a number of weaknesses: methodological for the former and political for the latter. More successful was the PWB in modernizing the organization and transforming the role of the council in its oversight of planning and budgeting. Is also contributed to change the nature of budget discussions between the divisions and between the secretariat and the council (Bourgon 2009).

A strong and committed leadership from the secretary-general, and a clear and urgent need to change were the main strengths. Still, the absence of a clearly defined strategy on how the performance management system would develop has weakened the support of mid-level managers.

Notes

1. Past attempts to evaluation—such as the Vinde reviews—have failed due to the lack of a corporate framework, a focus on processes rather than outputs, no clear planning, limited involvement of senior officials in capitals and other stakeholders, unclear accountability arrangements, a "one-off process" approach.

Cf. for example, Woodward (2007): "Much of the initial reform programme consisted of little more than minor tinkering with committee system, reforms to the financial and budgetary systems, and instituting more
scientific, output-oriented management techniques. These minor reforms
did not address the problems of legitimacy, intensified competition, and the
organization's tarnished image that had led to the initial calls for reform.
Johnston thus endorsed a bolder set of more substantive reforms which
would involve the expansion of OECD membership and the fortifying relations with non-members and civil society".

2. Cf. for example Woodward (2007): "Much of the initial reform programme
   consisted of little more than minor tinkering with committee system,
   reforms to the financial and budgetary systems, and instituting more scientific, output-oriented management techniques. These minor reforms did
   not address the problems of legitimacy, intensified competition and the
   organization's tarnished image that had led to the initial calls for reform.
   Johnston thus endorsed a bolder set of more substantive reforms which
   would involve the expansion of OECD membership and the fortifying relations with non-members and civil society".

3. They include the Development Centre, the Financial Action Task Force,
   International Energy Agency, the International Transport Forum, the
   Nuclear Energy Agency, the Sahel and West Africa Club

4. See http://webnet.oecd.org/oecdgroups/

5. They are (1) Promote Sustainable Economic Growth, Financial Stability
   and Structural Adjustment, (2) Provide Employment Opportunities for All,
   Improve Human Capital and Social Cohesion and Promote a Sustainable
   Environment, (3) Contribute to Shaping Globalization for the Benefit of all
   Through the Expansion of Trade and Investment, (4) Enhance Public and
   Private Sector Governance, (5) Contribute to the Development of Non-
   Member Economies, (6) Efficient and Effective Corporate Management
   (OECD 2003d).

6. Letter of the secretary-general, accompanying the MTO survey, to all
   Permanent Representatives. 2 August 2005.

REFERENCES

AIV – Advisory Council on International Affairs. *The OECD of the future*. Report
    No. 54. 2007.
Balint, Tim, and Christoph Knill. "*The limits of legitimacy pressure as a source of
    organizational change: The reform of human resource management in the
    OECD.*" University of Konstanz. Department of Politics and Management.
    Chair of Comparative Public Policy and Administration. Working Paper n. 1.
    (2007): 117–131

Bourgon, Jocelyne P. C. *International Institutions Reform and Modernization of the OECD.* Working Paper No. 42. The Centre for International governance Innovation. (2009).

Carroll, Peter, and Aynsley Kellow. The OECD: A study of organisational adaptation. Edward Elgar Publishing, 2011.

Clifton, Judith, and Daniel Díaz-Fuentes. "The OECD and phases in the international political economy, 1961–2011." *Review of International Political Economy* 18, no. 5 (2011): 552–569

Davies, Michael DV. *The administration of international organizations: top down and bottom up.* Routledge, 2017.

Hunter, Carrie Patricia. "The Organization for Economic Cooperation and Development's changing (?) discourse on higher education." PhD diss., University of British Columbia, 2013.

Marcussen, Martin. "OECD governance through soft law." In *Soft law in governance and regulation*, pp. 103–128. E. Elgar, 2004.

OECD. *The Future of the Organization. Paris: Organization for Economic Co-operation and Development.* 1995.

———. *The Future of the Organization. Paris: Organization for Economic Co-operation. The OECD: Challenges and Strategic Objectives 1997. Note by the Secretary General.* 1997.

———. *Annual Report.* 2001.

———. *Annual Report.* 2002.

———. *Report by the Chair of the Budget Committee on the new system for developing the OECD's Programme of Work and Budget (PWB).* 2003a.

———. *Reform and Modernisation of the OECD. HOD (2003)3.* 2003b.

———. *Reform and Modernization of the OECD, C/MIN (2003)6.* 2003c.

———. *Annual Report.* 2003d.

———. *Annual Report.* 2004.

———. *Implementing In-Depth evaluation of OECD Committees. Evaluation Sub-Group. C/ESG(2005).* 2005.

———. *Financial Regulations of the Organization.* 2008.

———. *The Integrated Management Cycle, priority-setting, resource reallocations and performance evaluation at the OECD. General Secretariat. Council. Working Party on Priorities.* 2009a

———. *Implementing In-depth Evaluation of OECD Committees. Evaluation Sub-Group.* 2009b.

———. Annual Report. 2014.

———. Budget Committee Financial Statements of the Organisation for Economic Co-operation and Development. 2017.

OECD Council. *2009-10 Programme of Work and Budget. Report of the Budget Committee Chair. Organisation for Economic Co-operation and Development.* 2008.

Ougaard, Morten. "The OECD's global role: Agenda-setting and policy diffusion." In *Mechanisms of Oecd Governance*, pp. 26–49. Oxford University Press, 2010.

Pal, Leslie. *Frontiers of governance: The OECD and global public management reform.* Springer, 2012.

Salzman, James. "Labor Rights, Globalization and Institutions: The Role and Influence of the Organization and Development." *Mich. J. Int'l l.* 21 (1999): 769.

Woodward, Richard. "Offshore strategies in global political economy: small islands and the case of the EU and OECD harmful tax competition initiatives." Cambridge Review of International Affairs 19, no. 4 (2006): 685–699.

———. "Global governance and the Organization for Economic Cooperation and Development." *In Global Governance and Japan*, pp. 83–99. Routledge, 2007.

———. *The organisation for economic co-operation and development* (OECD). Routledge, 2009.

CONCLUDING REMARKS

Our evidence shows that many international organizations have started modernizing their internal management structures, experiencing more or less far-reaching changes. Although a systematic and comprehensive knowledge about the reasons, trajectories, and content of management reforms in international organizations is still missing. By contrast, there is no shortage of research and studies analyzing public sector management reforms providing useful comparative and theoretical frameworks to account and classify the observed changes. The attempts to apply such frameworks and models to international organizations are limited, despite the absence of relevant barriers preventing such undertaking. Based on such, we applied a comparative model analysis based on the ideal types to assess the relevance and directions of the recent management modernization reforms carried out within the European Union and the Organizations for Economic and Cooperation Development.

In the first part of our research work (RQ.1), we investigated the key characteristics (in terms of contents and process) of managerial reforms adopted by the selected international organizations, along four management areas, finance, human resources, organization as well as performance management systems, based on the following reform models: the New Public Management (NPM), the Neo-Weberian State (NWS), the New Public Governance (NPG) as well as the traditional model. Our analysis shows that the great majority of the observed changes in the two international organizations reflect the Neo Weberian State (NWS) paradigm of

© The Author(s) 2020
M. Amici, D. Cepiku, *Performance Management in International Organizations*, https://doi.org/10.1007/978-3-030-39472-1

reform. The trajectory from a traditional to a Neo-Weberian model is coherent with the prevailing traditional administrative culture shaping the administration of international organizations as well as with the main trends observed in the public sector[1]. A common element of the observed changes is linking performance information to traditional functions and management practices. This is observable mainly in the financial and personnel sector, where performance information has been added to the budget and staff appraisal systems. Other elements common to both organizations include the introduction of temporary contracts for specialists, the rationalization and centralization of recruitment procedures to increase openness and publicity, as well as the introduction of strategic planning cycles for setting priorities, assigning resources and define outputs standards. There are also differences in the direction and intensity of the changes observed. The OECD accounts for a higher number of NPM elements, including for budgeting and accounting systems, as well as in personnel policy, including the fixed-term contracts for all senior management contracts. This is a peculiar aspect adopted in the early 2000 and typical of the NPM administration model. According to this, even internal candidates promoted as Directors and Deputy Directors have to leave their indefinite time contract. The European Commission is the most compliant with the NWS model as most of the dimensions analyzed reflect a more or less extent, the features of the NWS model. These findings, from one side, are in line with several studies showing the reluctance of the European Commission to engage in NPM style management reforms (Levy 2004, 2003), and from the other, with the view of many external observers about the positive results led by the post-2000 management reforms in the Commission functioning (Nugent and Rhinard 2015).

The second part of the research specifically focused on the assessment of the performance management systems (RQ.2). The findings show that both performance systems display Neo-Weberian features, although with differences. The EU has a three-level performance management model much more suited to a network structure, while the OECD presides the organizational level. Given its nature, the OECD makes use of mostly qualitative and subjective performance measures, while the indicators included in the EU documents are more objective and structured according to the different organizational levels and perspectives. Nevertheless, within the EU, several disconnections still affect the performance chain across levels and perspectives. Among them, the different time-perspective of the EU strategic documents and the presence of multiple and overlapping strategic frameworks. Finally, considering the perspective of network performance, the EU performance structure is more network-oriented than OECD. Although the attitude of the European Commission to perceive national administrations as an external factor rather than an internal component of the network, still prevents an effective assessment of the network management strategy.

NOTE

1. According to Bouckaert and Halligan (2008), "traditional administration in continental Europe are shifting from a Weberian to a Neo-Weberian design" by an increasing focus on performance"

REFERENCES

Levy, Roger. "Confused expectations: Decentralizing the management of EU programmes." *Public Money & Management* 23, no. 2 (2003): 83–92.
———. "Between rhetoric and reality: Implementing management reform in the European Commission." *International Journal of Public Sector Management* 17, no. 2 (2004): 166–177.
Nugent, Neill, and Mark Rhinard. *The European Commission*. Macmillan International Higher Education, 2015.

Index[1]

---

[1] Note: Page numbers followed by 'n' refer to notes.

CPSIA information can be obtained
at www.ICGtesting.com
Printed in the USA
LVHW070116020520
654882LV00019B/388